CONVERSATIONS OF SOCRATES

XENOPHON was an Athenian country gentleman born *c.* 430 BC. He may have helped to publish Thucydides' *History* and certainly wrote his own *Hellenica* as a continuation of it. By his own (probably reliable) account he was a fine officer and outstanding leader, but his admiration for Sparta and devotion to Socrates led to his banishment. He was given an estate at Scillus and settled down to enjoy the life of a landed aristocrat under Spartan protection, and it was during this period that he began to write histories, biographies, memoirs and specialist treatises. Events forced him to move to Corinth in 371, but he was allowed to return to Athens in 365, where he lived until his death in *c.* 354.

HUGH TREDINNICK was born in 1899 and educated at King Edward's, Birmingham, and Trinity Hall, Cambridge, where he received a double first in Classics. He was Professor of Classics at Royal Holloway College from 1946 until 1966, and was also Dean of the Faculty of Arts at London University from 1956 to 1960. He was joint editor of the *Classical Review* from 1961 to 1967. He edited and translated works by Aristotle, as well as Xenophon's *Memoirs of Socrates* and Plato's *The Last Days of Socrates* for the Penguin Classics. Hugh Tredinnick died in 1982.

ROBIN WATERFIELD was born in 1952. He graduated from Manchester University in 1974 and went on to research ancient Greek philosophy at King's College, Cambridge. He has been a university lecturer, and both copy editor and commissioning editor for Penguin. He is now a self-employed writer with publications ranging from academic articles to children's fiction. He has translated various Greek philosophical texts, including several for Penguin Classics: Xenophon's *Hiero the Tyrant and Other Treatises*, Plutarch's *Essays*, Plato's *Philebus* and *Theaetetus* and (in Plato's *Early Socratic Dialogues*) *Hippias Major*, *Hippias Minor* and *Euthydemus*. His biography of Kahlil Gibran, *Prophet: The Life and Times of Kahlil Gibran*, is published by Penguin. He has also edited *The Voice of Kahlil Gibran* for Penguin Arkana.

XENOPHON

CONVERSATIONS OF SOCRATES

Translated by Hugh Tredennick and Robin Waterfield, and edited with new material by Robin Waterfield

PENGUIN BOOKS

PENGUIN BOOKS

Published by the Penguin Group
Penguin Books Ltd, 80 Strand, London WC2R 0RL, England
Penguin Putnam Inc., 375 Hudson Street, New York, New York 10014, USA
Penguin Books Australia Ltd, 250 Camberwell Road, Camberwell, Victoria 3124, Australia
Penguin Books Canada Ltd, 10 Alcorn Avenue, Toronto, Ontario, Canada M4V 3B2
Penguin Books India (P) Ltd, 11 Community Centre, Panchsheel Park, New Delhi – 110 017, India
Penguin Books (NZ) Ltd, Cnr Rosedale and Airborne Roads, Albany, Auckland, New Zealand
Penguin Books (South Africa) (Pty) Ltd, 24 Sturdee Avenue, Rosebank 2196, South Africa

Penguin Books Ltd, Registered Offices: 80 Strand, London WC2R 0RL, England

www.penguin.com

Published in Penguin Classics 1990

047

Printed and bound in Great Britain by Clays Ltd, Elcograf S.p.A.
Filmset in Linotron Bembo

ISBN-13: 978–0–140–44517–6

To T. J. S.

CONTENTS

PREFACE

The chief reason, and sufficient justification, for my wanting to translate Xenophon's Socratic writings is that there is today a distinct danger of imbalance for English readers of ancient literature. To judge by what is available in bookshops, one would think that Plato was the only person who had ever written about Socrates. This is far from being the case: after Socrates' death in 399 BC, a number of his followers, and some others, wrote dialogues with Socrates as the protagonist. As it happens, we have only the titles of most of these works and a few fragments of others. But we do possess the complete Socratic works not only of Plato, but also of Xenophon. Socrates was arguably one of the most important people in the history of mankind. In case we think that the portrait we find in Plato is the one and only Socrates – the true Socrates – it makes sense to have available Xenophon's portrait as well. I say this without prejudging the question of which of these portraits is the more interesting or the more accurate; this is an issue to which I will return.

A less scholarly and more idiosyncratic reason for wanting to make Xenophon's Socratic work available is somewhat as follows. It will soon become clear to the reader that Xenophon's moral code is loosely describable as 'Victorian': at any rate, he is a staunch advocate of the quest for 'a healthy mind in a healthy body', to use Juvenal's phrase. It seems to me that today, in the late 1980s, both the moral and political pendulum in a great many Western countries is swinging away from the flux of earlier years, and back to a desire for a secure way of life. The reader will find in the pages of Xenophon the modern world's concerns for, among other things, physical fitness, healthy eating, self-restraint, self-responsibility and, of particular relevance given the threat of an AIDS epidemic, sensible sex. What is important in Xenophon, however, and why a new edition of his Socratic work seems to be timely, is not just the apparent contemporaneity of his thought, but the fact that his ideas are not based on unthinking acceptance of a conservative code or due simply to a swing of the pendulum in the collective unconscious; they are based on his own reflection on moral principles, which he derived from his acquaintance with Socrates. Whether or not this particular thesis is true, it is certain that reading Xenophon's Socratic works can offer a different perspective on moral and political notions which are fast becoming idealized today.

This volume contains the complete Socratic works of Xenophon:[1] *Socrates' Defence* (traditionally referred to under its Anglicized Greek title as *The Apology of Socrates*), *Memoirs of Socrates* (which is traditionally called by its Latin name, *Memorabilia*), *The Dinner-party* (*Symposium*), and *The Estate-manager* (*Oeconomicus*). The translations of *Memoirs* and *The Dinner-party* are revisions of a version by Hugh Tredennick, which Penguin published in 1970, but which has long been out of print; the other two translations and all the introductions are original to this volume; in *Memoirs* and *The Dinner-party*, some of the footnotes are Tredennick's, but the rest are original. Where Tredennick's translations are concerned, my policy has been to change as little as possible. I have altered the translation of quite a number of words and sentences, but rarely whole passages; that is, I have not made alterations gratuitously, but only where sentences seemed to me to contain infelicitous or (rarely) inaccurate translations; moreover, Tredennick had sometimes omitted phrases and, in one or two cases, whole sentences. One peculiarity of Tredennick's version is that despite being published in 1970, he

1. There is another work of Xenophon's, *Hieron*, which is classifiable as philosophy, and uses the dialogue form to have the fifth-century Syracusan tyrant Hieron discuss tyranny with the lyric poet Simonides; but I have restricted myself to Xenophon's writings which have Socrates as the protagonist.

appears to have used the first edition (1901) of E. C. Marchant's Oxford Classical Text (*Xenophontis Opera*, vol. 2), although the better second edition (1921) should have been available to him: the second edition is a reprint of the first edition, but with emendations listed in an 'Addenda et Corrigenda' section at the beginning of the book. I have taken the second edition of the Oxford Classical Text as my standard (though I have also consulted the relevant texts in the Loeb, Teubner and Budé series), and this too occasioned a number of changes to Tredennick's version. Where I prefer a different reading to that of Marchant, this has been mentioned in a footnote; this applies not only to the revisions of Tredennick's work, but also to my translations of *Socrates' Defence* and *The Estate-manager*.

Not for the first time, I must thank Professor Tony Woodman for his patient and prompt checking of the translations: his eye for 'translationese' is truly remarkable and I constantly profit from it. Especial thanks are also due to Zorine Roy-Singh, for taking the strain at a critical time, and to Charles Drazin for copy-editing over and above the call of duty. The book is dedicated to Professor Trevor Saunders for debts which go back many years and include benefiting not just from his advice, but from reading his own paradigmatic translations of ancient Greek philosophical texts.

R. W.

whereas it introduced the first edition (1907) of [illegible] Classical Texts [illegible] with [illegible] [illegible] (1910) [illegible] separately [illegible] [illegible] of the first edition, [illegible] [illegible] Although [illegible] [illegible] the second edition of the Oxford Classical Texts [illegible] (1908) I have [illegible] [illegible] and [illegible], and this [illegible] [illegible] [illegible] to that of [illegible] [illegible] applies not only to [illegible] [illegible] translations of [illegible] and [illegible]

Not for the first time, I must thank [illegible] for [illegible] [illegible] also due [illegible] [illegible] The book is dedicated to [illegible] for [illegible] advice [illegible]

E. W.

INTRODUCTION

Xenophon, son of Gryllus, was born in Athens *c.* 428 BC and died *c.* 354; he was therefore an exact contemporary of Plato (429–347), the other author whose Socratic writings survive. Xenophon's family was fairly well off, but we must take into account Athens' stormy political history in the last decade of the fifth century, and the fact that the Peloponnesian War, which Athens eventually lost, began in 431 and ended in 404. Under such circumstances, and particularly during the formative years of one's life, wealth does not necessarily imply security.

Nevertheless, many of the details of Xenophon's life, and the topics on which he wrote, reflect the concerns of the well-to-do. He wrote, among other things, on hunting, horsemanship and cavalry command, on estate-management and military history. It is important to note this right from the start, so that when we find these topics peppering Socrates' conversations as reported by Xenophon, we avoid the temptation to think that these were Socrates' interests and experiences rather than Xenophon's.

In 401 Xenophon left Athens, and soon afterwards (possibly in 399) he was formally exiled. What were the reasons for this official disfavour? The last couple of years of the fifth century saw a fervent return to democracy in Athens, following the arbitrary and tyrannical rule of the Thirty Oligarchs in 404–403. Quite possibly, then, Xenophon had, or had been suspected of, oligarchic inclinations. The historian Thucydides, whom Xenophon held in great esteem (Xenophon continued Thucydides' unfinished history in his *Hellenica*, or *A History of My Times*, as the Penguin edition has it), expressed admiration for the moderate oligarchy of 411, and the young Xenophon too may well have been impressed by this form of government. Certainly his portrait of Theramenes, one of the leaders in 411, who was also appointed one of the Thirty Oligarchs in 404, is favourable (*Hellenica*, 2.3.15–56); and further evidence of his sympathies may be found in his approval of the laws of Draco and Solon (*The Estate-manager*, 14.3–10; p. 337) – 'restoring the laws of Draco and Solon' was the slogan of the oligarchs of 411. Moreover, Xenophon's life and writings reflect an admiration for Athens' enemy Sparta, and such admiration was often expressed by those in Athens who tended towards oligarchy. However, it is probably more true to say that Xenophon was not particularly passionate about politics; rather, he commended the traditional virtues wherever he found them and, as a soldier, particularly the military virtues of Sparta. In his view, although Athens' past reveals these virtues, Sparta's present more closely conformed to the ideal (see especially p. 149). But when Sparta acted viciously, he was prepared to condemn it (*Hellenica*, 5.4.1).

The question of Xenophon's unpopularity in Athens cannot be separated from his association with Socrates.[1] The duration and depth of this association can only be guessed, but it was there, and in a town as small as Athens was at the time it would have been well known. Not only were several members of Socrates' circle overt or covert oligarchs, but they were all, without exception, members of the upper classes,[2] which in divided political times are always suspected of seeking dominion in one way or another. And the restored democracy was to put Socrates himself to death in 399 (on the reasons for his trial and execution, see pp. 32–40).

In short, while there are reasons to think that Xenophon was not especially committed to politics, the charges which led to his

1. See also Aristophanes, *Birds*, 1281–2: 'Everyone was mad about Sparta in those days – growing their hair long, starving themselves, never washing, Socratizing . . .'
2. A great many of them were closely related too: see J. K. Davies, *Athenian Propertied Families, 600–300 BC* (Oxford University Press, 1971), Table I.

formal exile are likely to have been based on suspicions of oligarchic and pro-Spartan tendencies.[1]

The rest of Xenophon's life can be briefly chronicled. On leaving Athens in 401, he joined (apparently not with Socrates' wholehearted approval: see *Anabasis*, 3.1.4–7) Cyrus the Younger's expedition to wrest the Persian throne from his brother Artaxerxes. The attempt failed; Xenophon chronicles the expedition and his own part in leading – if he is to be believed – the Greek mercenary troops back to Greece in *Anabasis* (published by Penguin as *The Persian Expedition*). After a short period as a mercenary in Thrace, from 399 to 394 Xenophon fought for Sparta; however, it is not clear whether he actually fought against Athens in the battle of Coronea in 394. For the next thirty years he lived, with his wife and two sons, the life of a country gentleman under Spartan protection, until he returned to Athens in 365 (his exile had been repealed in 368), where he lived until his death.

Not surprisingly all his writing was carried on in the last, more secure, forty years of his life. It should be noted that the process of publication was a far more haphazard affair than it is today, and it is arguable that Xenophon wrote chiefly for his own and his intimates' pleasure, and his sons' education; where he crusades, however, as when he is defending Socrates, he doubtless wanted to reach as wide an audience as possible. All the same, he not infrequently completed books started many years earlier. The datable parts of *Hellenica* were written as much as twenty years apart; the first two books of *Memoirs* were possibly written *c.* 380, but the last two books may have been as late as *c.* 355; the beginning of *The Estate-manager* (the conversation with Critobulus) seems to be contemporaneous with the last two books of *Memoirs*, whereas the conversation with Ischomachus, as is evident to even a casual reader, is a later addition.

Xenophon's writings have undergone variations in popularity. The Romans admired him a great deal and, for reasons that will

1. See also Diogenes Laertius, 2.51.

become apparent, Europe in the seventeenth to nineteenth centuries found him edifying;[1] in between, however, opinions have not always been favourable. Those ages and those people who dislike moral earnestness will not find Xenophon attractive. Xenophon's Socrates is bound to come across as one of those people who tell you how to live your life. This is particularly annoying when, like Socrates, they are 'right'. Nor does good philosophy arise out of such an attitude: philosophy should be a form of inquiry – it is generated by curiosity, as both Plato and Aristotle said. Xenophon's Socrates, however, is plainly more interested in conclusions than in the process of reaching them.

Xenophon's literary style should become clear from the translations in this volume with little need for comment. At his best – and he is often at his best – he is plain and readable, though perhaps somewhat repetitious; at his worst he descends into awkwardness or embarrassing rhetoric (e.g. *Memoirs*, 2.4.5–7, 4.8.3; *The Estate-manager*, 5.1–17). His eulogies too can be overdone (*Agesilaus* and *Cyropaedia* are good examples of this). He is neither as great a historian as Thucydides, nor as great a philosopher as Plato (though we will find philosophy wherever we look in Xenophon), nor as outstanding a writer as either of these two. But he has a style which is all his own, whether one loves it or loathes it. He is informative and, when he tries, he tells a good story; and he does all this with writing which can afford pleasure and is always easy to read. Certainly, he is not an original thinker or writer: the conservatism of his thought is matched by the plainness of his style, and both are apparent on every page. But to us he is unique because he is our best and most accessible witness to events and attitudes without which our knowledge of ancient Greece would be considerably less. For more on Xenophon's style, see pp. 55–9, 282–4.

★

1. For a typically favourable Victorian estimate of Xenophon, see H. G. Dakyns, 'Xenophon', in E. Abbott (ed.), *Hellenica* (Rivingtons, 1880), pp. 324–86.

As already mentioned, Xenophon's own interests and experiences are reflected in his Socratic writings, and often even put into the mouth of Socrates. This raises the question to which I shall devote the rest of this general introduction: Who was Socrates? In so far as approaching this question involves considering Socrates' philosophy as described by Xenophon, I will reserve some of the discussion until later, when introducing *Memoirs* (pp. 59–67); here I shall outline the extant portraits of Socrates with a view to answering the question whether any one of these portraits is to be preferred as more accurate than the others.[1] We have to rely on other portraits because, as must never be forgotten, Socrates himself wrote nothing (but perhaps only because writing was not widespread at the time).

The first portrait which needs considering, and the only one which is contemporary with Socrates, is that of the comic playwright Aristophanes, who in 424 BC wrote *Clouds* and chose Socrates as one of the main characters. The play is great fun. In it Socrates is shown running a fee-paying school, teaching philosophical mysteries. The teaching is largely of rhetoric, to enable a person to argue an opponent down, even if the opponent has the morally stronger case. But Socrates and his students also research subjects such as astronomy, geometry and meteorology; they have a novel and off-beat approach: a geometry lesson, for example, involves considering how many flea-feet fleas can jump (see *The Dinner-party*, 6.8). Socrates and his students are also religious non-conformists, who substitute natural explanations for the traditional gods. They are ragged and dirty, work-shy, impecunious and thieving. What they concern themselves with is at best hair-splitting and time-wasting, at worst absurd and subversive.

Fully to rehearse the arguments for and against regarding all or some of this as an accurate portrait of Socrates would be simply to repeat the work of Sir Kenneth Dover, in his edition of *Clouds*

1. See A. R. Lacey, 'Our Knowledge of Socrates', in G. Vlastos (ed.), *The Philosophy of Socrates* (Anchor Books, 1971), pp. 22–49.

(Oxford University Press, 1968). The portrait is so starkly opposed to that of Plato and Xenophon that the issue is polar: either Plato and Xenophon were engaged in a massive cover-up or Aristophanes is wrong. The former alternative is both difficult to entertain, and is disproved by other fragmentary evidence about Socrates, which also contradicts Aristophanes' portrait. Therefore, Aristophanes is not providing us with a true likeness of Socrates.

What is Aristophanes up to then? The answer should already be clear from the timeless nature of some aspects of the portrait (though others are peculiar to ancient Greece). He is using Socrates as a figurehead for intellectuals of all types; the sophists and natural scientists of fifth-century Greece are particularly represented. Socrates in *Clouds* is a catch-all character who displays features which popular prejudice and the collective unconscious attribute to intellectuals; he can hardly, therefore, be used as evidence for what the historical Socrates was really like. There was considerable fear of intellectualism at the end of the fifth century; Aristophanes is playing up to that fear.

We might still ask, however, why Aristophanes picked on Socrates. The answer is simply that Socrates was visible.[1] Not only was he one of the very few native Athenian philosophers of the time, but his work carried him on to the streets, into the agora and other crowded meeting-places. Athens was a small enough town for Socrates to have been easily recognizable by a large number of Athenians. It is noticeable that just about the only aspect of Aristophanes' portrait which can be securely attributed to Socrates is asceticism (albeit in the comically exaggerated form of scruffiness), which would, of course, have been his most visible trait.

As a sad postscript, we should note the following possibility. In his *Symposium*, Plato has Aristophanes and Socrates together at a party, and on good terms. Supposing this to be the truth, then

1. The comic playwrights Ameipsias and Eupolis also wrote plays (now lost to us) with Socrates as a leading character at much the same time as Aristophanes' *Clouds*.

Aristophanes' portrait of Socrates was mere jest, with little or no underlying malice. Nevertheless, both Plato, in his *Apology of Socrates*, and Xenophon (especially *Memoirs*, 1.1.11–16, 4.7), feel that Socrates was implicitly on trial as an archetypal intellectual (that is, a religious non-conformist etc.). This is precisely Aristophanes' portrait of Socrates, and Plato, at least, alludes to *Clouds*. No doubt the issue would have arisen in Socrates' trial anyway; but Aristophanes' *Clouds* cannot have helped. If it was mere jest, then, the joke turned extremely sour.

There are other occasional comic references to Socrates, which, for the reasons discussed above, can be dismissed as unreliable evidence; there were also others who wrote Socratic dialogues. Among Socrates' disciples, apart from Plato and Xenophon, the following are known to have written such *Sokratikoi logoi* (as Aristotle calls them at *Poetics*, 1447b11): Aeschines, Antisthenes, Aristippus, Cebes, Crito, Euclides, Phaedo and Simmias. At the beginning of *Defence*, Xenophon refers vaguely to 'others' who have written versions of Socrates' defence. It is clear that writing Socratic dialogues constituted a minor industry and a sub-genre of Greek prose literature at the time. It is also clear that there were even stock settings in which Socrates was portrayed: for instance, we have both Plato's and Xenophon's *Symposium* (*Dinner-party*) and their *Apology of Socrates* (*Defence*). It is less surprising, of course, to find that there were standard characters with whom Socrates was regularly portrayed as conversing, since these would be the members of his circle.

The probable nature of these *Sokratikoi logoi* is something I shall come back to. For the present, it need simply be noted that we possess only a few disconnected fragments of most of them. Their evidence is, therefore, almost worthless for our present concerns, and we have to concentrate on the two major surviving proponents of the genre – Plato and Xenophon. Having dismissed Aristophanes' evidence, can we decide which of their portraits, in so far as they differ, is the more accurate?

★

It would take a book in itself to list and fully discuss the points of similarity and difference between Xenophon's and Plato's portraits of Socrates; here I restrict myself to more general argument.

Let us start with the parameters. By 'Xenophon's Socrates', I mean simply Socrates as he is found in any or all of the works in this volume; despite the fact that these works were written sometimes years apart, there is no sign of any changes in the ideas that Socrates is made to express. By 'Plato's Socrates', however, I mean Socrates as he is found in Plato's earlier dialogues.

Few, if any, scholars would disagree that it is in his earlier dialogues that Plato approximates more closely to a portrait of the historical Socrates. Socrates remains the protagonist in some of Plato's later dialogues, but increasingly becomes a mouthpiece of Plato's own ideas. Here are four of the most important philosophical issues which make the point. A consideration of these issues will give us an idea as to the nature of Socrates and his thought, and also be relevant later, when we come to compare Xenophon and Plato.

First, in Plato's early dialogue *Protagoras* (352b–e, 355a–357e, 358b–d; see also *Meno*, 77b–78a), Socrates provocatively denies the existence of *akrasia*, which may be roughly translated as 'weakness of will'. It is the state that causes one to 'see the better course and approve of it, but follow the worse course', as Seneca's Medea would later put it. Socrates claims that everyone always follows the course which is perceived as better, and that no one can see a course as worse and yet follow it. People can be wrong, but this is an intellectual error, not weakness of will – that is, they can be wrong in what they perceive as good for themselves. In a later dialogue such as *Republic*, however, Socrates admits without argument that appetites and emotions can lead a person to act against even a perceived better course.

Second, and most remarkably, there is no sign in the early dialogues of the standard Greek, pre-Christian tenet that it is acceptable, and even morally sound, to do good to one's friends and harm to one's enemies. Instead, Socrates argues in *Crito*,

49a–d that if someone does wrong to me, I should not do wrong back, and 'doing wrong' is identified with harming in any way. However, in later dialogues, Socrates is made to mouth the standard tenet (e.g. *Republic*, 471b; *Philebus*, 49d).

Third, the Socrates of Plato's early dialogues is content with trying to define moral terms. He is concerned with trying to find out what courage or justice are, for instance, but not with theoretical questions such as what properties they must have in order for me to be able to know them and even ask the question in the first place. His pungent method of questioning and his thought centre entirely on getting people to try to change their lives for the better. In the later dialogues, however, Socrates is made to have an interest in metaphysics, the theory of knowledge, astronomy, mathematics, politics and a whole host of subjects foreign to the earlier Socrates.

Fourth, and finally, with one or two outstanding exceptions, in Plato's early dialogues Socrates is constantly, both explicitly and implicitly, denying that he himself knows anything; from this profession of ignorance ('Socratic irony') stems his questioning method, his mission to rid people of the illusion that they know anything important, and all his philosophy. Whether or not we think that this profession of ignorance is sincere, it is the cardinal characteristic of Socrates in the early Platonic dialogues.[1] In later dialogues, however, Socrates teaches from a standpoint of *certain* knowledge.

So, 'Plato's Socrates' means the Socrates of Plato's early dialogues. His portrayal of Socrates differs markedly from that of Xenophon. There are many differences of substance between the two pictures and, even where there are similarities, many differences of emphasis. I shall illustrate these differences of emphasis and substance using the four philosophical issues outlined above as both foundations and test-cases.

1. See G. Vlastos, 'Socrates' Disavowal of Knowledge', *Philosophical Quarterly*, 35 (1985), pp. 1–31. This article must be read in order to understand Socratic irony; and generally, anyone working on Socrates is constantly indebted to Professor Vlastos' many writings and lectures on the subject.

These four issues are important: the very fact that there are such differences between the earlier and later Platonic portraits makes it highly plausible to claim that here, if anywhere, we have a starting-point – we can assume that the Socrates of the early dialogues is, if not the 'historical Socrates' (who I believe to be irrecoverable – see below), at least Plato's version of Socrates.

First, then, Plato's Socrates denies the existence of moral weakness, on the grounds that no one deliberately chooses what is perceived as bad for them. This is the famous Socratic paradox that 'No one deliberately goes wrong' (which, given an ambiguity in the Greek, also means 'No one deliberately does wrong'). This paradox goes hand in hand with another famous Socratic paradox, that 'Virtue is knowledge'. The two paradoxes are related in the sense that, if virtue is knowledge, then plainly no one can deliberately or knowingly do wrong (act unvirtuously). Where the paradox 'Virtue is knowledge' is concerned, we often find in Plato that this knowledge is assimilated to knowledge of crafts: virtue, and all its branches (courage, justice, etc.) could and should have experts who have been taught and can teach others; virtue has products, just as a cobbler's product is shoes; a virtuous person can explain his actions, just as a craftsman can.

Like Plato, Xenophon has Socrates discuss moral weakness (*Memoirs*, 3.9.4); he has Socrates claim that the basis of the denial of such weakness is that 'everyone acts by choosing from the courses open to him the one which he supposes to be most expedient', which is to say that 'No one deliberately goes wrong' (see also *Memoirs*, 4.6.6 and *The Estate-manager*, 20.29); in the very next paragraph he has Socrates claim that 'virtue is wisdom'; and we find the Craft Analogy referred to here and there (for example, *Memoirs*, 4.2.12, 4.4.5; *The Estate-manager*, 6.13–14; and more obliquely at *Memoirs*, 1.2.37).

So here we have a difference of emphasis. Xenophon has all the tools, but doesn't make anything very much with them – certainly, nothing as philosophically stimulating as Plato's Socrates does. There are signs of philosophical muddle. For instance, as we have seen, he has Socrates pronounce the principle which denies moral weakness, but at another point (*Memoirs*, 4.5.6) has Socrates affirm the existence of such weakness.

It is also interesting to see how Plato and Xenophon diverge on the consequences of the paradox that 'Virtue is knowledge'. In *Hippias Minor* Plato has Socrates implicitly adopt the extreme position that such knowledge is sufficient for virtue: anyone with the relevant knowledge will by definition be virtuous. He has Socrates take this route as a consequence of a possible flaw in the Craft Analogy. A craftsman makes a product, but it is beyond his sphere of responsibility, *qua* craftsman, to guarantee that the product is used for good rather than ill. The products of virtue, however, must necessarily be good: the analogy is in danger of breaking down at this point. There are two possible responses: one is the Platonic response, that knowledge is sufficient for virtue, which keeps the Craft Analogy central to Socrates' thought; the other is Aristotelian, that the virtuous man naturally desires good. This Aristotelian option relegates the Craft Analogy to the sidelines, since the desire for good is now just as important as the bare knowledge. Whereas Plato takes the former response, Xenophon attributes to Socrates the Aristotelian response (*Memoirs*, 3.9.5: those who know how to act justly 'would choose to do nothing else').

However, Plato and Xenophon do agree on a political consequence of Socrates' intellectualism. They both show Socrates as critical of the Athenian political system in which people who are merely rich, charismatic or persuasive can be appointed to positions of power and responsibility; according to Socrates, positions of responsibility in all spheres, including politics, should be open only to experts with the appropriate knowledge. In Plato, see for example, *Protagoras*, 319b–320b (and later, of course, Plato's ideal of the philosopher-king); in Xenophon, see especially *Memoirs*, 3.6 and 3.9.10–11 – and note that this aspect of Socrates' thought was well enough known for it to be used against him: *Memoirs*, 1.2.9.

*

Second, we have seen that Plato's Socrates appears not to hold the normal Greek view that it is morally sound to do good to one's friends, but harm to one's enemies. Xenophon's Socrates, however, is constantly reiterating this tenet (for example, *Memoirs*, 2.1.19, 2.1.28, 2.3.14, 2.6.35, 4.2.16, 4.5.10). Here we have a difference of substance, rather than merely one of emphasis.

Third, Plato's Socrates is far more concerned with the moral life of the individuals he meets than with theoretical issues. Here there are points of both similarity and difference between Xenophon and Plato. On the one hand, Xenophon's Socrates expresses more certainty about matters such as religion (*Memoirs*, 1.4, 4.3) than is conceivable for Plato's Socrates. On the other hand, his concern, even when expressing such theoretical views, is likewise to improve the life of the people he is talking to. The very fact that both Plato and Xenophon only ever show Socrates at work on individuals or, at the most, small groups, suggests that they both agree that individuals are Socrates' concern. Moreover, in Xenophon we find Socrates recommending theoretical studies such as mathematics and astronomy only in so far as they are of practical application (see *Memoirs*, 4.7, especially).

Fourth, not only does Xenophon's Socrates never profess ignorance, but also he constantly persuades his interlocutors of views which he himself holds: in fact, for Xenophon this is the whole point of Socrates' teaching – that he was a good man and taught others the good things he knew. Yet Socrates' profession of ignorance is central to Plato's portrayal of Socrates, and leads to the whole Platonic picture of his having not so much a philosophy in the sense of a system of ideas as a valuable philosophical method of inquiry. This difference, therefore, between Xenophon and Plato is striking.

It is true that in Xenophon we find some aspects of Socrates which in Plato we would associate with his profession of ignorance – Socrates invariably asks questions, and stresses the importance of self-knowledge (for example, *Memoirs*, 4.2.24) and of people acknowledging their own ignorance (for example, *Memoirs*, 1.7) – but these aspects are not made three-dimensional by being centred on the Socratic profession of ignorance. To take the last aspect: acknowledging ignorance for Xenophon's Socrates is merely prudential – so that one doesn't make a fool of oneself and harm those one shouldn't harm. Plato's Socrates, however, knows from his own experience that an awareness of ignorance is the only way to make life a quest for moral improvement rather than being content with the notions and attitudes one already has. Knowing the value of this, he uses his profession of ignorance as the excuse for constant questioning; the result is not to arrive at definite conclusions, as it is in Xenophon, but to reduce the interlocutor to the same awareness of ignorance as Socrates. Xenophon's Socrates merely pays lip-service to the educational value of questioning (*Memoirs*, 4.6.15; *The Estate-manager*, 19.15), but the tone and purpose of his questions are entirely different.

Besides those which centre upon the four philosophical issues, there are other differences of emphasis. For instance, Plato's Socrates devotes whole dialogues to attempting (but failing) to define certain moral terms; Xenophon alludes to this aspect of Socrates' work only in *Memoirs*, 3.9, and, more explicitly, in *Memoirs*, 4.6, where he implies that Socrates was invariably successful in reaching definitions of such terms. Again, Xenophon's Socrates is rarely as subtle or brilliant in dealing with people as Plato's Socrates – *Memoirs*, 4.2, is the closest Xenophon comes to a Platonic episode. There is also less humour, intellectual sparkle and biting irony – though humour does occasionally struggle through his earnestness. Xenophon emphasizes far more Socrates' personal self-discipline, the differences between slavishness and freedom, and the characteristics of a man of virtue.

We must now face the question of how to explain these frequent differences of emphasis and occasional (but important) differences of substance between Plato's and Xenophon's portraits of Socrates. Evidently, neither portrait is right, or one is right, or both are right.

A great many scholars choose the middle option – that only one portrait is right – and nowadays invariably choose Plato's Socrates as the true likeness.[1] They do this either explicitly (by arguing that Xenophon is wrong) or implicitly (by ignoring Xenophon when claiming to describe 'Socrates' philosophy'). Unfortunately, those who argue explicitly in favour of Plato are rarer than those who simply ignore Xenophon. There are good reasons for this, however: it is difficult to argue objectively that one portrait is preferable, because there is no objective, or even external, evidence to support the claim. The only plausible means of doing so is to argue that Aristotle's remarks about Socrates side with Plato against Xenophon. The most relevant Aristotelian passages are *Nicomachean Ethics*, 1145b23–27; *Magna Moralia*, 1182a15–25; *Metaphysics*, 987b1–4, and 1078b23–32; *De Sophisticis Elenchis*, 183b7–8: there is nothing in Aristotle, however, on the important issue of whether Socrates claimed that it was never right to cause harm.

Yet, even if Aristotle's remarks did support Plato's picture, this would prove very little. Aristotle may simply have chosen to rely on Plato's early dialogues for his evidence about Socrates: he never met Socrates and, after all, Plato was his teacher. He might not even have had access to Xenophon's works.

I believe that, ultimately, the choice of Plato over Xenophon is largely a matter of prejudice. Plato's Socrates is simply a far more provocative and brilliant character. It is sometimes said that Xenophon's portrait must be wrong, because his Socrates is so conventional that it is impossible to believe the Athenians could ever have put him to death. Even if this were true, it would not

1. See especially G. Vlastos, 'The Paradox of Socrates', in G. Vlastos (ed.), op. cit. (p. 9, n. 1), pp. 1–21. For a recent attempt to reinstate Xenophon, see D. Morrison, 'On Professor Vlastos' Xenophon', *Ancient Philosophy*, 7 (1987), pp. 9–22.

follow that Plato's portrait is right, because there is equally little reason for the Athenians to have killed Plato's Socrates: even at their most intolerant, the Athenians never executed anyone simply for being brilliant. Both our authors are avowed followers of Socrates, whose purpose was to defend their mentor posthumously; both succeeded so well that the question of why Socrates was put to death is still an open one (see pp. 32–40).

In short, to prefer Plato's portrait to Xenophon's is just to compare Xenophon unfavourably with Plato as both a writer and a thinker. But this is only to say that not everyone is a genius. There is also a fairly obvious sense in which Plato's greater intellectual stature is likely to make him *less* slavishly dependent on Socrates and more his own man. The conclusion that Plato's brilliance leads him to understand Socrates' philosophy, when Xenophon didn't, is no more or less plausible than the conclusion that his brilliance makes him more to be mistrusted, since he is more likely to put his own ideas into Socrates' mouth. We might just as well argue that Xenophon's is the minimal portrait, and as such is more likely to be true than any exaggerated and larger-than-life portrait.

Others argue, more plausibly, that *both* portraits are correct. Guthrie puts this point of view well (*Socrates*, p. 9):

> He [Socrates] was a complex character, who did not and could not reveal every side of himself equally to all his acquaintances, since by reason of their own intellectual powers and inclinations they were not all equally capable of observing and appreciating them. If, then, the accounts of, say, Plato and Xenophon seem to present a different type of man, the chances are that each by itself is not so much wrong as incomplete, that it tends to exaggerate certain genuine traits and minimize others equally genuine, and that to get an idea of the whole man we must regard them as complementary.

In other words, the practical, conservative Xenophon, whose professed aim was to defend Socrates against the charges brought against him, highlights the prudential, conservative side of Socrates; the brilliant, philosophical Plato brings out this side of Socrates. Even a great philosopher is not always a philosopher; he will also give more practical advice and homilies to his friends: this is the Socrates Xenophon shows us. We glimpse in Xenophon the side of Socrates that Plato develops; but largely Xenophon deals with aspects of Socrates in which Plato has little interest.

The accuracy of this approach, however, is bound to be a question of degree: both portraits cannot be correct in all their details, because some details are contradictory. Apart from philosophical contradictions (we have already noted one), there are contradictions in the fine detail. A trivial example springs to mind: Plato's Socrates, like the Taoist sage, has no desire to leave the city and only does so when compelled by military service (*Phaedrus*, 230d), whereas in *The Estate-manager* Xenophon's Socrates sings the praises of a healthy life in the country. Once we start admitting that both portraits cannot be right in all details, it is impossible to know where to draw the line. And once we start dismissing the details, we are left with the view that neither portrait is correct, except at the most general level. This is the view to which I now turn.

For obvious reasons, the possibility that neither Xenophon's nor Plato's (nor Aristophanes', nor Aristotle's, etc.) portrait is correct has not been highly favoured. Nobody *wants* Socrates to become more invisible; but if that is the case, then we have to face it. Those who have taken this view, however, have invariably done so from a position of despair; I think, however, that we can be more positive.

We can begin by reminding ourselves of some facts. First, Xenophon certainly put his own military, agricultural and hunting expertise into Socrates' mouth; similarly, Plato in his later dialogues certainly put his own philosophical notions into Socrates' mouth. Is there any good reason to think that Plato was not doing the same in his earlier dialogues? On the contrary, there are good reasons for thinking that he was. I have already said that *Sokratikoi logoi* constituted a genre of literature: since the surviving examples of the genre present us with startlingly different portraits of Socrates, and since the majority of the surviving examples (Xenophon's work and Plato's later dialogues) are clearly fictional, or 'factional' – to use the modern term for a blend of fact and fiction – then there is good reason for supposing that the remainder of the genre (Plato's early dialogues) was equally 'factional' – that this was the nature of the genre.[1] A parallel is provided by Xenophon's other biographical works – *Agesilaus* and *Cyropaedia* – which are so eulogistic that no one denies they are 'faction'. We mustn't suppose that our own more scrupulous standards of biographical accuracy apply to the seeds of biography at the start of the fourth century BC.[2]

We must similarly shed our modern preconceptions before we can understand the next point. Nobody supposes that Plato and Xenophon were actually present at all or even the majority of the Socratic conversations they describe. But Xenophon, at any rate, does claim to have been present at some (see also p. 58). One of them, however, he certainly could not have attended. At the beginning of *The Dinner-party*, he claims to have been present, but since the dramatic date of this dialogue is 422 BC, when Xenophon was eight years old at the most, he could not have been. The statement 'I was there' is often a literary flourish, to reassure the reader of the accuracy of what follows: it is a lie by our modern standards, but not by those of ancient Greece. I am not saying that Plato and Xenophon were not present at *any* of the conversations they report; but I am saying that the facts make it safer to regard their works as quasi-fictional accounts – 'What Socrates might have said' rather than 'What Socrates actually said'. And as soon as the modality of 'might' is allowed to enter, it is clear that we are dealing with subjective portraits rather than hard and true likenesses. In this context it must also not be

1. Aristotle, it should be noted, classifies *Sokratikoi logoi* with types of poetry (*Poetics*, 1447b), as if it were poetic prose: this becomes significant when one remembers that in Aristotle's view it was the job of poetry to be fictional.
2. Or – an interesting parallel – that our standards of historical accuracy apply to ancient historiographers either: see A. J. Woodman, *Rhetoric in Classical Historiography* (Croom Helm/Areopagitica Press, 1988).

forgotten that both Plato and Xenophon are partisan followers of Socrates.

We can illustrate the subjective nature of the portraits as follows. We are fortunate to have not only Plato's and Xenophon's accounts of what Socrates said on luck, but also that of another writer in the genre, Aeschines of Sphettus. Plato's occurs at *Euthydemus*, 279c–280a; Xenophon's at *Memoirs*, 3.9.14–15; and Aeschines' in Fragment 8a. The reader will by now probably not be surprised to learn that there is little immediate unanimity. Plato's Socrates denies the existence of luck altogether: 'In every walk of life, then,' he says, 'wisdom causes luck.' Xenophon's Socrates conventionally describes luck as totally random. Aeschines' Socrates says that luck comes from the gods, but is not random: it is one of the gods' ways of rewarding good men.

No doubt one could argue for a reconciliation between these views, but that is precisely the point: the reconciliation would have to be at a higher, more general level than the particular ideas we find expressed in our sources.

To proceed by means of analogy, suppose we assume, for the sake of argument, that the basic function of law is to preserve organized communities. It is evident that a wide variety of secondary rules can fulfil this primary function and that the differences between these rules can range from the trivial to the profound. Some communities choose to drive on the right, some on the left; some choose to execute certain classes of criminal, some do not. Even while communities may agree on the basic function of law (principle), they may disagree over their rules (applied principle).

In order to make sense of the idea that neither Plato's nor Xenophon's portrait of Socrates is correct, we need only assume that Socrates taught principle rather than applied principle. This seems to me to make sense of the disagreements that we find between our sources for Socrates' work. Socrates' followers took the principles that Socrates taught and applied them; on this level of applied principle there is room for disagreement, and yet any or all of Socrates' followers, even while disagreeing, may still claim that they are true Socratics. There is some evidence for arguments between Socrates' followers: we know, for instance, that Antisthenes wrote an abusive dialogue against Plato. Plato had argued that the denial of the possibility of contradiction was self-defeating (see, for example, *Euthydemus*, 283e–288a); Antisthenes, who denied the possibility of contradiction, wrote his dialogue in reply.

This thesis, if correct, would lead to an interesting methodology for recovering Socrates' ideas. Wherever possible, we would have to consider what his followers said on any issue, and then generalize what they said to discover the underlying principle. Needless to say, the results of such a methodology will always be speculative. Let us consider the subject of pleasure. We have a pretty good idea of what several Socratics said about pleasure, and so, inasmuch as they disagree with one another on this issue, rather than arguing that one of them is right and the others wrong, we might be able to uncover a basic Socratic principle about pleasure.

In brief, Plato presents Socrates as an out-and-out hedonist (*Protagoras*, 351b–357e): wherever the word 'good' is used with human reference, 'pleasant' could be substituted, and wherever 'bad' is used, 'distressful' could be substituted. Xenophon presents Socrates as a modified, moral hedonist (see, for example, *Memoirs*, 1.3.5–7, 1.6.4–10, 2.1.21–33, 4.5). Xenophon's Socrates takes precisely the position which Protagoras in Plato's dialogue tries to take, but is argued down by Socrates – that some pleasures are good, but some are bad. For Xenophon's Socrates, good pleasures are those which arise from moral, self-disciplined activity, and bad pleasures are the opposite. It is more difficult to recover the views of other Socratics, but we can be fairly sure of the following. Antisthenes was vehemently anti-hedonistic; he comes close to Xenophon's Socrates when he says in *The Dinner-party* (4.39) that his asceticism affords him greater pleasure than indulgence, but he adds a rider that he could wish that this were not so, since so much pleasure cannot be good for one. Later sources report Antisthenes as claiming that the only worthwhile pleasures are those derived from hard work, or even that he would rather go mad than feel pleasure. At any rate, it is clear that not only does Antisthenes not take pleasure to be the goal of life, but it is not even a yardstick of the goal of life, as it is for Xenophon's Socrates. As for Aristippus, it is difficult to separate his views on pleasure from those of later hedonists who claimed his authority. It is probable that he did not go as far as saying that a life of indulgent luxury was best, but that the views attributed to him at *Memoirs*, 2.1, are closer: that avoidance of trouble of any kind is pleasant and is the goal of life.

Here then are four opinions on pleasure attributed to Socrates. Can we recover Socrates' actual views on the matter?

There is little doubt that it was a Socratic principle that the goal of life, whatever it may be, must be beneficial to oneself as a human being. This raises a number of questions, such as what it is to be a human being, and what is beneficial for such a being. Now suppose, as regards the latter, Socrates had suggested that pleasure and its lack are natural or god-given guidelines as to what is beneficial for a person. This principle, or something like it, I believe, is what we are looking for. It is open to interpretation whether pleasure is understood as itself the goal of life, or rather as a concomitant of the goal of life; it is open to interpretation whether all or only some pleasures are worth pursuing; it is even possible to interpret the principle as denying that the goal of life is accompanied by pleasure at all.

This view of Socrates as concerned only with the higher principles runs the risk of making him out to be a pontificating dogmatist. I am not claiming, however, that Socrates spent the whole time teaching in this way. Both Plato and Xenophon show him questioning most of the time, and that no doubt was his main activity. The advantage of questioning is that, if carried out consistently, it encourages others to think for themselves – to make up their minds about their own views. This is one reason, surely, why his followers came up with so many different applications of Socratic principles.

Another reason – less historical, more philosophical – why one need not think that Socrates spent the thirty or forty years of his mission spouting dogma is connected with the general nature of the principles he espoused. Because they are general, they have far more potential: they do not close doors by giving answers, but open them by being capable of being spelled out in many different ways. Hence, the picture of a dogmatic Socrates is wrong even if he did pronounce principles, because principles, as defined here, cannot be dogma. Moreover, such is the power of principle that someone like Socrates need not enunciate very many to generate a lot of philosophical discussion – not only enough for the thirty or forty years of his mission, but also enough for the next two and a half thousand years, so far! Socrates has often been compared with Jesus, but never, as far as I know, in this respect: principle has the power to change the ways in which people think. Both Jesus and Socrates, in their respective ways, used principle to such effect.[1] What I am trying to express here is not just the truism that ideas are powerful, but that certain ideas – 'general principles' – can be called creative: they open things up and allow the minds of those who are receptive to them to expand into *new* areas, rather than merely to reformulate old areas.

My view, therefore, is that Socrates taught 'principles' and these principles may be recoverable by a judicious abstraction from the extant Socratic texts. I should make it clear how this position differs from that of W. K. C. Guthrie (see p. 19), since it could quite easily collapse into Guthrie's view. Guthrie argues that details of thought found in the Socratic writings are attributable to the 'historical' Socrates. I believe, however, that few, if any, of the details are so attributable; where they are, it is because those details are in fact principles. Guthrie's methodology is bound to be subjective, especially where there are contradictions between details found in different Socratic writers: 'This detail

1. The innovatory impulse of Socrates' work is often brought out by writers on the subject, but perhaps nowhere so eloquently as by Bruno Snell, *The Discovery of Mind in Greek Philosophy and Literature* (Dover Publications, Inc., 1982).

strikes me as Socratic, so I'll accept it; that one does not, so I'll reject it.' A methodology which attempts to abstract Socratic principle out of the Socratic writers, however, could be more objective. It could not only provide guidelines for Guthrie's methodology, but also account for the varying portraits of Socrates we receive in the different Socratics.

As I have already said, however, certainty is impossible – and perhaps there is a sense in which historical certainty is unnecessary with figures like Socrates. To continue the parallel with Jesus, there are contradictions both of detail and of general portrait between the Gospels (consider, for instance, the different accounts of his birth and his last words on the cross); but people who initiate events are what they become. From this point of view, while the argument outlined above has the consequence that the 'true' Socrates starts to fade into invisibility, it might still be said that the 'true' Socrates is the Socrates we see in Plato and Xenophon, despite and because of all the differences between the two portraits. But my conclusion, and my warning to the reader, is that you are more likely to learn about Xenophon in the following pages than about Socrates.

SOCRATES' DEFENCE

TRANSLATED AND INTRODUCED BY ROBIN WATERFIELD

INTRODUCTION

It seems a good idea to begin a presentation of Xenophon's Socratic works with his *Socrates' Defence*, for two reasons. First, I suspect it is the earliest of Xenophon's Socratic writings. Second, it creates the opportunity to discuss the charges which were brought against Socrates at his trial; since it is Xenophon's express purpose in his Socratic writings, especially *Memoirs*, to defend his mentor against these charges, it helps us to be aware of them from the start.

Socrates' Defence is a rather scrappy little work, but not without interest. It inevitably invites comparison with Plato's work of the same title (usually known as the *Apology of Socrates*). The comparison, however, does nothing to improve one's impression of Xenophon's piece. Plato is eloquent and often, in a wry, ironical fashion, extremely funny; he is also highly interesting philosophically. Xenophon lacks these qualities. Plato's work is longer, but has a narrower scope: he presents a version only of Socrates' speech at the trial. Xenophon's piece, however, falls into three parts: (a) Socrates' thoughts immediately before the trial; (b) some of Socrates' speeches at the trial; (c) Socrates' behaviour after the trial. The style, in common with much of Xenophon's Socratic work, is anecdotal and eulogistic: it is a pamphlet rather than a philosophical tract.

To describe Xenophon's work as inferior to Plato's in these respects is not to say that his version of what Socrates said is necessarily less accurate than Plato's. Indeed, the very qualities which make Plato's *Apology* marvellous reading give us cause to doubt its historical accuracy. Xenophon was not in Athens at the time of the trial in 399 (see p. 5), but he takes more than the usual care to assure the reader that he is being accurate by constantly referring to Hermogenes, his source for the information. However, Xenophon's report of Socrates' speech at the trial is too brief and too full of Xenophontic themes to inspire confidence, and we must look to coincidences between his and Plato's accounts for any hope of historical accuracy.

These points of coincidence are as follows:[1]

1 That the charges brought against Socrates were as Xenophon states (compare Plato, *Apology*, 24b–c; and p. 32).
2 That Socrates did not prepare a speech for the trial (compare Plato, *Apology*, 17c; if this is historical, then the eloquence and rhetorical flourishes in Plato's version are clearly Platonic).
3 That, in some form or other, 'the divine' – Socrates' inner voice – implied that he would benefit from the trial (compare Plato, *Apology*, 40a–c, 41d).
4 That Socrates attributed part of the indictment to the fact that 'the divine' communicated with him (compare Plato, *Apology*, 39c).
5 That Socrates thought it better for him to die when he did (compare Plato, *Apology*, 41d).
6 That Socrates referred to Chaerephon's consultation of the Delphic oracle about him (compare Plato, *Apology*, 20e–21a).
7 That Socrates engaged in dialogue with Meletus in the course of the trial (compare Plato, *Apology*, 24c–28a).
8 That Socrates refused, or all but refused, to propose a counter-penalty (compare Plato, *Apology*, 36b–37a).
9 That Socrates refused to escape from prison (compare Plato, *Crito*).

1. I find unconvincing the attempts to show that Xenophon's *Defence* is dependent on Plato's *Apology*: there are far too many discrepancies, and even the points of similarity receive different treatment and are better explained otherwise than by dependency.

10 That Socrates insisted that he had never wronged anyone (compare Plato, *Aplogy*, 37a, for instance).

11 That Socrates made some reference to the view that those about to die gain prophetic powers (compare Plato, *Apology*, 39c).

12 That Socrates compared himself to the legendary hero Palamedes (compare Plato, *Apology*, 41b).

It is chiefly the brevity and scrappiness of Xenophon's *Defence* that lead me to regard it as the earliest of his Socratic writings. There are no hard and fast objective criteria for this view, however. The following facts are relevant, but not conclusive evidence. First, there are echoes in *Memoirs* of *Defence* (but which echoes which?); in particular, whole sentences of *Defence* are repeated more or less verbatim in *Memoirs*, 4.8. Second, *Memoirs*, 1.1–2, constitutes a far more polished defence of Socrates. Third, *Memoirs*, 1.1–2, has as its target not just the charges brought against Socrates at his trial, but also (and perhaps mainly) a pamphlet written in *c.* 392 by a certain Polycrates,[1] in which a broader range of charges were brought against him. These factors incline me to think that it is an early piece, but we must take into account the fact that Xenophon refers to other versions of Socrates' defence (1), and to the death of Anytus, one of Socrates' accusers (31).[2] These things considered, we could tentatively date it to around 394. I believe that it is quite plausible to see *Defence* as a kind of trial run; it may not have started out as such, but may none the less have led Xenophon to conceive of defending Socrates on a grander scale, especially once he got hold of Polycrates' pamphlet. It is possible that *Defence* was not intended for publication in any formal sense, but, rather, to be

1. A.-H. Chroust's book, *Socrates, Man and Myth: The Two Socratic Apologies of Xenophon* (Routledge & Kegan Paul, 1957) is often not to be trusted; but it does include a reasonable and detailed reconstruction of Polycrates' pamphlet (pp. 69–100).
2. I assume, therefore, that the Anytus mentioned at Lysias, 22.7, and therefore alive in the mid-380s, is not our Anytus. We do in fact know of six different people with this name between 445 and 329.

read aloud to friends and visitors (see p. 7). Its date of composition (assuming I am correct) coincides with the time when Xenophon was fighting for Sparta, and must therefore have been at the height of his unpopularity in Athens (see p. 7): he can hardly have hoped that his work would be widely circulated in Athens, although if it was intended for publication, Athenians must have been meant to be its primary audience, since Xenophon wanted to make them regret having executed Socrates.

The other issue that claims our attention is the charges against Socrates at his trial. Needless to say, these have been much discussed, and little of what I have to say on the matter is original.[1] In *Defence* Xenophon says that the charges were as follows: Socrates was accused of 'not recognizing the gods recognized by the State, but introducing new deities, and corrupting the young'. This version could make it sound as though the way in which Socrates corrupted the young was by his religious non-conformism; but the other versions we have of the charges (Xenophon, *Memoirs*, 1.1.1; Plato, *Apology*, 24b–c; Diogenes Laertius, 2.40)[2] make it clear that there are two separate, but interrelated, main charges: religious non-conformism, and corrupting the young.

Almost inevitably, those who write about Socrates often attempt to whitewash him and claim that he could not have been guilty. However, among the shifting sands of all the issues surrounding Socrates, the hard facts stand out that he *was* indicted and found guilty. Of course, justice is not always done in

1. I cannot claim to have read all the available literature, but among what I have read the following can be recommended: R. E. Allen, *Socrates and Legal Obligation* (University of Minnesota Press, 1980); K. J. Dover, 'The Freedom of the Intellectual in Greek Society', *Talanta*, 7 (1976), pp. 24–54; M. I. Finley, 'Socrates and Athens', in *Aspects of Antiquity* (Chatto & Windus, 1968). I do not, of course, agree with everything all these writers say.
2. Diogenes Laertius, despite writing late in the third century AD, is a valuable independent witness, and claims to preserve the original wording of the official indictment. Note also that the better version of the charges, in *Memoirs*, again suggests that *Defence* is earlier.

lawcourts: juries can be swayed and the legal system may not be beyond reproach. But I do not propose to defend Socrates because I find it difficult to define guilt in a vacuum outside the society in question; we are left with the fact that Socrates was tried and found guilty according to the due process of Athenian law.

The only trouble with assuming that Socrates was guilty is that it is difficult to know why he was guilty. Plato's and Xenophon's portraits appear to give us no reason to convict Socrates on these charges (or on any others). Where religion is concerned, Plato's Socrates scarcely touches on the subject, except, as might be expected, in *Apology*. Xenophon's Socrates has interesting things to say (*Memoirs*, 1.4, 4.3), but they are views about the traditional gods, not 'new deities'. Neither Plato's brilliant philosopher nor Xenophon's moral conservative could easily be said to have corrupted anyone. Either Plato and Xenophon are involved in a massive cover-up, or there were factors peculiar to Athenian State religion which make Socrates guilty as charged. We can only hope that the former alternative is not the case, since Plato's and Xenophon's accounts are practically our only evidence on Socrates' views.

In order to make the following discussion clearer, I shall break the charges down into: (1a) not recognizing the gods recognized by the State; (1b) introducing new deities; (2) corrupting the young.

(1a) *Not recognizing the gods*

There is important background to sketch in. In short, Greek State religion required the performance and avoidance of certain actions, but, unlike a religion such as Christianity, there were few tenets of belief by which one could accuse someone of being heterodox: orthodoxy is not a Greek religious notion. So this would be an extremely difficult charge on which to secure conviction. Moreover, our surviving evidence is that Socrates did perform and avoid the proper actions.

It is clear, then, that the brunt of the charge of religious non-conformism lies in introducing new deities (1b) rather than in not recognizing the gods (1a): (1a) simply leads up to (1b). But before leaving (1a), we should note that the charge is couched in terms which would be highly emotive for an ancient Athenian. The Greek word translated 'recognize' ('acknowledge' would do just as well) is *nomizein*, a verb from the noun *nomos*, which means 'custom', 'law', 'convention', 'tradition' or even 'society'. *Nomos*, whether written down and codified as a legal system or present in the collective unconscious of the Athenian people, was the absolute foundation of Athenian society; and religion cannot be separated from the proper working of that society. By this I mean not just that religion pervaded it in the form of festivals, statues all over the city, and each individual's daily private and public worship of the gods, but also that each individual's worship was part of his duty as a citizen. By worshipping the gods according to *nomos*, the individual was keeping his community under the protection of the gods; and irreligion became a prosecutable offence because it threatened this link between the gods and the State.

(1b) *Introducing new deities*

It is also difficult to understand why the charge of introducing new deities was brought against Socrates. At the end of the fifth century, as often happens when a society is just beginning to undergo a transformation, Athens saw many new cults being introduced: not only were the superstitious aspects of folk religion resurrected, but the cults of Sabazios and Cybele, the Great Mother, both from the Middle East, and Bendis from Thrace, all either flourished or were introduced. Not only is there no suggestion that Socrates was involved in any such movement, but more importantly, these cults received official State recognition. Under these circumstances, how could Socrates or anyone be prosecuted for introducing new deities?

The only possible reason is Socrates' inner voice, which Xenophon introduces in the context of rebutting this charge (*Defence*, 12–13, *Memoirs*, 1.1.2–5), as does Plato, though more vaguely (*Apology*, 31c–d; see also *Euthyphro*, 3b). Socrates calls it *to daimonion*, 'the divine', and claims that it communicates with him. It communicates mainly by warning him if he is about to do something that is not to his advantage; it seems never to have told him what to do, but only what not to do (though that, of course, can lead one to know what to do). We should be wary of assimilating it too closely to our concept of 'conscience', if by that we mean a moral force, because Socrates' little voice appears to have no moral function, nor indeed to consider the future consequences of actions, but only to be an immediate intuition. The relevant references are: Xenophon, *Defence*, 12–13; *Memoirs*, 1.1.2–5, 4.3.12–13, 4.8.1, 4.8.5–6, 4.8.11; *Dinner-party*, 8.5; Plato, *Apology*, 31c–d, 40a–b, 41d; *Theages*, 128d–130e; *Alcibiades I*, 103a–b; *Euthydemus*, 272e; *Republic*, 496c; *Phaedrus*, 242b; *Theaetetus*, 151a.

Now, as we have already noted, both Plato's and Xenophon's versions of Socrates' defence agree that he attributed this part of the indictment to his belief that the divine communicated with him. We are, therefore, on reasonably safe ground in regarding this claim as historical fact. No doubt, in the nature of things, this belief of Socrates would not have been known to many people prior to the trial; but, during the trial, no doubt, the prosecutors could have made great play with it.

So, given Socrates' claim that the divine communicated with him, was he guilty as charged? Xenophon says no: he says that Socrates was doing no more or less than any conventional Greek who consulted oracles and diviners. I think, however, that the prosecutors here have a stronger case than Xenophon. We have seen that the *nomos* of State religion is founded on the belief that the good of the community is paramount. Socrates, however, was claiming not just to be specially favoured by the gods (as opposed to being just one member of the citizen body), but also that the communications he received were private and for his benefit alone (*Defence* 13, repeated at *Memoirs*, 1.1.4, is the only place in either Xenophon or Plato where the communications are said to be for the benefit of people other than Socrates himself, and I believe that here Xenophon is making a special plea in his eagerness to defend Socrates). To make matters worse, in a direct democracy like that of ancient Athens, it was every citizen's duty to play a part in politics – the system depended on this. Plato and Xenophon are forced to make great play with the few occasions on which Socrates did his civic duty; nevertheless, at *Apology*, 31d, Plato has Socrates admit that the divine stopped him from helping the State in this respect.

(2) *Corrupting the young*

Suppose, given what has already been said, that the prosecutors could plausibly argue that Socrates was subversive of State *nomos*. It would then be even easier for them to argue that he corrupted the young. Socrates gathered around himself a circle of rich (and therefore potentially influential) young men. I have discussed at length (pp. 22–6) the difficulty of knowing what the Socratic groups did; but certain facts are clear, and centre around a single, simple core. This is that he trained people to be individuals. We have seen how he claimed to be a special individual as far as the gods were concerned, but that is less than half the story. His questioning method was (and is) designed to get people to think for themselves and to prick the illusory conceit of knowledge. And what is the most common source for thinking that one knows something? It is *nomos*, the unwritten conditioning that any society imposes on its members. Since Socrates was particularly concerned with morality, which is the heart of *nomos*, he could easily be made out to be subversive: justice was regarded as a State issue, not a matter of private knowledge. Moreover, although Socrates' political views are as irrecoverable in detail as the rest of his views, it is clear that he had, or he inspired in his followers, little love for democracy (see p. 15). Any organization has reason to fear individuality (witness the Church and its heretics), and Athenian society in particular had a history of fearing tyranny and oligarchy.

In short, within the context of the restored democracy of 399, and within the context of Greek *nomos*, a good case could be made out that Socrates was guilty as charged. Presumably the prosecutors did make a good case, because Socrates was found guilty and condemned to death.

There were, almost certainly, subtexts to the trial – background factors which would have influenced its outcome. This seems inevitable, given the emotive nature of the charges. Thus we could make a distinction between 'formal' and 'informal' charges against Socrates, or, as Plato does, between the 'old' and the 'new' accusers.

The Athenian legal system was wide open to the covert entry of such subtexts. Socrates was tried by 501 of his peers (if Socrates can be said to have that many peers!): they constituted possibly 2.5 per cent of the total citizen body. A large number would have known about Socrates for many years, and made up their minds about him long ago; most of the others would have discussed him in the days immediately prior to the trial. And these people – the jurors – were also the judges: no separate judge presided over an Athenian lawcourt. Furthermore, there were no professional barristers (though there was a rising class of professional speech-writers). The State never prosecuted anyone: private individuals brought actions on behalf of the State, which was in itself a vague concept. Socrates' prosecutor was Meletus, backed by Anytus and Lycon. We have no certain knowledge concerning Meletus and Lycon,[1] but we do know that Anytus was a prominent democrat. If Arthur Scargill were to take anyone to court over any matter, that person would inevitably be seen as a political opponent.

In Socrates' trial, there were two main subtexts – one political, the other intellectual and religious. The political subtext has already been noted in passing, namely Athens' fear of individuals. Not only had being a member of Socrates' circle long been linked

1. Lycon is described as an 'orator' in Plato, *Apology*, 23e; on the question whether he is the Lycon who appears in Xenophon's *The Dinner-party*, see p. 221, n. 1. If our Meletus is the Meletus who prosecuted Andocides for impiety also in 399 BC, this may be significant: Meletus may have been a champion of traditional piety.

in Athenian minds with being pro-Spartan and oligarchic (see p. 6), but also Critias, Charmides and Alcibiades, at least, had at one time or another been, and been known to have been, members of Socrates' group. Critias was the prime mover of, and Charmides prominent in, the dreadful oligarchy of 404–403 only a few years previously. As for Alcibiades, the Athenians had a love–hate relationship with him: they felt that his undeniable talents could help them win the war, but were terrified lest his charisma, influence and egotism led him to autocracy. In *Memoirs*, 1.2.12–47, Xenophon defends Socrates' association with such people at great length. At the trial this could remain only a subtext because a general political amnesty had been granted in 403, of which Anytus himself was one of the promoters. Afterwards, however, the anti-Socratic literature exemplified by the pamphlet of Polycrates (see p. 31) brought the subtext out into the open. Fifty years later the orator Aeschines could say (1.173) that Socrates was killed 'because it was shown that he had educated Critias'.

The second subtext is intellectual and religious. Particularly because of the war, but more generally because society as a whole was in a period of transition, there was considerable questioning of the traditional values by a number of intellectuals. Yet, in any period of flux and insecurity, the majority cling for safety on to convention. Comic playwrights and orators were constantly harping on the corruption caused by the new intellectuals.[1] A revolution had occurred in education. Up until *c.* 450, *nomos* – one's parents and society – had been the teachers; but gradually (and peaking *c.* 420) professional teachers began to encroach. They taught those rich enough to pay their fees to argue, to govern, to speak in public as well as a host of more particular subjects ranging from music to martial arts. Inevitably, given the context, they also taught that *nomos* was relative, not absolute; and their teachings were thought to subvert the fabric of society.

1. For example Aristophanes, Fragment 490: 'He's been corrupted by a book or by Prodicus or some windbag or other.'

Here are two examples of this assault on conventional morality. Critias wrote a play in which one of the characters suggested that the gods were a human invention to keep people toeing the line. And in 415 most of the statues of Hermes, which overlooked every road junction in the city, were mutilated (the statues were ithyphallic, and probably had their phalluses broken off). This desecration was attributed to Alcibiades, who promptly went over to the Spartans (with catastrophic consequences for Athens in the war). Alcibiades was already under suspicion of having mocked the Eleusinian mysteries, which were central to Athenian State religion, by having imitated them in company with some friends.[1]

I have, of course, picked out the parts, or alleged parts, that Critias and Alcibiades played in this period of moral turmoil. There is, however, an enormous amount of other evidence that *nomos* was under fire, and that intellectuals were blamed for the attack. It is noticeable that both Meletus' remarks on pp. 45–6 stress *nomos*.

So the second subtext to Socrates' trial is that he became the butt on whom the Athenians vented their pent-up fury at the assault on *nomos*: despite later stories to the contrary, there had probably been no earlier trials of intellectuals, although a certain Diagoras of Melos was banned from the city for his atheism. Hence both Plato and Xenophon have Socrates defend himself against the implicit charge of being a sophist or a natural scientist (see also pp. 9–10). Not only was Socrates seen as a dangerous intellectual himself, but he was also seen as the teacher of other dangerous intellectuals. As few people were aware that Socrates actually taught people to think for themselves, the common Greek belief (but of course it is not only Greek) that anything a pupil says is attributable to the teacher was of significance.

In conclusion, I believe that Socrates was guilty as charged, but

1. Other acquaintances of Socrates were also implicated in one or both of these scandals; and Andocides, one of the mockers of the mysteries, who returned from exile to Athens under the general amnesty of 403, was also tried in 399, the same year as Socrates.

his condemnation was assisted by both political and moral subtexts in the trial. It follows that in so far as Xenophon portrays Socrates in *Defence* (and more especially in *Memoirs*) as a conventional moralist, he is whitewashing him. However, I do not believe he intended a cover-up. It is probably closer to the truth to say that, like all Socratics, as far as we can tell, the limitations of his own intellectual capacities and perceptions led him to see no more in Socrates than himself reflected.

In the context of differences between Socratics, we should note that one of the most striking differences between Xenophon's and Plato's Socrates occurs forcefully in *Defence*. Anyone coming to *Defence*, 5, who has met only Plato's Socrates will be astonished at the confidence – even arrogance – with which Socrates assesses his own importance. A similar difference occurs in the two versions of Chaerephon's consultation of the Delphic oracle. In Plato's *Apology*, the oracle says that there is no one wiser than Socrates, but Socrates interprets this as meaning that he is wisest because he alone knows that he is ignorant – in other words, the humblest man is the wisest; in Xenophon's version, however, the oracle declares that Socrates is 'the most free, upright and prudent of all people', and Socrates goes on to justify this with little sign of humility.

It is perhaps some slight mitigation of Xenophon's portrait in this regard that he expressly sets out in *Defence* to justify the 'arrogance' of Socrates' tone during his trial. He does this by explaining that it was due to Socrates' conviction that it was better for him to die at that time; given this, the selections he makes from Socrates' speech during the trial can be seen as being guided by the principle of illustrating precisely this arrogance.

One might legitimately think that the reason Plato gives for Socrates' conviction that death was preferable is more plausible than the reason Xenophon gives: Plato claims that Socrates did not wish to live if that entailed his being required to curb his philosophical mission; Xenophon more weakly claims that Socrates wished to avoid senility.

SOCRATES' DEFENCE

I think it is worth recording what Socrates thought about his defence and the end of his life, once he had been summoned for trial. Now, others have written about the trial, and they have all touched upon his arrogant tone;[1] so it is clear that this is how Socrates actually spoke. But what they didn't make clear – and without it the arrogance of his tone is bound to appear rather foolish – is this: he had already decided that for him death was preferable to life. However, Hermogenes the son of Hipponicus was a companion of Socrates and he has divulged information about him which shows that his haughtiness was in keeping with his thinking.[2]

Hermogenes reported that he noticed Socrates discussing anything rather than the trial, and that he said to him: 'Really, Socrates, ought you not to be considering your defence?'

Socrates at first replied: 'Don't you think that my whole life has been a preparation for my defence?'

'How?'

'Because I have consistently done no wrong, and this, I think, is the finest preparation for a defence.'

Hermogenes tried another tack: 'Don't you see that the Athenian courts have often been prevailed upon by argument to put

1. See, for example, Plato, *Apology of Socrates*, 35e–38b. The word translated 'arrogance' should ideally not carry too many negative connotations: the Greek word can simply imply 'talking from a high standpoint'.
2. There are verbal echoes of what follows in *Memoirs*, 4.8 (pp. 215–16). On the issue of which was written first, see pp. 31–2. See also pp. 197 and 330 for further echoes of this passage.

innocent men to death, and equally have often acquitted wrong-doers, either out of pity aroused by the speeches or because they've been flattered?'[1]

'Yes, but as a matter of fact,' he said, 'twice now, when I was trying to consider my defence, the divine opposed me.'[2]

'That's remarkable,' said Hermogenes and Socrates replied: 'Do you really think it's remarkable that God should decide that it is better for me to die now?[3] Don't you realize that up to now I would not have conceded to anyone that he had lived a better life than I? I mean, nothing could be more pleasant than knowing that I have lived my whole life respecting the gods and acting morally towards men. And not only has this integrity of mine caused me to be extremely proud of myself, but I have also found that my associates recognize it in me. Now, if my years are prolonged, I'm sure that I shall have to pay the penalties of old age: impaired vision and hearing, and increasing slowness at learning and forgetfulness of what I have learned. And if I am aware that I am deteriorating and find fault with myself, how could I live pleasantly then?

'Perhaps, you know,' he went on, 'God in his kindness may even have my interests at heart and be arranging for me to be released from life not only at exactly the right age, but also in the easiest way possible. For if I am condemned now, then obviously I will be able to die in a way which those who have studied the matter judge to afford not only the least discomfort, but also the least trouble to friends, and which most makes them miss those who have died. For when a person leaves behind in the minds of those around him no blot or ache, but passes away with a sound body and a mind capable of happiness, then it is inevitable that such a person will be missed, isn't it?

'The gods were right to oppose me,' he continued, 'and prevent

1. In the Athenian lawcourts, tactics to arouse pity became so blatant that they were made illegal not long after Socrates' trial. See also p. 195.
2. See pp. 34–6.
3. Notice how Socrates speaks throughout as if his death was inevitable, rather than dependent on the trial.

me from working on my speech, when we thought that we ought to find some way to secure my acquittal, whatever it took. Suppose I had achieved this goal: clearly the result would have been that instead of facing the cessation of life as I am now, I would have guaranteed for myself a death made burdensome by illness or old age – and old age is a pit into which flows everything which is intolerable and devoid of pleasure. I swear, Hermogenes,' he added, 'I will not go out of my way for that, especially since the alternative, as I see it, is that I will benefit at the hands of both gods and men; and if revealing the opinion I have of myself annoys the jurors, then I will be choosing to die rather than to remain alive without freedom and beg, as an alternative to death, a vastly inferior life.'[1]

Hermogenes reported that those were Socrates' thoughts and that therefore, when he was faced with his adversaries accusing him of not recognizing the gods recognized by the State, but introducing new deities, and corrupting the young, he came forward and said: 'You know, gentlemen, the first thing I find puzzling is what evidence Meletus[2] can be using to claim that I do not recognize the gods recognized by the State. For, leaving aside all the possible eyewitnesses, Meletus himself could, if he had chosen, have seen me sacrificing during the communal festivals and at the public altars. As for my claim that a divine voice comes to me and communicates what I must do, how in claiming this am I introducing new deities? Those who rely on bird-calls and the utterances of men[3] are, I suppose, receiving guidance from voices. Can there be any doubt that thunder has a voice or that it is an omen of the greatest significance? And take the priestess who sits on the tripod at Pytho[4] – doesn't she too use a voice to

1. Under Athenian law, in certain cases, including Socrates', the defendant had the right to propose an alternative penalty to that proposed by the prosecutors. This alternative might well be accepted by the court, if it was reasonable, but Socrates' proposal was so outrageous (Plato, *Apology of Socrates*, 35e–38b) that, as he says here, he deliberately courted death.
2. One of Socrates' accusers: see p. 37.
3. That is, men like prophets.
4. The district around Delphi, where Apollo's famous oracle was.

announce messages from the god? Moreover, that God[1] has knowledge of the future and communicates it in advance to whomever he wishes – this too, as I say, is a universal claim and belief. But whereas others state that it is birds and utterances and chance meetings and oracles which forewarn them, I call it divine, and I think that in using this description I am being both more accurate and more devout than those who ascribe the power of the gods to birds. Furthermore, I have evidence to show that I am not attributing things falsely to God: I have often told friends what God has advised and I have never been found to be wrong.'

There was uproar from the jurors at this speech: some of them didn't believe what he was saying, while others were jealous that he might have had more from the gods than they. So Socrates continued: 'Listen: if some of you are inclined to disbelieve that I have been honoured by deities, I can tell you more, to increase your disbelief. Once, when Chaerephon made an inquiry about me in Delphi, Apollo replied – and there were many witnesses – that I was the most free, upright and prudent of all people.'[2]

When there was, not surprisingly, even greater uproar from the jurors at these words, Socrates said: 'But, gentlemen, what Apollo said about me is less than what he pronounced in oracular utterances about Lycurgus, who established Sparta's laws.[3] The story goes that when Lycurgus entered the shrine, Apollo said to him: "I am considering whether to call you god or man." In my case, Apollo didn't liken me to a god, although he thought I by far outshone the rest of mankind.

'All the same, rather than just take the god's word for it, you

1. Despite their usual polytheism, the Greeks often spoke of 'God' in the singular as well, as if all the many gods were aspects of one God, or the divine, which is sometimes identified with Zeus.
2. Chaerephon was a devoted follower of Socrates. In his *Apology of Socrates*, Plato makes Apollo's reply to Chaerephon the impetus for Socrates' mission: he set out to test whether or not the god was right (and found that, in a sense, he was!).
3. Lycurgus' dates are uncertain, and he seems to belong as much to legend as to history. For a longer version of the oracle, see Herodotus, 1.65.

should analyse his statement and examine it. So, do you know anyone who is less of a slave to bodily desires than I am? Do you know anyone more free, since I accept no gratuities or payment from anyone? Could you plausibly regard anyone as more upright than the man who is so in tune with his immediate circumstances that he has no need of anything extraneous? Mustn't it be reasonable to describe me as wise, seeing that, ever since I began to understand speech, I have never stopped investigating and learning any good thing I could? Don't you think that the success of my efforts is proved by the fact that many Athenians and non-Athenians, who have made virtue their goal, choose to associate with me rather than anyone else? To what shall we attribute the fact that although everyone knows that repayment is entirely beyond my means, nevertheless people often want to give me something? What about the fact that there is not a single person to whom I owe a debt of service, but there are many people who admit that they are in my debt for services rendered? What about the fact that during the blockade,[1] although others were filled with self-pity, I was no worse off than when the city's prosperity was at its peak? What about the fact that while others acquire their shop-bought luxuries at a high price, I arrange for greater, mental luxuries at no cost at all? Suppose that all I've said about myself is irrefutably true: doesn't it follow that I deserve congratulations from gods and men alike?

'But do you still claim, Meletus, that I am corrupting the young by these practices? Now, we know, of course, what corruptions the young are liable to; so you tell me if you know of anyone who has stopped worshipping the gods because of me, or who has substituted arrogance for humility, or extravagance for economy, or drunkenness for moderate drinking, or flabbiness for exercise, or who has given in to any base indulgence because of me.'

'No,' said Meletus, 'but I most certainly know of those whom you have persuaded to listen to you rather than to their parents.'

1. Of Athens by Sparta in 405–404.

'I admit it,' said Socrates, 'at least where education is concerned; people know that I have made a special study of the matter. But when health is at stake, people listen to doctors rather than their parents, and when the Assembly meets,[1] all Athenians listen, as you know, to those speaking the best sense rather than to their relatives. Don't you, after all, elect as military commanders – in preference to your fathers, in preference to your brothers, and yes, even in preference to yourselves – those who you think know the most about military matters?'[2]

'True, Socrates,' said Meletus, 'since that is both to our advantage and in accordance with custom.'

'So don't you think it strange,' Socrates continued, 'that whereas those who are outstanding at other activities get not only appropriate compensation, but even conspicuous recognition, I am prosecuted by you on a capital charge because there are people who think I am an expert at education, which is the greatest of human goods?'

Now, obviously this was not all that he said, and his friends spoke on his behalf too. But I have not been concerned to report all the details of the trial; I am satisfied with having made it clear that, although Socrates considered it of crucial importance that he was neither irreligious towards gods nor did he give the slightest impression of being unjust towards men, he still did not believe that he should beg to be allowed to live; but indeed thought that the time had come for him to die. That this was his point of view became even clearer when the verdict went against him. In the first place, when he was told to propose a counter-penalty,[3] he both refused to do so himself and forbade his friends to do so either, but claimed that to propose a counter-penalty would be an

1. In the Athenian democratic system, there were two main organs of the people: the Council of 500 members annually chosen by lot from the ten tribes into which citizens were divided, and the Assembly, which every male citizen over eighteen could attend. The Council debated and prepared the Assembly's agenda.
2. Military command was at least partly a political post at Athens and was therefore subject to annual election.
3. See p. 43, n. 1.

admission of guilt. In the second place, when his friends wanted to get him secretly away, he refused to go, but instead seemed to make fun of them, asking them whether they knew of some spot beyond Attica's borders which was inaccessible to death!

At the end of the trial, he said: 'Well, gentlemen, there are two sets of people who must be conscious in themselves of a high degree of impiety and injustice – those who instructed the witnesses that they must, though under oath, testify falsely against me and those who were prevailed upon to do so; but as for me, why should I have a lower opinion of myself now than I did before the guilty verdict? After all, it has not been proved that I committed any of the crimes mentioned in the indictment. It has not been shown that I sacrifice to any new deities, or swear by them, or recognize other deities instead of Zeus and Hera and their divine companions. Moreover, how could I corrupt the young by making endurance and economy second nature to them? Death is the prescribed penalty for acts such as temple-robbery, burglary, enslavement and high treason, but even my adversaries do not accuse me of any of these deeds. So I am left wondering how on earth you gained the impression that any action I have done merited the death penalty.

'Nor should the injustice of my death cause me to have a lower opinion of myself, for the shame falls not on me but on those who condemned me. The example of Palamedes, whose death was similar to mine, encourages me to think like this: for even now he inspires far greater eulogies than Odysseus, who unjustly put him to death.[1] I have no doubt that the future, just as the past has done, will attest that I never wronged or harmed anyone, but benefited those I conversed with by freely teaching them any good thing I could.'

After this speech he was led away; his features, the way he held

1. Palamedes was a Greek hero at Troy against whom Odysseus contrived a charge of treason, because Palamedes had exposed Odysseus' attempt to evade military service. The Palamedes myth of a wronged innocent had been boosted in the fifth century by plays by Aeschylus and Euripides and a rhetorical defence by the sophist Gorgias of Leontini.

himself and the way he walked were all cheerful, which was in keeping, of course, with what he'd said. When he saw tears on the faces of those who accompanied him, he said: 'What's this? You're crying *now*? You should have realized long ago that ever since I was born I have been condemned to death by my nature. As it is, either I am facing death while blessings are still pouring in on me, in which case I and my friends obviously ought to be distressed; or I am being released from life when troubles are in store for me, in which case I think you should all be glad at my good fortune.'

One of those present was Apollodorus, who was a great devotee of Socrates, but was not particularly bright. He said, 'But the most difficult thing for me to bear, Socrates, is that I see you being unjustly put to death.' Socrates (as the story goes) stroked Apollodorus' head and replied with a smile: 'You're a good friend, Apollodorus, but would you rather see me put to death justly or unjustly?'

Socrates is also said to have spotted Anytus[1] passing by and to have said: 'Well, here is a man who is swaggering as if he had achieved something important and excellent: he is having me put to death because when I saw that he was under consideration by the State for the most important offices, I suggested that he oughtn't to educate his son in a tannery.[2] He's in a bad way because he apparently doesn't realize that, of the two of us, the one whose achievements are the more beneficial and excellent is the victor, and will remain so for all time.

'Moreover,' he went on, 'according to Homer, some people at the end of their lives have foreknowledge of the future.[3] I too want to make a prophecy. My brief acquaintance with Anytus' son led me to believe that he was a person of some calibre: therefore, my prediction is that he will not remain in the servile occupation his father has arranged for him; but because there is no

1. One of Socrates' accusers: see p. 37.
2. Tanning was the family business.
3. See, for example, *Iliad*, 16.851–61.

one of principle to take him in hand, he will succumb to some base motivation and make considerable progress as a degenerate.'

This prediction of his was quite right: the young man became an alcoholic, spent his days as well as his nights drinking, and finally became utterly worthless to his country, his friends and himself.[1] So Anytus, even though dead, has acquired a bad reputation – for bringing up his son badly as well as for his heartlessness.

Socrates was so arrogant in court that he invited the jurors' ill-will and more or less forced them to condemn him. Anyway, it seems to me that his fate was proper to one loved by the gods, because he both avoided the most difficult part of life and gained the easiest of deaths. His fortitude was obvious: since he had decided that death was better for him than further life, he showed no weakness in the face of death (just as he had never turned his back on any other good thing either), but awaited it cheerfully and discharged his final duty in good spirits.

When I consider how wise the man was, and how high-minded, I am bound to remember him; and when I remember him, I am bound to admire him. If anyone in his search for virtue has encountered a more helpful person than Socrates, then he deserves, in my opinion, to be called the most fortunate of all men.

1. These are awful crimes in Xenophon's view: see pp. 59–61.

one competent to take him in hand, he will fall into some base propensity and make considerable progress towards degeneracy.'

[illegible]

MEMOIRS OF SOCRATES

TRANSLATED BY HUGH TREDENNICK
TRANSLATION REVISED AND INTRODUCED BY
ROBIN WATERFIELD

INTRODUCTION

The *Memoirs of Socrates* is Xenophon's major Socratic work. It is divided into four books of roughly equal length, which portray Socrates either conversing with one interlocutor after another or (infrequently) delivering a homily. There are signs of some organization of the material. For instance, 1.1–2 makes a suitable introduction, and 4.8 a fitting epilogue; the second book is dedicated to showing Socrates dealing with his acquaintances' personal problems and affairs; the first seven sections of the third book are devoted to public and military matters. But otherwise, the reader is often asked to jump from topic to topic, and from style to style, as he or she moves from one section to the next. Sometimes the lack of order is disconcerting. For instance, 4.2, 3, 5 and 6 show Socrates in conversation with one of his followers, Euthydemus. 4.2 is a good introduction to this sequence, since it shows how Socrates attracted Euthydemus in the first place; 4.3, 5 and 6 could come in any order, since they merely show Socrates at work on various topics, and 'Euthydemus' is a stand-in for any of his followers. But the four sections all belong together, so why are they interrupted by 4.4, which is a conversation with Hippias, the sophist from Elis?[1] It may well be that the arrangement was not the work of Xenophon himself, but some later editor, who collated the anecdotes. But even if we were to rearrange the material (by theme, say), it would still read somewhat like a literary lucky dip.

1. It has been suggested that 4.4 is spurious, but the fact that it interrupts the Euthydemus sequence is inadequate evidence of this, given the lack of order of the rest of the *Memoirs*.

This feature of the work makes it impossible to date. It is quite possible that anecdotes were jotted down by Xenophon at widely different times. However, as I have remarked elsewhere, the crusading nature of the work – to defend Socrates – argues that it was intended for publication. If so, there is nothing to prevent it having been published in two parts: Books 1 and 2 are more overtly defensive of Socrates than the last two books. Books 3 and 4 are more organized and contain more signs of borrowing from Plato; and 4.3 effectively repeats 1.4. So perhaps the first two books were published separately from the last two. That either the whole or some parts of *Memoirs* were written relatively late in Xenophon's life (which again suggests historical unreliability: see pp. 21, 57–9) is shown by a singular anachronism. In 3.5 Socrates is seen conversing with the younger Pericles. This is not impossible (see p. 145, n. 1), but the background to the conversation is formed by a military event which occurred long after both Socrates' and Pericles' deaths: the Boeotians are threatening Attica's northern borders. In 3.5.4 Pericles comments that the Boeotians used not to dare to face the Athenians without Spartan support: this is a reasonably accurate summary of the situation in the Peloponnesian War when Socrates and Pericles were alive. Pericles goes on, however, to say that now the Boeotians are prepared to attack by themselves. This is only relevant to the situation *c.* 370–362 after the battle of Leuctra (371), when Epaminondas' Boeotian army decimated the Spartans and established Theban supremacy in southern Greece. Thebes then remained a severe threat to Athens until Epaminondas' death in 362.[1]

I have advanced the thesis (pp. 17–21) that Xenophon's Socratic works can be described as quasi-fictional. Some slight qualification now needs to be made by comparing *Memoirs* (and *Defence* and *The Dinner-party*) with *The Estate-manager*. The latter work

1. Xenophon had good reason to remember this, since his son Gryllus had died fighting for Athens against Boeotia in 362.

is more obviously fictional than the others. The biographical trimmings of *The Estate-manager* are hardly prominent, and Xenophon was, one hopes, not intending to fool anyone about the historicity of the conversations he records there. The biographical element, however, of *Memoirs* is more important. Although there are overt anachronisms and Socrates discusses topics which were undoubtedly closer to Xenophon's heart than his, there is a residuum of genuine Socratic material (see, for example, pp. 12–17). Above all, by the very variety of the anecdotes, Xenophon presents us with a picture of Socrates at work: this is the strength of what I have called the 'lucky-dip' nature of the work. We see Socrates conversing with a varied sample (excluding the very lowest classes) of types of people in Athens at the time: sophists, politicians, military leaders, artisans, businessmen – even on one occasion a courtesan. As well, there are his loyal followers. We are encouraged by this variety to imagine Socrates haunting the public places of Athens, casually dressed and shoeless, being sought out by some, and himself seeking others.

However, Xenophon does not present us with a *vivid* picture. It is I who have to tell you to imagine Socrates in the agora; Xenophon, at the most, merely encourages us to do so. One of the charms of Plato's Socratic writings is that he often makes the locations real and characters come alive as flesh-and-blood actors in a philosophical drama. Xenophon's characters, however, are more often stooges for Socrates' moral earnestness; and, no matter to whom he is talking, Socrates' tone and method of approach change very little. But Xenophon's defects are self-evident, and it is far easier to condemn than to praise.[1] A great

1. The most extreme condemnation I have come across is by H. J. Rose (*A Handbook of Greek Literature*, 4th edn (Methuen, 1951), pp. 305–9), who in the space of a few pages dismisses Xenophon in excessively severe terms: Xenophon has 'a mind which it would be flattery to call second-rate'; the *Cyropaedia* is 'one of the dullest writings in any tongue'; Ischomachus in *The Estate-manager* is 'a prig of the first water'; as for *Memoirs*: 'it is surprising how little is made of its fascinating subject' and 'the reader is very apt to find the four books much too long'.

many intellectual writers find that well-rounded phrases trip easily off the tongue in disparagement, whereas praise sounds somewhat insipid. So here, to correct the balance, are some examples from *Memoirs* of Xenophon at his best.

Memoirs, 1.1–2, whatever one may think about its historicity or the picture it presents of Socrates, constitutes a well-constructed defence. The charges – whether those of the trial or those of Polycrates – are clearly stated, and the refutation of each point is also lucid and relevant. In fact, nobody accuses Xenophon of lack of clarity; rather, his weakness is to overdo it – he tends to lack subtlety (but see below), is over-fond of repetition to get a point across, and presents us with a portrait of Socrates that is so easy to digest that it may seem bland.

Xenophon does not always lack subtlety, however. There is, for example, his nicely muted humour in 2.7. Aristarchus is depressed because of his financial difficulties: the civil war means that he is supporting a large number of refugee relatives, but has no income and cannot raisc a loan. Socrates suggests that he put his relatives to work to create an income; he points out that a number of traders are doing well despite the war. The humour here lies in the obvious practical soundness of the advice, which Aristarchus had failed to think of as a solution to his problems. Aristarchus is an aristocrat: he expects a ready-made income from his estates, and that is why he had not thought of this solution himself. His attitude resembles the British aristocracy's traditional attitude towards 'trade' and the *nouveaux riches*; trade is *infra dig* and it is unthinkable that one would do it oneself. Socrates gently pricks this conceit and makes Aristarchus wish to emulate traders. The underlying more serious point is that, when it comes to the crunch, aristocrats are no different from artisans. Furthermore, it is interesting to note how, although Xenophon is not in this passage overtly defending Socrates against any of the charges against him, none the less he does place him in the Piraeus at a time when this was a democratic stronghold – a clever, indirect rebuttal of the accusations that Socrates was an oligarch. Thus Xenophon's defence of Socrates is not always crudely obvious; other elements of the defence are taken in subconsciously by the reader.

So 2.7 portrays Xenophon's Socrates as having the provocative sense of humour which we find more obviously in Plato. It is possible, without too much effort, to take quite a few of the dialogues in this vein. The trouble is that the frequent ponderousness of Xenophon's style tends to obscure such humour. But sometimes the pricking of conceits is overt, as when Socrates is dealing with the pretensions of would-be military leaders (3.1, 3.4) or Glaucon's political aspirations (3.6).

Memoirs, 3.6, shows that Xenophon is also occasionally capable of accomplished characterization. Under Socrates' ironic prodding, Glaucon moves from vanity to evasiveness born of uncertainty, and finally to realization of the enormity of the task he faces and his own inadequacy. He cannot even manage his uncle's household, so how does he expect to manage the whole city? Again, of course, there is an underlying serious point – that Athenian politics requires knowledge and expertise, and not another amateur demagogue. Other good examples of characterization of the interlocutor are 2.1 (Aristippus), 3.11 (Theodote) and 4.2 (Euthydemus). Many readers of *Memoirs*, in fact, think that 4.2 is the pick of the entire work. It achieves an almost Platonic blend of scene-setting, characterization, wicked humour, and philosophy.

In short, a reader with a sense of humour and a little charity will probably find quite a bit to enjoy in *Memoirs*, if he or she does not try to read too much at a time. Indeed, it is important to appreciate that a sense of humour can change one's reading of Xenophon. Consider, for example, *Memoirs*, 2.5, where Socrates suggests that the value of friends can be assessed in strict financial terms: the idea is likely to seem rather obnoxious, unless one assumes that Socrates has his tongue at least partially in his cheek.

In considering Xenophon's style, some comment must be passed on one of the most noticeable features – his constant assurances to the reader that his information for these Socratic conversations is reliable. In *Memoirs* he uses several phrases to convey this impression. Sometimes he actually claims to have been present at the conversation (1.3, 1.4, 1.6.11–14, 2.4, 2.5, 4.3); more often he says something like: 'I know that he had the following conversation with —' Only once does he refer to a source for the information (4.8). The majority of the dialogues or homilies are simply presented as factual by the method of confidently plunging the reader straight into the conversation: 'This is what he said to —' is the style, and it is, of course, scarcely different from the 'I know that —' formula.

I have mentioned in another context (p. 21) that Xenophon's claim to have been present at the occasion recorded in *The Dinner-party* is demonstrably false; this fact alone goes a long way towards undermining any confidence that these reassurances to the reader are guileless. Moreover, although Greek memories were generally better than ours (since they rarely relied on the written word), no Greek's memory was good enough to recall so accurately that many conversations – and this applies not only to Xenophon, but also to his putative sources. There is no indication that, when Xenophon left Athens in 401, he knew he was not going to return for thirty-six years, nor can he have foreseen Socrates' trial and death; so why, before leaving, should he have bothered to go round all Socrates' friends and take notes on their conversations with Socrates? Is it really possible to imagine Xenophon as a silent witness to so many of the conversations, especially the more personal ones in Book 2, such as Socrates ticking off his son Lamprocles (2.2)? There is a sense in which Xenophon's lack of characterization of the interlocutors (see p. 53 and p. 205, n. 2) suggests that they are mere literary artifices, rather than recreated participants in a historical discussion; and sometimes the interlocutor becomes anonymous – 'one of his companions' or the like (3.1–3, 3.14). Once the floodgates of doubt are opened, there is no stopping extreme scepticism about Xenophon's claim to historical veracity. Nor would he be the only writer to use this literary device; recent work has suggested, for instance, that the historian Herodotus' claims to be an eyewitness are invariably examples of exactly the same artifice, namely to reassure the reader of the accuracy of his account.[1]

Given what I have already said about the loose organization of *Memoirs*, it would make little sense to discuss the work chapter by chapter. A thematic discussion ('Socrates on religion', 'Socrates on self-discipline', etc.) would be possible, but I propose, for the purpose of this brief introduction, to restrict myself to a single broad topic.

A conclusion to be drawn from the discussion of pp. 9–26 is that we should not expect Xenophon's Socrates to be anything other than Xenophon's ideal in dramatized form. The values and character of 'Socrates' are really those of Xenophon.[2] But what are Xenophon's moral values? The phrase which recurs throughout *Memoirs* and the other works in this volume, and which sums up Xenophon's ideal, is 'truly good'. What is it, in Xenophon's view, to be 'truly good'?

The Greek phrase for 'truly good' is *kalos kagathos*. But this gives us little insight, since it is as vague a phrase as the English words used to translate it. It is a compound formed of two common commendatory adjectives, *kalos* ('fine') and *agathos* ('good'): the phrase literally means 'fine and good' (see also p. 310, n. 1). Both *kalos* and *agathos* can be used extremely widely: *kalos* refers to physical attractiveness, but also to moral goodness and the appropriateness of anything – animate or inanimate – in its setting; *agathos* does not, in Xenophon's time, directly refer to external qualities, but has much the same extension as the English

1. See also p. 21. On Herodotus, see S. West, 'Herodotus' Epigraphical Interests', *Classical Quarterly*, 35 (1985), pp. 278–305; on the same device in Greek fiction-writers, see J. Morgan, 'Lucian's *True Histories* and the *Wonders Beyond Thule* of Antonius Diogenes', fortuitously in the same volume of *Classical Quarterly*, pp. 475–90.
2. A striking confirmation of this is that the general picture we acquire of Socrates in Xenophon's Socratic writings is much the same as the ones we acquire from other writings about his other heroes, such as Cyrus and Agesilaus. There are so many similarities between views attributed to Socrates (and Ischomachus) in the four works in this volume and views attributed to Cyrus in *Cyropaedia* that I have not bothered to mention them in footnotes.

'good', which we use for everything from moral goodness ('He's a good man') to utilitarian value ('That's a good knife'). Both terms are discussed in *Memoirs*, 3.8 and 4.6.

Xenophon did not invent the phrase (though the abstract noun *kalokagathia*, 'true goodness', first occurs in his works); yet its past history is of little help in understanding its use in Xenophon, since, not surprisingly, what one person sees as true goodness, another does not. However, it is generally true to say that before Xenophon it was applied as much to external as to internal qualities. Until recently, a reasonable English translation was 'gentleman', with all its connotations of correct behaviour and a certain moral code, usually backed by wealth and standing in the community.

In order to see what Xenophon means by the phrase, then, we must see how it is spelled out. Here is a thorough, but not necessarily complete, list of its occurrences in *Memoirs*: 1.1.16, 1.2.2, 1.2.7, 1.2.17, 1.2.23, 1.2.29, 1.2.48, 1.3.11, 1.5.1, 1.5.14, 1.6.13, 1.6.14, 2.1.20, 2.3.16, 2.6.16–28, 2.9.8, 3.5.15, 3.9.4, 3.9.5, 4.2.23, 4.7.1, 4.8.11.

A survey of these passages in their contexts reveals that a 'truly good' person, like Socrates, has the following qualities:

1 Freedom (as opposed to slavishness) as a result of self-discipline.
2 Certain knowledge and a certain degree of education.
3 The ability to make good friends and get on with people.
4 The ability to do good to friends (and harm to enemies).
5 The ability to manage one's estate and, if need be, one's country.
6 The ability to do good to one's country.
7 The traditional virtues, such as wisdom, justice, self-control and piety.

In Socrates' case, there is an eighth item: the ability to teach and make others truly good.

This list constitutes a summary of Xenophon's values. I have restricted the references to *Memoirs*, but the conversation with

Ischomachus in *The Estate-manager* is important corroborative evidence: Socrates goes in search of a 'truly good' person, finds Ischomachus and learns from him how he has earned this description (pp. 309–38). The emphasis in *The Estate-manager* is inevitably on the ability to manage one's estate, but all the other features of the list, including the ability to teach, play a part. The fact that Ischomachus is obviously the type of a country gentleman reminds us that Xenophon's *kalos kagathos* is never far removed from that conception: indeed, one might almost say, were it not for Socrates' poverty, that Xenophon is portraying him as a country gentleman!

There is a sense in which 'freedom' is almost synonymous with 'true goodness' in Xenophon's mind. Thus, for instance, knowledge of certain truly good things is a mark of a truly good person, but ignorance of them is equated with slavishness (e.g. 1.1.16). Further, all the abilities numbered 3–6 in the list are contrasted at 2.1.18–20 with lack of self-discipline which is often described as slavishness (for example, *Memoirs*, 1.5, 2.6, 4.2.22, 4.5; *The Estate-manager*, 1.16–23). And since all the traditional virtues are knowledge, and ignorance is slavish, then a free person is virtuous and a virtuous person is free.

Freedom, we see, depends on self-discipline, and it is a refrain throughout the *Memoirs* that Socrates was the most self-disciplined of men. He was ruled by neither his instinctive appetites nor his emotions, but *he* ruled them. Self-discipline is presented as the foundation of true goodness.

The emphasis throughout is practical, prudential and result-oriented. Thus, self-discipline is important not just for itself, but because it enables a person not to be distracted by his appetites from doing his duty. Education is desirable provided it stops short of useless theoretical studies. You do good to your friends so that they stick by you, defend you from your enemies, and otherwise repay you.[1] The purpose of estate-management is to

1. This will appear realistic or selfish, depending on how far the reader subscribes to the more sentimental attitudes towards friendship which are current in the Western world today.

create wealth, and the purpose of benefiting one's country is partly to achieve recognition.

Once more it must be said that anyone coming to Xenophon after having absorbed Plato's portrait of Socrates is likely to be disappointed. As Saunders remarks (p. 16): 'There is nothing here to make the blood race', and, in Xenophon, Socrates' strong point is 'massive horse-sense, not philosophical acumen'. But it is arguable that Xenophon's portrait provides a useful, and not entirely false, counterbalance to Plato's. On the whole, Plato's Socrates is otherworldly: he wants to help people to act well, but otherwise is not concerned with the things of this world. The best summary of his attitude is given in a late dialogue, *Theaetetus*. In the course of a long, brilliant and often savage comparison of philosophers with the worldly-wise (172c–177b), Plato has Socrates describe philosophers as free, while other men are slaves, and as unaware of trivial day-to-day events. At one point he says (175d–176a):

> So there are the two types, Theodorus. There's the one you call the philosopher, whose upbringing has been genuinely free and unhurried, and who can't be blamed for looking simple and being useless when he is confronted with menial tasks – if, for instance, he doesn't know how to make the bed or sweeten a sauce or a flattering speech. Then there's the other one, who can do all these things keenly and quickly, but who doesn't know how to strike up an elegant and free-spirited song – no, nor how to play his part in the harmony of discussion and properly celebrate the life of gods and happy men.

This, as I say, is from a late dialogue, but it is not untrue to the spirit of earlier dialogues. At *Gorgias*, 521c–522e, for instance, Socrates admits that he would be useless in court: if he were brought to trial, it would be like a doctor being accused by a confectioner before a jury of children!

Now, no doubt Socrates in his philosophical moments was 'impractical'; more importantly, no doubt it was the philosophical side of Socrates that someone like Plato saw and valued, and/or that Socrates himself revealed to pupils like Plato. But there is no reason to think that Socrates was always like that, and would not have been seen by a follower like Xenophon as teaching prudential goals. It is quite possible that Xenophon's innate conservatism has to a large extent coloured his descriptions of Socrates' practicality; but perhaps Socrates did teach practical goals too.

If there is any reluctance to accept this, it is, I suspect, largely due to the ethical dichotomy enshrined in our Western conditioning as 'Ye cannot serve God and Mammon'. This is certainly a view to which Plato would subscribe, and he would probably dismiss Xenophon as a Mammon-server. But there is no reason to think that Socrates accepted the dichotomy. The Socratic principle underlying both Plato's and Xenophon's descriptions of Socrates' ethical thought is that virtue is knowledge of what is good for oneself. This principle, which is universally recognized by commentators on Socrates and has been called 'moral egoism', is, as with all Socratic principles, open to interpretation. To Plato, what is really good for oneself is to shun the world as much as possible; to Xenophon, the principle is a reflection of traditional morality.

We must, however, be wary of directly equating the God–Mammon dichotomy with the Plato–Xenophon dichotomy. There is a middle way, which, arguably, is reflected in both Plato and Xenophon, namely, to be *in* the world, but not *of* the world. This requires some explanation.

Broadly speaking, Socrates' philosophical predecessors had, by a process of reductionism, attempted to make the world comprehensible. Instead of viewing it as the playground of fickle, or at least unintelligible, gods, they tried to see the world as explicable by as few physical elements and processes as possible. At the same time great advances were made in technology, and several fifth-century writers celebrated man's control over his environment (see Guthrie, *The Sophists*, pp. 79–84).

Man's mind was beginning to be seen as the means for understanding and then controlling the world.[1] Socrates played an important part in this process: his original contribution was to stress that the rational mind controls the world by governing the choices we make (see Snell, pp. 182 ff.). People had always made decisions, of course, but Socrates puts such decision-making firmly within the province of reason, rather than, for example, passion or appetite. This is evident particularly in his denial of *akrasia* (which both Plato and Xenophon describe; see pp. 12–15), and in the emphasis on self-discipline (more prominent in Xenophon than in Plato). To take a simple example, suppose I am offered a sixth glass of wine at a party. The denial of *akrasia* means that, whether I accept or refuse it, the choice will be dictated by what I believe to be good for me,[2] and self-discipline means that I will probably choose to refuse the wine!

Again, in both Plato and Xenophon, Socrates emphasizes that deliberate, knowing action is preferable to involuntary action (see, for example, Plato, *Hippias Minor*; Xenophon, *Memoirs*, 4.2.19–23), and in Xenophon, at any rate, involuntary action, which is based on ignorance, is described as slavish; and slaves, obviously, have fewer choices than free men.[3] It is clearer in Plato than in Xenophon that what governs choice is the rational mind's knowledge of oneself, which is knowledge of what is good and bad for oneself, as a human being and as an individual. Armed with this knowledge, we will always act virtuously.

If this is the ideal, what is the opposite? What constitutes involuntary, unknowing and therefore unvirtuous action? Socrates' answer is that it is action which is governed by ig-

1. It is hard for us to comprehend this revolution – but that is only because the revolution succeeded, and we are its heirs. To put it in context, if a similar revolution were to start today, it would have to establish some human faculty other than the rational mind.
2. Hence, in both Plato and Xenophon, Socrates stresses the importance of self-knowledge; see, for example, Plato, *Alcibiades I*; Xenophon, *Memoirs*, 4.2.24–29.
3. See *The Estate-manager*, 1.16–23; as Plato says in *Hippias Minor*, a knowledgeable person can choose to use his knowledge for either good or bad results, but an ignorant person is restricted to bad results.

norance, which either precludes or restricts choice. Hence, his mission (see pp. 13, 17, 36) was to show people that they were ignorant by pricking the bubble of illusory knowledge. We have already seen that this is a dangerous practice, of which only tolerant societies can approve (see p. 36), because what normally governs choice is *nomos*, the conditioning of our society. To get people to think about their conventional rules is revolutionary.

Now, even according to Plato, it may be that an action based on knowing choice will coincide with an action based on *nomos*, although the difference between the two *superficially* identical actions is as wide as the difference between awareness and blind adherence to rules. In Plato's *Crito* Socrates says that he has chosen to live in Athens: if he did not like it, he could have gone elsewhere; and the choice to stay entails a decision to obey the Athenian laws. This is the most striking Platonic evidence that knowing action may coincide with conventional action.[1] We can also consider the following: Socrates' astonishment that Euthyphro is prepared to go against conventional morality and prosecute his father (*Euthyphro*, 4a–e); his insistence, even in the legal context of an Athenian lawcourt, that he has never wronged anyone (*Apology*, 37a), and therefore it would be his prosecutor who was wrong (*Gorgias*, 521d; compare *Meno*, 94e–95a); and the view implicit in *Hippias Minor* that a knowing, virtuous person will not, although he could, choose to lie and do wrong.

These are the parameters of the 'middle way' which I believe Socrates taught, and is reflected in both Plato and Xenophon. The Socratic ideal is to know what is good for oneself and to base one's actions on rational choice derived from that knowledge. One's

1. There is, however, a crucial twist to this sort of Platonic evidence where Socrates is talking about himself, owing to Socrates' constant disavowal of knowledge in Plato's dialogues. Can we then say that Plato's Socrates tells us anything at all about knowing action? But (see Vlastos' article cited on p. 13, n. 1) Socrates' disavowal of knowledge only means that he disclaims absolutely certain knowledge and leaves the door open for development and improvement. He can, therefore, base his actions and views on knowledge of a less rigid kind.

actions are, naturally, *in* the world, but because they are not based on blind adherence to *nomos*, they are not *of* the world.

The point is that these speculations (as remarked on p. 23, any attempt to uncover Socrates' thought is bound to be speculative) are based equally on the accounts of both Plato and Xenophon. As I said, even in Plato knowing action may coincide with traditionally moral action; from this point of view Xenophon's values can appear less humdrum. Since the foundations of the 'middle way' – the denial of *akrasia*, the ideal of voluntary action and the notion that virtue is knowledge – are all present in Xenophon, it is possible that his presentation of a conservative and conventional ideal is because, for a person like himself, knowing action will always be conventional action. As Anderson says: 'Throughout his life, Xenophon remained the sort of conservative whose acceptance of the doctrines and principles that he has inherited seems either unintelligent, or dishonest, or both, to those who do not share them.'[1] In this extract, I would be inclined to stress 'seems': more thought may underlie Xenophon's values than he is often credited with.[2]

Two final words of warning related to the above thesis. First, Xenophon's flat, matter-of-fact tone will tend to encourage the reader to treat as banal issues which bear thinking about, and which perhaps Xenophon had thought about. Second, it is too easy for us today to dismiss Xenophon as not much better than a bad Victorian writer. This applies not just to his style of writing, which may seem Victorian to us, accustomed as we are to racy colloquialisms in our fiction, but also to his morals. It is quite reasonable to describe his moral code as 'Victorian' in the lay sense given in my dictionary: 'strict but somewhat conventional in morals, inclining to prudery and solemnity'. But the fact that this morality was reinstated in nineteenth-century Europe and is now

1. J. K. Anderson, *Xenophon* (Duckworth, 1974), p. 34.
2. D. Morrison, op. cit. (p. 18. n. 1), selects a few passages from Xenophon's writings and argues that these, at least, have philosophical interest. By contrast, I am arguing that there could be philosophy buried underneath the whole of Xenophon's picture of Socrates.

past history to us should not make us forget that Xenophon may have reached *his* conventional position by original routes. Xenophon's portrait of Socrates may be only a pale reflection of the historical Socrates, but it is still a reflection, and Socrates was killed for what he said and did.

MEMOIRS OF SOCRATES

BOOK ONE

I have often wondered what arguments Socrates' accusers can possibly have used to convince the people of Athens that he deserved execution. The indictment against him ran something like this: Socrates is a malefactor, firstly, in that he does not recognize the gods recognized by the State, but introduces new deities; secondly, in that he corrupts the young.[1]

With regard to the first charge, that he did not recognize the gods recognized by the State, on what evidence can they possibly have relied? Everyone could see that he sacrificed regularly at home and also at the public altars of the State; and he made no secret of using divination; in fact it was common gossip that Socrates claimed that the divine communicated to him.[2] This, I imagine, was the chief reason for accusing him of introducing new deities. Yet he was no more heretical than any other people who believe in divination and rely on portents and omens and chance meetings and sacrifices. They do not suppose that the birds they see or the people they meet know what is the right course for those who are consulting the diviner; they believe that these things are simply means used by the gods to communicate, and Socrates took the same view. But whereas most people say that it is the omen or the encounter that dissuades or encourages them, Socrates asserted what he actually believed: he said that the divine

1. See pp. 32–6 on the charges against Socrates.
2. See pp. 34–5.

does the communicating. He often warned his associates to do this or not to do that, at the prompting of the divine, and those who took his advice benefited from it, while those who did not were sorry for it afterwards. Surely anyone would agree that Socrates did not want to seem either a fool or an impostor to his companions; and he would have been thought both if he had been manifestly mistaken in making what he claimed to be divine revelations about the future. It seems obvious, then, that he would not have predicted the future if he had not been sure that his statements would come true; and who could base this trust on anything other than a god? And if he trusted in gods, he surely must have believed in gods.[1]

Besides, towards his intimate friends he adopted the following line: if an action was unavoidable, he advised them to carry it out as they thought best, but where the result of an action was uncertain, he sent them to consult a diviner to see if the action should be taken. He said that anyone who proposed to run an estate or a country efficiently needed the help of divination. Skill in carpentry or metalwork or farming or government, or critical ability in these subjects, or proficiency in mathematics or estate-management or military science – all these attainments he considered to be within the scope of human choice and judgement; but he said that the most important aspects of these subjects the gods reserved for themselves, and none of them were revealed to mortals.[2] A man who has sown a field well cannot tell who will reap the harvest; and a man who has built a house well cannot tell who will live in it. A general cannot tell whether it is to his advantage to hold his command, and a politician cannot tell whether it is to his advantage to be the head of the State. The man who has married a beautiful wife for his pleasure cannot tell whether she will cause him pain, and the man who has secured influential connections in his native land cannot tell whether they

1. This misses the point, since Socrates was not charged with atheism, but with religious non-conformism.
2. See *The Estate-manager*, 5.18–20 (pp. 307–8) for an example.

will result in his banishment from it. To suppose that such consequences are all a matter of human judgement and contain no element of the divine was, he said, superstition; and he also said it was superstition to consult diviners about questions which the gods had enabled us to decide by the use of our wits (for example, supposing one were to ask whether it is better to engage a qualified or an unqualified driver for a carriage, or helmsman for one's ship), or to which the answers can be found by calculation or measuring or weighing. People who put this sort of question to the gods were, in his opinion, acting wrongly. He said that where the gods have given us power to act by the use of our intelligence, we ought to use it; but where the outcome is concealed from human beings, we should try to discover it from the gods by divination; for the gods communicate to those whom they favour.

Then again, Socrates was always in the public eye. Early in the morning he used to make his way to the covered walks and the recreation grounds, and when the agora became busy he was there in full view; and he always spent the rest of the day where he expected to find the most company. He talked most of the time, and anyone who liked could listen. But nobody ever saw Socrates do, or heard him say, anything that was heretical or irreverent. He did not discourse about the nature of the physical universe, as most other philosophers did,[1] inquiring into the constitution of the cosmos (as the sages call it)[2] and the causes of the various celestial phenomena; on the contrary, he pointed out the foolishness of those who concerned themselves with such questions. In the first place, he inquired whether they proceeded to these studies only when they thought they had a sufficient knowledge of human problems, or whether they felt that they were right in disregarding human problems and inquiring into divine matters.

1. According to Plato (*Phaedo*, 96a–99d), Socrates, when young, was interested in natural science, but became disillusioned with it and pioneered his new philosophy. See also Plato, *Apology of Socrates*, 19b, 26b–d; Aristotle, *Metaphysics*, 987b; and p. 255, n. 3.
2. The word 'cosmos' literally means 'order' or 'beauty'.

He expressed surprise that it was not obvious to them that human minds cannot discover these secrets, inasmuch as those who claim most confidently to pronounce upon them do not hold the same theories, but disagree with one another just like lunatics. He pointed out that some lunatics don't even fear what is fearful, and others are terrified of things that aren't terrible; some don't scruple to say or do anything even in a crowd, and others feel that they can't even show themselves in public; some show no respect for temples or altars or anything else that is sacred, and others worship stones and odd pieces of wood and animals. In the same way, he said, some of those who ponder about the nature of the universe think that reality is one, and others that it is infinitely many; some think that everything is always in motion, and others that nothing can ever be moved; some think that everything comes to be and passes away, and others that nothing can come to be or pass away.[1]

He also raised this further question about them: whether, just as those who study human nature expect to achieve some result from their studies for the benefit of themselves or of some other selected person, so these students of divine matters expect that, when they have discovered the laws that govern the various phenomena, they will produce at will winds and rain and changes of season and any other such required effect;[2] or whether they have no such expectation, but are content with the mere knowledge of how these various phenomena occur.

That is how he spoke about people who occupied themselves with these speculations. He himself always discussed human matters, trying to find out the nature of piety and impiety, honour and dishonour, right and wrong, sanity and lunacy, courage and cowardice, State and statesman, government and the capacity for government, and all other subjects the knowledge of which he thought marked truly good men, while those who were ignorant of them might fairly be called slavish.

1. The followers of Parmenides claimed that everything was one, unmoving and unchanging; the followers of Heraclitus held the opposite.
2. Empedocles promised such abilities to his students (Fragment 111).

In so far as his views were not clearly known, it is no wonder that the jury formed a wrong estimate; but is it not extraordinary that they should have taken no account of what was common knowledge? On one occasion, when he had been elected to the Council and had taken the councillor's oath, which included the clause 'I will act in accordance with the law', he was chosen to preside in the Assembly.[1] The people were bent on putting Thrasyllus and Erasinides[2] and all their colleagues to death by a single resolution in defiance of the law. But Socrates refused to put the motion to the vote, although the people were angry with him and a number of influential men threatened him; he thought it more important to keep his oath than wrongfully to curry favour with the people and defend himself against intimidation.

He believed that the gods care for men, but not in the way that most people believe they do. They suppose that the gods know some things but not others; but Socrates believed that they know everything, both words and actions and unspoken intentions, and that they are present everywhere and communicate to people about all kinds of human affairs. So I cannot understand how the people of Athens were persuaded that Socrates was heretical in his religious beliefs, when he never said or did anything irreverent, but on the contrary, in his relationship to the gods, said and did only what was recognizably consistent with the deepest reverence.

2

It also seems extraordinary to me that any people should have been persuaded that Socrates had a bad influence upon young men. Besides what I have said already, he was in the first place the

1. In spite of this statement, echoed in 4.4 (p. 195), Socrates was probably not presiding at the time, and merely voted against the illegal motion (see also Plato, *Apology of Socrates*, 32b–c; *Gorgias*, 473e; Xenophon, *Hellenica*, 1.7.15). On the Council and the Assembly, see p. 46, n. 1.
2. Two of the Athenian commanders at the battle of Arginusae in 406. Although victorious, they were prosecuted for negligence in rescuing the crews of sunken warships.

most self-disciplined of men in respect of his sexual and other appetites; then he was most tolerant of cold and heat and hardships of all kinds; and finally he had so trained himself to be moderate in his requirements that he was very easily satisfied with very few possessions. So if he himself was like this, how could he have made others irreverent or criminal or greedy or sensual or work-shy? On the contrary, he rescued many from these states by inspiring them with a desire for goodness and offering them hope that, if they took themselves in hand, they would become truly good. At the same time he never undertook to teach how this could be done; but by obviously *being* such a person, he made those who spent their time with him hope that, if they followed his example, they would develop the same character.

He neither neglected the body himself nor commended others for doing so. He disapproved of over-eating followed by violent exercise, but approved of taking enough exercise to work off the amount of food that the mind accepts with pleasure; he said that this was quite a healthy practice and did not hinder the cultivation of the mind. He was certainly not foppish or ostentatious either in his clothing or in his footwear or in the rest of his daily life. Nor again did he make his associates money-lovers: he rid them of all other desires except for his company, and for that he charged no fee.[1] In eschewing fees, he considered that he was protecting his own independence; those who accepted a fee in return for their services he nicknamed 'self-enslavers', because they were obliged to converse with those who paid the fee. He expressed surprise that a man who offered to teach goodness should demand to be paid for it and, instead of anticipating the greatest possible gain through obtaining a good friend, should be afraid that the person who has become truly good will feel less than the deepest gratitude to his supreme benefactor. Socrates never made any such offer to anyone, but he believed that those of his associates who accepted the principles which he himself approved would be good friends all their life long to himself and to one another.

1. Unlike the sophists, who were professional teachers.

How, then, could such a person have a corrupting influence upon the young – unless the cultivation of goodness is a form of corruption?

But it is a fact, according to his accuser,[1] that he encouraged his associates to make light of constitutional practice by saying that it was foolish to appoint political leaders by lot,[2] and that nobody would employ a candidate chosen by lot as a pilot or a carpenter or a musician or for any other such post – although if these posts are badly filled, they cause far less harm than bad political appointments; and the accuser said that this sort of talk encouraged the young to despise the established constitution and made them unruly. But *I* think that those who exercise reason and believe that they are capable of teaching their fellow citizens what is for their good are most unlikely to become unruly, since they know that violence involves enmity and danger, whereas persuasion produces the same results without danger and in a friendly spirit; for the victims of violence feel that they have been deprived, and are resentful, while those who have yielded to persuasion are appreciative of having received a kindness. So violence is not to be expected of those who exercise reason; such conduct belongs to those who have strength without judgement. I may add that anyone who ventures to use violence will also need not a few accomplices, while the man who can persuade will need none, because he will be sure of his power to persuade even if he is single-handed. Also, such people are most unlikely to commit murder. Who would choose to kill a man rather than have him alive and acquiescent?

However, according to Socrates' accuser, Critias and Alcibiades, who had belonged to Socrates' circle, did more harm to their country than any other persons. Critias developed into the most avaricious and violent of all the oligarchs, and Alcibiades in

1. This prosecutor is probably not one of those who indicted Socrates at his actual trial, but Polycrates, who wrote a pamphlet, probably shortly after Socrates' death, attacking him. However, Xenophon returns to Socrates' actual trial at the end of this chapter (1.2.62).
2. This was the Athenian system for the majority of political appointments.

his turn became the most dissolute and arrogant of all the democrats. For my part, I shall not defend any wrong that these men did to the State; I shall merely explain how their connection with Socrates came about.[1]

These two men were by nature the most ambitious persons in all Athens, determined to have personal control over all State affairs and to be famous above all others. They knew that Socrates lived quite contentedly on very slender resources, and that he was absolutely self-disciplined in respect of all pleasures, and that he could do as he liked in argument with anyone who conversed with him. Given that they were aware of these facts, and were men of the kind that I have described, should one say that they courted Socrates' society because they desired his way of life and the self-discipline which he had, or because they thought that by associating with him they would acquire the highest efficiency in speech and action? My opinion is that if God had offered them the choice between living out their lives as they saw Socrates living his, and dying, they would have preferred to die. They showed as much by their conduct: as soon as they felt superior to the rest of the company, they broke away from Socrates and took up politics, the object for which they had courted his society.

Perhaps it might be objected that Socrates should not have taught his associates politics before he taught them self-discipline. I do not dispute this, but I observe that all teachers show their pupils how they themselves practise what they preach, and lead them on by reasoned argument. I know that Socrates in the same way made it clear to his companions that he was a truly good man, and excelled in discussing ethical questions and all other human problems. And I know that both those men too were self-disciplined so long as they associated with Socrates – not because they were afraid of being punished or hit by him, but because they thought then that it was best to behave so.

No doubt many professed philosophers[2] would say that a just

1. For more on these two, see pp. 37–9.
2. Including Antisthenes, a Socratic who became a substantial philosopher in his own right.

man can never become unjust, nor a self-disciplined man a bully, just as one who has learned any other subject can never become ignorant of it. But this is not my view of the matter. It seems clear to me that just as those who do not exercise their bodies cannot carry out their physical duties, so those who do not exercise their characters cannot carry out their moral duties: they can neither do what they ought to do nor avoid what they ought to avoid. That is why fathers keep their sons (even if they are right-minded) away from bad men, because they believe that the company of good people is a training in virtue, while the company of bad men is the ruin of it. Witness to this fact is borne by the poet who says:

> Good company will edify you; bad
> Will rob you even of the wits you had.[1]

And the one who says:

> But good men are by turns both base and brave.[2]

And I can add my testimony to this. For I observe that just as epic poetry fades from the minds of those who fail to rehearse it, so those who neglect what their teachers tell them are liable to forget it. Now, when a person forgets the advice he has been given, it means that he has also forgotten the influences that set his heart on self-discipline; and when he has forgotten these, it is not surprising that he should forget self-discipline too. I observe also that those who have developed a taste for drinking, or have become involved in love affairs, are less capable of attending to what they ought to do and of abstaining from what they ought not to do.[3] I mean, often those who were able to control their spending before they were in love, after they have fallen in love, can do so no more; and when once they have run through their money, they no longer reject in disdain the sources of profit which they rejected before. So how can it be impossible for one

1. Theognis 35–6.
2. The line is also quoted by Plato, *Protagoras*, 344d; but the author is unknown.
3. Compare *The Estate-manager*, 12.10–12 (p. 333).

who was self-disciplined before to be undisciplined later, or for one who was formerly able to act rightly to be unable later? On the contrary, it seems to me that every truly good thing needs to be exercised, and not least self-discipline; for the appetites that are implanted with the soul in the same body encourage it not to be self-disciplined, but to gratify both them and the body in the quickest possible way.

Critias and Alcibiades, then, as long as they kept company with Socrates, were able by his help to master their ignoble desires. But when they had parted from him, Critias was banished to Thessaly and attached himself to men who indulged more in law-breaking than in upright conduct. Alcibiades, on the other hand, was courted because of his good looks by many women of rank, and, because of his prestige in the city and among the allies, he was pampered by many influential men and held in honour by the people, and enjoyed an easily won supremacy; and just as athletes who easily achieve supremacy in athletic competitions neglect their exercises, so he neglected himself.

Since this is what happened to Alcibiades and Critias, and since they were exalted by their birth, elated by their wealth, puffed up with their power, and spoiled by many people, is it any wonder that, when they were corrupted for all these reasons and long separated from Socrates, they became overbearing? Socrates' accuser holds him responsible for all their faults; does he find nothing creditable in the fact that in their youth, when it was natural that they should be most irresponsible and undisciplined, Socrates made them behave decently? That is not how other cases are decided. If the teacher of a wind or string instrument or of some other art has made his pupils proficient, and they then attach themselves to other teachers and deteriorate, is the first teacher blamed for this result? If a man's son through attaching himself to some teacher becomes self-disciplined, and later through associating with somebody else becomes vicious, does the father blame the first teacher? Surely he gives him the greater credit in proportion as the son shows himself worse in the company of the latter. In fact, when fathers themselves look after their sons, if the sons go wrong, the fathers are not blamed for it, if they themselves have been impeccable in their conduct. Socrates ought to be judged in the same way. If he himself had done anything bad, he might reasonably have been regarded as a bad person; but if he was consistently scrupulous, how can he justly be held responsible for a fault which he did not possess?

However, even though he himself did nothing discreditable, if he had expressed approval of these men when he saw them behaving badly, he would have deserved censure. Well, when he noticed that Critias was in love with Euthydemus and was trying to seduce him, like one seeking to gratify his sexual appetite, Socrates tried to dissuade him by insisting that it was slavish and improper for a truly good man to solicit his favourite, to whom he wishes to appear in a creditable light, importuning him like a beggar and entreating him to grant his favours, especially since those favours are far from honourable. And when Critias paid no attention to these protests and was not diverted from his purpose, Socrates is reported to have said, in the presence of several persons including Euthydemus himself, that Critias seemed to be suffering from pig's itch: he wanted to scratch himself against Euthydemus like a piglet scratching itself against a stone. This made Critias take a dislike to Socrates, so that when as one of the Thirty[1] he became a legislator along with Charicles, he held it against Socrates and introduced a law against teaching 'the art of debate'. He did this out of spite towards Socrates, since he had no means of attacking him other than misrepresenting him to the public by applying to him the usual layman's allegation against all philosophers.[2] I never heard Socrates do this myself, nor did I ever know anyone else claim to have heard him do so.

He made his position quite clear. When the Thirty were putting to death many of the citizens (and those not the worst among

1. The Thirty Oligarchs seized power in Athens in 404, but were soon overthrown.

2. Probably 'making the worse argument appear the better case': cf. Aristophanes, *Clouds*, 112 ff., 872 ff.; Plato, *Apology*, 18b, 19b. See also *The Estate-manager*, 11.25 (p. 331).

them) and were inciting many others to do wrong, Socrates observed on one occasion that it seemed extraordinary to him that a man appointed to look after a herd of cattle who made them fewer and worse than they were before should not admit that he was a bad herdsman, and still more extraordinary that a man appointed as a political leader who was making the citizens fewer and worse than they were before was not ashamed and did not consider himself a bad political leader. This was reported to the tyrants, and Critias and Charicles summoned Socrates, and, calling his attention to the law, forbade him to converse with the young. Socrates asked them if he was allowed to ask for information about anything in their proclamation that he did not understand. They said he could.

'Well,' said he, 'I am prepared to obey the laws; but in order that I may not unconsciously offend through ignorance, I want you to make this point clear to me. When you order abstention from the art of debate, is it because you think it is accompanied by correctness or by incorrectness of speech? If by correctness, clearly I would have to refrain from speaking correctly; and if by incorrectness, clearly I would have to try to speak correctly.'

Charicles was annoyed with him and said, 'As you are so dense, Socrates, we issue you this warning, which is easier to grasp: do not converse with the young at all.'

'Well, then,' said Socrates, 'to prevent any misunderstanding, give me a definition of the age up to which one should regard people as young.'

Charicles replied, 'As long as they are considered too immature to serve on the Council; on this principle you are not to converse with men below the age of thirty.'

'Not even if I am buying something,' asked Socrates, 'and the seller is below the age of thirty? Can't I even ask what the price is?'

'Yes, of course you can ask that sort of question,' said Charicles. 'But Socrates, most of the questions *you* like to ask are ones to which you know the answers. That is the kind you must stop asking.'

'Am I not to reply either, then,' said Socrates, 'when a young man asks me something, if I know the answer – like "Where does Charicles live?" or "Where's Critias?"?'

'Yes, of course you can answer that kind,' said Charicles.

Critias interposed, 'The people you will have to keep off, Socrates, are the cobblers and carpenters and smiths. They must be worn out by now with all your talk about them.'[1]

'Then must I also keep off the topics that they lead to,' said Socrates, 'morality and piety and so on?'

'Certainly,' said Charicles, 'and from herdsmen. Otherwise you had better take care that you don't decrease the number of the herd yourself.'

This made it plain that their hostility to Socrates was due to their having been told of his remark about the cattle.

So much for the nature of the association of Critias with Socrates and the relations between them.

I myself would deny that anyone can be instructed by a person of whom he disapproves; and it was not because they approved of him that Critias and Alcibiades associated with Socrates while they did associate with him, but because from the very first they had set out to be supreme in the State. Even while they were still in Socrates' company, they tried to converse with the leading politicians in preference to anybody else. There is a story that when Alcibiades was still under twenty, he had the following conversation about the laws with Pericles, who was his guardian and the head of the State.

'Tell me, Pericles,' he said, 'could you explain to me what law is?'

'Most certainly,' said Pericles.

'Then please do so,' said Alcibiades. 'I hear people being praised for being law-abiding, and I presume that nobody can rightly win this praise if he does not know what law is.'

'Well,' said Pericles, 'it's not at all a difficult object that you're seeking, Alcibiades, if you want to find out what law is. When the

1. Socrates used to support his arguments by analogies drawn from the trades and professions. On this Craft Analogy, see p. 14.

people, meeting together, approve and enact a proposal stating what should or should not be done, that is a law.'

'On the assumption that good actions should be done, or bad ones?'

'Good ones, of course, my boy, not bad ones.'

'Supposing that instead of the whole people a small section of it (as happens when there is an oligarchy) meets and enacts what ought to be done – what is that?'

'Everything that the powers that be in the State enact, after deliberating what should be done, is called a law.'

'Then supposing a despot, being in power in the State, enacts what the citizens are to do, is that a law too?'

'Yes, even the enactments of a despot in power are called laws.'

'And what is violence and lawlessness, Pericles? Isn't it when the stronger party compels the weaker to do what he wants by using force instead of persuasion?'

'So I believe,' said Pericles.

'Then anything that a despot enacts and compels the citizens to do instead of persuading them is an example of lawlessness?'

'I suppose so,' said Pericles. 'I retract the statement that what a despot enacts otherwise than by persuasion is law.'

'And if the minority enacts something not by persuading the majority but by dominating it, should we call this violence or not?'

'It seems to me,' said Pericles, 'that if one party, instead of persuading another, compels him to do something, whether by enactment or not, this is always violence rather than law.'

'Then if the people as a whole uses not persuasion but its superior power to enact measures against the propertied classes, will that be violence rather than law?'

'You know, Alcibiades,' said Pericles, 'when I was your age I was very clever too at this sort of thing; I used to practise just the same sort of ingenuity that I think you practise now.'

'I wish I could have met you when you were at your cleverest, Pericles,' said Alcibiades.

Well, as soon as they thought that they were a match for the politicians, they stopped associating with Socrates – because, apart from their general lack of sympathy with him, whenever they came into his company they had the annoyance of having their mistakes exposed – and took up politics, which was the very object for which they had attached themselves to Socrates.

But Crito was Socrates' companion, and so were Chaerephon, Chaerecrates, Hermogenes, Simmias, Cebes, Phaedondas and others, who associated with him not because they wanted to become politicians or barristers, but because they wanted to become truly good men and to be able to behave properly towards their family, servants, relatives and friends, their State and their fellow citizens. Not one of these men at any period of his life did anything wrong, or was accused of doing so.

But Socrates, according to his accuser, taught children to treat their fathers with contempt by claiming to make those who associated with him wiser than their fathers, and asserting that it was legal to put even one's father in confinement after first getting him certified insane, and citing as evidence that it was lawful for the ignorant to be kept under restraint by the wise. Actually, Socrates thought that anyone who imprisoned people on the ground of ignorance might fairly be confined himself by those who understood what he did not. Such reflections led him often to examine the difference between ignorance and madness; and he considered that, whereas for mad people to be confined would be an advantage both to themselves and to those who were fond of them, the right thing for those who lacked necessary knowledge would be to learn from those who had it.

Socrates' accuser said that he lowered the regard of his associates not only for their fathers, but also for their other relatives, by saying that it is not their relatives that help the victims of disease or litigation, but doctors in the one case and competent advocates in the other. Still on the subject of friends, Socrates said, according to his accuser, that their goodwill is useless, unless there was a prospect of their being actually able to help one; and that the only friends who deserved to be esteemed were those who knew what was right and could make it clear to others. In this way, the accuser said, Socrates, by prevailing on the young to believe that he was the wisest of men and best qualified to make others wise, so influenced his associates that nobody else had any position in their eyes by comparison with himself.

I know that Socrates did express these views both about fathers and other relatives and about friends; and what is more, that he said that when the soul, which is the one and only seat of the intelligence, had departed, people lose no time in carrying out and putting away the body of the person dearest to them. He used to say that even in life, although everyone is especially fond of his body, he is ready to give up any part of it that is useless or unprofitable, either removing it himself or getting someone else to do it. People cut their own nails and hair and corns, and allow surgeons to amputate and cauterize with consequential pain and suffering, and feel bound to show them gratitude and pay a fee; and they spit out phlegm from their mouths as far as they can, because its presence there does them no good and is much more likely to harm them. It was not with the object of instructing his friends to bury their fathers alive or cut themselves to pieces that Socrates stated these facts; by showing that what is without intelligence is without value, he was appealing to people to take pains to be as intelligent and helpful as possible, so that if a person wished for the regard of father or brother or anyone else, he might not rely on the relationship and take no trouble, but try to be of service to those whose regard he wished to obtain.

Another charge against Socrates was that he used to pick out the most immoral lines of the most famous poets and by using their evidence, taught his associates to be criminals and autocrats. The line of Hesiod, 'No work is shame, but idleness is shame,'[1] he is supposed to have explained as meaning that the poet bids us shrink from no kinds of work, not even such as are wicked or discreditable, but to do even these for the sake of gain. Actually, when Socrates had agreed that to be a worker was beneficial to a person and a good thing, while to be an idler was harmful and a

1. *Works and Days*, 309.

bad thing – in other words that to work was good and to be idle was bad – he used to add that only those who performed a good action were working and were good workers, while those who played dice or performed any other kind of worthless and punishable action he denounced as idlers. On this basis, 'No work is shame, but idleness is shame' would be quite correct.

He was also accused of constantly quoting the passage from Homer[1] which says about Odysseus:

Whenever he met some king, or man of distinction,
He would stand there and try to stop him with gentle words:
'Sir, you ought not to be scared, like any base coward;
Keep a grip on yourself and check the rest of the people . . .'
But when he came across a common man and found him wailing,
He would lash out with his staff and address him imperiously:
'Sir, stop your trembling and listen to the words of others
Who are your betters – you unsoldierly weakling,
Worthless in battle and in council.'

It was alleged that he interpreted this as meaning that the poet commended the beating of commoners and poor people. But that was not what Socrates meant. If it had been, he would have thought that he ought to be beaten himself. What he did say was that any people who could neither say nor do anything useful, and who were incapable, if the need arose, of helping the army or the State or even the citizen body, ought to be placed under every kind of restraint (especially if they are presumptuous too), even if they happen to be very rich. No; on the contrary, Socrates was obviously a friend of the people and well disposed towards all mankind. Although he gained many admirers, both native and foreign, he never charged any of them a fee for his company, but shared his resources unhesitatingly with everyone. Some people, after getting some scraps of wisdom from him free, sold them to others at a high price, and were not as democratic as he was,

1. *Iliad*, 2.188–91, 199–203. The Greeks are considering abandoning the siege of Troy. Comparison with Plato's *Protagoras* and *Hippias Minor*, for instance, suggests that Socrates used to imply that you could make poets mean anything you want.

because they refused to converse with those who could not pay. But Socrates, even in the eyes of the world at large, brought greater honour to his city than the celebrated Lichas did to Sparta. Lichas used to give a dinner to the foreigners who visited Lacedaemon for the festival of the Gymnopaedia,[1] but Socrates spent his life conferring the highest benefits at his own expense upon all who wanted them, for he never let his associates go without improving them.

Since Socrates was as I have described him, in my opinion he deserved to be honoured by the State rather than executed.[2] Consideration of the law would lead one to the same conclusion. According to law, death is the penalty for conviction as a thief or pickpocket or cutpurse or housebreaker or kidnapper or temple-robber: but Socrates was the last man on earth to commit these crimes. Moreover, in his public life he was never guilty of involving his country in an unsuccessful war, or in sedition or treason or any other calamity; and in his personal dealings he never deprived anyone of a benefit or got anyone into trouble, and he was never even accused of any such action. How, then, could he be guilty of the charge? So far from being an atheist, as was alleged in the indictment, he was obviously the most devout of men; and so far from corrupting the young, as he was accused of doing by his prosecutor, he obviously rid his associates of any wrong desires that they had and urged them to set their hearts on the finest and most splendid form of excellence, which makes both countries and estates well managed. By acting in this way he surely deserved high honour at the hands of his country.

3

I said above that in my opinion he actually benefited his associates, partly by practical example and partly by his conversation. I shall record as many instances as I can recall.

1. The 'Festival of Unarmed Dancing' (or possibly 'The Festival of the Naked Boys') was the most splendid of the Spartan festivals. All male Spartans participated by age-groups in the singing, dancing and sport.
2. Compare Plato, *Apology of Socrates*, 36b–37a.

As regards religion, anyone can see that Socrates' behaviour accorded exactly with the Pythia's advice to those who inquire what they ought to do about sacrifices or showing respect to ancestors or any other such observance.[1] The Pythia replies that they will show proper piety if they act in accordance with the law of the land. Socrates both acted on this principle himself and urged others to do so; and he thought that those who acted otherwise were acting excessively and foolishly.

He prayed to the gods simply to give him what was good, recognizing that they know best what is good for us. He thought that to pray for gold or silver or unlimited power or anything of that sort was just like praying for a throw of dice or a battle or anything else with an obviously unpredictable sequel. He thought that in offering small sacrifices to the gods from small resources he was in no way falling behind those who offered ample ones from ample resources. He said that it was a poor thing for the gods if they took more pleasure in great sacrifices than in small ones, because then they would often be better pleased with the offerings of the wicked than with those of the good; and for human beings life would not be worth living if the offerings of the wicked pleased the gods better than those of the good. On the contrary, he believed that the gods appreciated most the honours paid to them by the most devout people. He also used to commend the line 'Offer your utmost to the immortal gods',[2] and he said that it was also a sound maxim to offer one's utmost to friends and strangers and in all other departments of life. If he thought that he was receiving any communication from the gods, he could no more have been persuaded to act against it than if someone had tried to persuade him to accept a blind guide who didn't know the way in preference to one who could see and did know it. And he denounced the folly of others whose actions go against the gods' communications because they are trying to avoid the

1. The Pythia is the priestess of Apollo at Delphi: see p. 43, n. 4.
2. Hesiod, *Works and Days*, 336.

disapproval of men. He himself disregarded all human opinions in comparison with the advice of the gods.

He disciplined both his mind and his body by a way of life which would enable any mortal human being who followed it to live with confidence and security, and to have no difficulty in meeting his expenses. In fact, he was so economical that I doubt whether anyone could work so little as not to earn enough for Socrates' needs. He took only so much food as he could eat with pleasure, and he was so ready for a meal when he came to it that his appetite was sauce enough. Any drink was agreeable to him, because he drank only when he was thirsty. If he ever accepted an invitation to dinner, he very easily resisted what costs most people the greatest effort – namely, the temptation to fill oneself beyond repletion. Those who could not resist this he advised to avoid anything that impelled them to eat when they were not hungry or drink when they were not thirsty; for that, he said, was what ruined stomachs and heads and characters. He used to say jokingly that he believed Circe turned people into pigs by entertaining them with this kind of fare; and that the reason why Odysseus was not turned into a pig was partly the prompting of Hermes and partly the fact that he was self-controlled and refrained from partaking of the dishes beyond the point of repletion.[1] Such were the views that he expressed on this subject humorously but seriously.

He urged resolute avoidance of sexual relations with beautiful people, because it was not easy for one who became involved with them to preserve self-control. Indeed on one occasion, when he had discovered that Critobulus the son of Crito had kissed the handsome son of Alcibiades, he said to Xenophon in Critobulus' presence: 'Tell me, Xenophon: didn't you think that Critobulus was the sort of person to be more sober than reckless, and more prudent than thoughtless and foolhardy?'

'Yes, indeed,' said Xenophon.

'Well, now you must look on him as a thorough hot-head and

1. For the story of Circe the witch, see Homer, *Odyssey*, 10.

desperado. He would turn somersaults over sword-points[1] and jump into a fire.'

'Why,' said Xenophon, 'what have you seen him do to make you accuse him of this?'

'Isn't it a fact,' said Socrates, 'that he dared to kiss Alcibiades' very handsome and attractive son?'

'Well, really,' said Xenophon, 'if that's the type of a foolhardy act, I think I might face such a risk myself!'

'Very rash of you,' said Socrates. 'What good do you think you would do yourself by kissing him? Don't you realize that you would instantly be a slave instead of a free man, and spend a lot of money on harmful pleasures, and have no time to take an interest in anything truly good, and be forced to exert yourself for ends that not even a lunatic would bother about?'

'Good heavens!' exclaimed Xenophon. 'What a sinister effect a kiss has, according to you!'

'Does that really surprise you?' asked Socrates. 'Don't you know that spiders not a quarter of an inch long by the mere contact of their mouths distract people with pain and drive them crazy?'

'Yes, of course,' said Xenophon, 'because they inject something in the act of biting.'

'You *are* dense,' said Socrates. 'Do you think that good-looking people inject nothing in the act of kissing, just because you can't see it? Don't you realize that this creature which they call the bloom of youth is even more dangerous than spiders? They produce their effect by contact, but this needs no contact; if one looks at it, even from quite a distance, it can inject a kind of poison that drives one crazy. No; I advise you, Xenophon, when you see an attractive person, to take to your heels as fast as you can; and I advise you, Critobulus, to go away for a year. That may give you just enough time to recover.'

In the same way, he thought that those who are not proof against sexual attraction should confine their relations to such as the mind would not tolerate unless there were strong physical

1. See *The Dinner-party*, 2.11 (p. 232).

need, and such as would not disturb the mind by being needed. He himself was obviously so well schooled in this respect that he could avoid the best-looking and most attractive people more easily than others could avoid the ugliest and most unattractive.[1]

This, then, was his attitude towards food, drink and sex; and he considered that in this way he would obtain no less satisfaction, and would suffer much less discomfort, than those who devoted a large part of their energy to these objects.

4

If anybody thinks, as some of the spoken and written accounts of him have held, that Socrates, though excellent at setting people on the road to goodness, was incapable of leading them to their goal, I invite him to consider not only the way in which Socrates used to question and refute (by way of correction) those who thought they knew everything, but also the way in which he used to spend the whole day in conversation with the members of his circle; and then to decide whether Socrates was capable of making his companions better men.

I shall relate first a conversation about religion which I once heard between him and Little Aristodemus, as he was called. Socrates had learned that this man was known for neither sacrificing to the gods nor praying nor using divination, and went so far as to scoff at those who did so. 'Tell me, Aristodemus,' he said, 'have you ever admired any people for their artistry?'

'Yes,' he replied.

'Tell us their names.'

'Well, in epic poetry the man I have most admired is Homer, and in dithyrambic Melanippides, and in tragedy Sophocles, and in sculpture Polyclitus, and in painting Zeuxis.'[2]

1. See also *The Dinner-party*, 8 (pp. 257–65) for Socrates on sex. For the famous story of Socrates' resistance to Alcibiades' attractions, see Plato, *Symposium*, 216c–219d.
2. Dithyrambic poetry was a form of choral lyric connected with the worship of Dionysus and very popular in the fifth and early fourth centuries. Melanippides of Melos, Sophocles, Polyclitus of Argos and Zeuxis of Heraclea in south Italy were all active in the fifth century.

'Which do you think is more admirable – the artist who creates senseless and motionless images, or the one who creates things that are alive and intelligent and active?'

'The one who creates live things, by far, provided that they are products of design and not of chance.'

'Some things have no purpose so far as we can tell, and others are obviously useful for some end. Which class do you assign to chance and which to design?'

'Those which are useful should be products of design.'

'Then don't you think that it was for their use that he who originally created men provided them with the various means of perception, such as eyes to see what is visible and ears to hear what is audible? Take the case of smells: what good would they be to us if we weren't supplied with noses? And how should we perceive sweet and bitter tastes, and all the pleasures of the palate, if the tongue had not been fashioned in us to distinguish them? And apart from these, don't you feel that there are other things too that look like effects of providence? For example, because our eyes are delicate, they have been shuttered with eyelids which open when we have occasion to use them, and close in sleep; and to protect them from injury by the wind, eyelashes have been made to grow as a screen; and our foreheads have been fringed with eyebrows to prevent damage even from the sweat of the head. Then our hearing takes in all sounds, yet never gets blocked up by them. And the front teeth of all animals are adapted for cutting, whereas the molars are adapted for masticating what is passed on to them. And the mouth, through which the things that living creatures like are admitted, is situated close to the eyes and nose, whereas the outlets for excrement, which is disagreeable, are directed as far as possible away from the senses. Are you in real doubt whether such provident arrangements are the result of chance or of design?'

'No, indeed,' he said. 'Looked at this way, they seem very much like the contrivances of some wise and benevolent craftsman.'

'And the implanting of the instincts to procreate, and the

implanting in the female parent of the instinct to rear her young, and in the young so reared an intense desire to live and an intense fear of death?'

'These provisions too really seem like the contrivances of someone who has determined that there shall be living creatures.'

'Do you believe that you have some intelligence?'

'Go on asking questions and you will get your answer!'

'Do you suppose that there is nothing intelligent anywhere else, knowing as you do that what you have in your body is only a small portion of all the earth there is, and only a little water out of a vast volume of it, and that your share of each of the other elements of which your body is composed is minute in proportion to the whole? Do you really believe that by some lucky chance you have appropriated mind for yourself, and that it alone exists nowhere else, and that the orderliness of these vast masses of infinite multitude is due, as you say, to a kind of unintelligence?'[1]

'Yes, to be sure, for I can't see who controls them as I can see that the processes of manufacture that go on around us are controlled by the craftsmen.'

'You can't see your own mind either, although it controls your body. On that principle, you can say that you do nothing by design and everything by chance.'

Aristodemus said, 'I assure you, Socrates, it isn't that I think little of the divine; I regard it as too magnificent to need my service.'

'Then,' said Socrates, 'the more magnificent the object that deigns to serve you, the more you ought to esteem it.'

'You can be sure,' he said, 'that if I thought the gods took any interest in human beings, I shouldn't neglect them.'

'So you don't think they take any interest? Well, in the first place, man is the only creature that they have set erect; and his erect carriage enables him both to see further in front of him and to observe better what is above him, and to be less liable to injury. Then, to all other terrestrial creatures they have given feet, which

1. See Plato, *Philebus*, 28c–30d.

supply only locomotion; but to man they have also given hands, which are the principal agents of our superior happiness. Again, while all animals have a tongue, the human tongue alone is so made that by touching different parts of the mouth at different times it can produce articulate sounds and enable us to communicate with one another whatever we like. And don't forget that whereas to other animals they have granted the pleasures of sex for a limited period of the year, for us they provide them continuously, and up until old age.

'Now, God was not content with merely caring for the body; what is far more important, he also endowed man with mind in its highest form. What other animal, in the first place, has a mind that is aware of the existence of the gods, who have set in order the greatest beauty on the grandest scale? What kind of creature except man worships the gods? What mind is better able than man's to make provision against hunger or thirst, cold or heat, to relieve disease or cultivate bodily strength or take pains to acquire knowledge, or to keep in memory all that it has heard or seen or learned? Isn't it quite evident to you that, compared with other creatures, men live like gods, naturally supreme both in body and in mind? A person with the mind of a man but the body of an ox would not be able to do what he wanted; and it is no advantage to have hands without intelligence. You are lucky enough to possess both these priceless gifts – how can you think that the gods have no concern for you?[1] What do you expect them to do before you believe that they care about you?'

'Send advisers, as you claim they do,[2] to tell me what to do and what not to do.'

'When they reply by means of divination to some inquiry made by the people of Athens, do you not believe that the message is intended for you as well? Or when by sending portents they give warning to the whole of Greece or to all mankind? Are you the

1. There is still room for doubt, however, whether the gods care for individual people, rather than mankind as a whole.
2. See pp. 34–5, 68–9.

one exception that they deliberately ignore? Do you suppose that the gods would have implanted in man the belief that they can do good and harm, if they were really unable to do so? Do you suppose that we men have been deceived all this time and never realized that fact? Can't you see that the most enduring and wise of all human things – States and nations – are the most devout, and that the most intelligent times of life are the ones which are the most full of regard for the gods?

'My good friend,' he went on, 'get it into your head that your own mind, which is inside you, controls your body as it wills; and in the same way you must believe that the intelligence which is in the universe disposes all things just as it pleases. If you accept that your vision has a range of several miles, you must not suppose that the eye of God lacks the power to see everything at once; and if you accept that your mind can take thought about affairs both here and in Egypt and in Sicily, you must not suppose that the wisdom of God is incapable of taking thought for all things at the same time. Indeed, if you make the experiment of doing services to the gods to see whether they will be willing to advise you about events concealed from human foresight – just as by doing services or favours to men you discover who are willing to do them back to you, and by seeking advice you find out who are clear-headed – you will discover that the divine is so infinitely great and potent that it can see and hear everything, and be present everywhere at the same time, and take care of everything at the same time.'

It seemed to me that by speaking in this way he made his associates abstain from irreverent and wrong and discreditable actions not only in public but also when they were by themselves, for the simple reason that they had made up their minds that none of their actions could ever escape the knowledge of the gods.

5

If self-discipline is a truly good thing for a man to possess, let us consider whether Socrates gave any impulse towards it by homilies of the following kind.

'Gentlemen, supposing that war had broken out, and we wanted to elect a man under whose leadership we were most likely to save ourselves and subdue our enemies, should we choose someone who had no power of resistance against appetite or wine or sexual desire or sleep? How could we possibly expect that such a person would either save us or overcome the enemy? Or suppose that we have reached the end of life and want to entrust someone with the education of our sons or the guardianship of our unmarried daughters or the safe-keeping of our money: are we likely to regard a moral weakling as worthy of our confidence? Should we entrust livestock, or management, or the supervision of labour to a weak-willed slave? Should we be prepared to accept a person of this kind in the capacity of agent or buyer, even as a free gift? But if we would not put up with even a slave of weak character, surely it is proper to guard against incurring this defect oneself. It is not the case that a weak-willed man benefits himself by harming others in the way that money-lenders are supposed to enrich themselves by taking money from others; no, he injures others, but he injures himself much more, because to ruin not only one's estate, but also one's body and mind, is to do oneself the greatest injury of all. And who would appreciate the company of such a person at a social function, if he saw him caring more about the food and wine than about his friends, and paying more attention to the whores than to his companions? Surely every man ought to regard self-discipline as the foundation of moral goodness, and to cultivate it in his character before anything else. Without it, who could either learn anything good or practise it to a degree worth mentioning? Or who could escape degradation both of body and of mind if he is a slave to his appetites? I assure you, it seems to me that a free man ought to pray that he may never happen upon a slave of this kind, while a man who is a slave to such pleasures ought to pray to the gods that he may find good masters; for that is the only way in which such a person can be saved.'

While expressing these sentiments, Socrates showed himself to be even more self-disciplined in practice than in theory. He overcame not only his physical appetites, but also the attraction of money; for he thought that the man who accepts money indiscriminately is setting up a master over himself and submitting to a peculiarly disgraceful form of slavery.

6

It is only fair to Socrates not to leave unrecorded the conversations that he had with Antiphon the sophist.[1] On one occasion, this man, wishing to transfer Socrates' associates to himself, went up to him in their presence and said: 'Socrates, I always thought that people ought to become happier through the study of philosophy, but it seems to me that you have experienced the opposite effect. At any rate, you lead the sort of life that no slave would put up with if it were imposed upon him by his master. You eat and drink the worst possible food and drink, and the cloak you wear is not only of poor quality, but is the same for summer and winter; and you never wear shoes or a tunic. Then, you never accept money, the receipt of which is cheering and the possession of which enables people to live with more freedom and pleasure. So if you are going to affect your associates in the same way as the teachers of other occupations, who turn out pupils after their own pattern, you should regard yourself as a teacher of misery.'

Socrates replied, 'You seem to have got it into your head that I live such a miserable life, Antiphon, that I really do believe you would rather die than live as I do. Come on, then: let us see what hardship you have detected in my way of life. Is it that those who accept payment are bound to do the work for which they've been paid, whereas I, since I don't accept it, am not compelled to converse with a person if I don't want to? Or do you depreciate my diet on the ground that it is less wholesome and sustaining than yours? Is it that my means of subsistence are harder to procure than yours, because they are rarer and more costly? Is it that you enjoy your provisions more than I do mine? Don't you

1. One of the leading lights of the Greek sophistic movement.

know that the more a man enjoys eating, the less he needs a stimulus for his appetite, and the more he enjoys drinking, the less he craves for a drink that he hasn't got? As for cloaks, you know that people change them because of cold or hot weather, and they wear shoes to prevent things from hurting their feet and so impeding their movements. Well, have you ever known me stay indoors more than anybody else on account of the cold, or compete with anyone for the shade on account of the heat, or fail to walk wherever I wanted because my feet were sore? Don't you know that those who are physically weakest by nature, if they train with a particular end in view, become better able to achieve that end, with less effort to themselves, than the strongest athletes who neglect their training? And if that is so, don't you think that I, who am always training myself to put up with the things that happen to my body, find everything easier to bear than you do with your neglect of training? As for my not being a slave to my stomach, or to sleep, or to lechery, what better reason for it can you imagine than that I have other more pleasant occupations, which cheer me not only when I am engaged upon them, but also as giving me ground for hoping that they will benefit me always? Besides, you must be aware of this, that those who feel that their farming or seafaring or any other occupation that they have is going well are cheered by the consciousness of success. Now then, do you suppose that all these feelings give as much pleasure as the thought that one is becoming better oneself, and acquiring better friends? Well, I have this belief all the time. And then, if one's friends or the State needs help, which has more leisure to attend to this duty – the man who passes his time as I do now, or the one whom you regard as fortunate? Which could more readily go on military service – the man who can't live without an expensive diet, or the one who is content with whatever is to hand? And which would be sooner reduced to surrender in a siege – the one whose requirements are most difficult to obtain, or the one who is satisfied with whatever he comes across? It seems to me, Antiphon, that you identify happiness with luxury and extravagance; but I have always thought that to need nothing is divine, and to need as little as possible is the nearest approach to the divine; and that what is divine is best, and what is nearest to the divine is the next best.'

On another occasion, when Antiphon was talking to Socrates, he said, 'You know, Socrates, I think that you are an honest man, but not at all a wise one. And it seems to me that you realize this yourself; at any rate, you don't charge anyone for your company. But if you thought that your cloak or your house or any other item of your property was worth money, so far from giving it away, you wouldn't even accept a price lower than its value. So obviously, if you thought that your company was worth anything, you would charge a fee for it no less than its value. Therefore, honest you may be, since you don't deceive with a view to your own advantage; but wise you cannot be, if your knowledge is worthless.'

To this Socrates replied, 'In our society, Antiphon, the same rules with regard to what is creditable and what is not are thought to apply equally to the disposal of physical attractions and of wisdom. A man who sells his favours for a price to anyone who wants them is called a catamite; but if anyone forms a love-attachment with someone whom he knows to be truly good, we regard him as perfectly respectable. In just the same way, those who sell wisdom at a price to anyone who wants it are called sophists; but if anyone, by imparting any edifying knowledge that he possesses, makes a friend of one whom he knows to be naturally gifted, we consider that he is behaving as a truly good citizen should behave. As for myself, Antiphon, I take as much pleasure in good friends as other people take in a good horse or dog or bird – in fact, I take more; and if I have anything good to teach them, I teach it, and I introduce them to any others from whom I think they will get help in the quest for goodness. And in company with my friends, I open and read from beginning to end the books in which the wise men of past times have written down and bequeathed to us their treasures; and when we see anything good, we take it for ourselves; and we regard our mutual friendship as great gain.'

When I heard him say this, it certainly seemed to me that he was a fortunate man himself, and that he was leading his audience on towards true goodness.

On another occasion, Antiphon asked him how it was that he expected to make others politicians when he himself did not take part in politics, if indeed he was capable of doing so. Socrates retorted: 'Which would be the more effective way for me to take part in politics – by doing so alone, or by making it my business to see that as many persons as possible are capable of taking part in it?'

7

Let us also consider whether in discouraging his associates from pretence he encouraged them to apply themselves to goodness; for he always said that there was no better road to distinction than that by which one could become good at the pursuit for which one wished to be distinguished. He used to demonstrate the truth of this statement in the following way.

'Let us consider,' he said, 'what a man ought to do if he wants to be thought a good musical performer although he is not. Surely he should imitate good performers in respect of the outward accessories of their art. First, as they possess imposing paraphernalia and take round with them a large retinue, he must do the same. Secondly, as there are many who express admiration of them, he must provide himself with plenty of admirers. But actual playing he must never attempt; otherwise he will immediately be exposed as a laughing-stock, and not merely a bad performer, but an impostor. And yet, if he spends a lot of money and gets no benefit from it, and has besides a bad reputation, surely his life will be laborious and unprofitable and ridiculous.

'Similarly, supposing that someone should wish to be regarded as a good general or a good pilot without actually being one, let us consider what would happen to him. If he really wanted to be thought capable of such a line of conduct, and could not convince people, wouldn't his position be distressing? And wouldn't it be still more wretched if he did convince them, because obviously if a man who did not know his job were appointed as a pilot or as a general, he would destroy those whom he least wished to destroy, and the consequences for himself would be shameful and disastrous.'

On the same principle he showed that it did no good to be thought rich or brave or strong if one was not in reality, because people who were in this position were faced with obligations that were beyond their powers; and, if they could not perform them although they seemed to be capable of doing so, they would get no sympathy. It was no slight deception, he said, even to deprive another person by persuasion of a sum of money or an article of value, but it was the grossest deception of all for a good-for-nothing person to convey the false impression that he was capable of directing the State. In my opinion, by conversations of this kind, he discouraged his associates from even making pretensions.

BOOK TWO

It seems to me that Socrates also encouraged his associates to practise self-discipline with regard to food and drink and sex and sleep and heat and cold and physical exertion by discourses like the one which follows. When he observed that one of his associates was rather undisciplined in these respects, he said: 'Tell me, Aristippus,[1] if you had to take charge of two young men and educate them, one to be capable of governing and the other not even to aspire to it, how would you educate each of them? Would you like us to consider this problem by starting with the basic question of their food?'

Aristippus replied, 'It certainly seems to me that food is the starting-point: one can't even live without taking food.'

'So it's natural that both of them should feel the desire to partake of food when the right time comes, isn't it?'

'Yes, it is.'

'Which of them should we accustom to choose to press on with an urgent duty rather than gratify his belly?'

'Definitely the one who is being educated to govern, so that the business of the State may not be neglected under his government.'

'Then similarly when they want to drink, the same one must be endowed with the ability to restrain himself when he's thirsty.'

'Certainly.'

'Which should we endow with self-discipline as regards sleep, so that he can go to bed late and get up early and stay awake if need be?'

'The same one ought to have this too.'

'What about not shirking hard work, but willingly putting up with it? Which should we endow with this quality?'

1. It is not clear whether it was this Aristippus, or his grandson of the same name, who founded the Cyrenaic school of hedonistic philosophy. The present dialogue suggests that this Aristippus had gone some way towards formulating his own thought. The dialogue is therefore probably anachronistic, since it is unlikely that Aristippus would have worked out his views until after Socrates' death.

'We should give this also to the one who is being educated for government.'

'What about acquiring any kind of knowledge that is conducive to defeating one's opponents – to which would this faculty be more appropriate?'

'Far more, of course, to the one who is being educated for government. None of the other qualities is any good without this sort of knowledge.'

'Don't you think that a person so educated would be less likely than other creatures to be caught by his opponents? Some creatures, as you know, are lured on by their greed, and are often attracted to the bait, in spite of their timidity, by their craving for food, and so get caught, while others are trapped by means of drink.'

'Quite true.'

'And isn't it true that others are trapped because of their lasciviousness, as for example quails and partridges are attracted by the cry of the female because of their desire and expectation of sexual intercourse and, losing all count of the risks, rush into the hunting-nets?'

He agreed that this was true too.

'Don't you think that it's shameful for a man to be affected in the same way as the stupidest of creatures? I am thinking of the way in which adulterers walk into the snare, although they know that an adulterer is in danger not only of incurring the penalty threatened by the laws, but of having a trap set for him and, if he is caught, of suffering physical violence. When the adulterer is liable to all these serious and shameful consequences, and there are plenty of means to relieve his sexual appetite with impunity, nevertheless to rush headlong into the paths of danger – isn't that the very acme of infatuation?'

'I think so,' he said.

'As most of the essential human activities – such as those which relate to warfare and farming, and not the least important of the rest – are carried out in the open air, don't you think that it is extremely irresponsible for most people to be untrained to endure cold and heat?'

He agreed to this too.

'Then, do you think that the prospective ruler ought also to practise enduring these things easily?'

'Certainly,' he said.

'Then, if we rate those who are self-disciplined in all these respects as fit to govern, shall we rate those who are incapable of such conduct as not even claiming fitness to do so?'

He agreed again.

'Very well, then: now that you know the rating of both types, I suppose you have considered to which class you would rightly assign yourself?'

'I have indeed,' said Aristippus, 'and I certainly don't put myself in the class of those who want to govern. In fact, considering that it's a serious task to provide for one's own needs, it seems to me to be quite crazy not to be content with this, but to pile on top of it the task of supplying the needs of the rest of one's fellow citizens as well. And when a person has to do without a great many things that he wants himself, surely it's the height of folly, by assuming responsibility for his country, to render himself liable to prosecution if he doesn't carry out all his country's requirements. States claim the right to treat their ministers as I treat the slaves in my own household. I expect my servants to make lavish provision for me, but not to touch anything themselves; and in the same way, States think that their ministers ought to provide them with as many benefits as possible without participating in any of them personally. So if there are any people who want to have a lot of trouble themselves and cause it to others, I would educate them in that manner and set them in the category of potential rulers; but I rank myself among those who want their lives to be as easy and pleasant as possible.'

Socrates said, 'Would you like us to consider this question too: who have the more pleasant life, the rulers or the subjects?'

'By all means.'

'Well, in the first place, of the peoples that we know, in Asia the

Persians are rulers and the Syrians, Phrygians and Lydians are subjects. In Europe the Scythians are rulers and the Maeotians subjects. In Africa the Carthaginians are rulers and the Libyans subjects.[1] Who of these do you think have the pleasanter life? Or take the Greeks, to whom you belong yourself: who seem to you to have the pleasanter life – the conquerors or the conquered?'

'But, you know,' said Aristippus, 'I don't assign myself to the slave category either. It seems to me that there is a middle path which I am trying to follow: the path not through rule nor through servitude, but through liberty, which is the surest road to happiness.'

'Well,' said Socrates, 'if this path of yours that avoids rule and servitude avoids mankind also, there may perhaps be something in what you say; but if while living among men you expect neither to rule nor to be ruled, and don't intend to defer willingly to authority, I presume you can see that the stronger know how to make the weaker suffer both collectively and individually, and to treat them as slaves. Don't you realize that there are people who cut the corn that others have sown, and chop down the trees that others have planted, and put every kind of pressure upon inferiors who refuse them deference, until they finally prevail on them to prefer slavery to war against a stronger power? And in private life too, don't you know that the bold and powerful reduce the timid and powerless to slavery, and then exploit them?'

'But I have an escape, you know,' he said. 'To avoid being treated this way, I don't confine myself to a nationality at all: I am a stranger in all countries.'

Socrates replied, 'Now, that really is a clever stroke: ever since Sinis and Sciron and Procrustes were killed,[2] nobody has done any harm to strangers! All the same, nowadays those who form the administration in their several countries pass laws to protect themselves against harm, and make friends, in addition to their

1. Here 'Asia' refers to Asia Minor, 'Europe' to the area north of the Black Sea, and 'Africa' to the north coast of Africa.
2. Legendary characters who brutally maltreated travellers until Theseus put an end to their exploits.

so-called intimate friends, to give them help; they also put fortifications round their cities, acquire arms to keep off aggressors, and, besides all this, procure external allies as well. And with all these assets they still incur harm. As for you, who have none of these assets, and spend a great deal of time in the streets, where most injuries are sustained – you who, whatever country you visit, are in a weaker position than any of the citizens, and a natural victim for intending wrongdoers – do you still imagine that you would not be harmed, because you are a stranger? Is your confidence based on official assurances of safety as you travel here and there in the country? Or is it based on the belief that you are the sort of person who would be useless as a slave to any master? I mean, who would care to have in his house a man who refuses to do any work and enjoys the most expensive diet?

'Now let us consider another point: what sort of treatment slaves of this kind receive. Isn't it true that their masters discipline their wantonness by starvation, and stop them from stealing by locking up any place or receptacle from which anything can be removed, and prevent them from running away by putting them in fetters, and drive out their idleness by beating them? Or what steps do you take when you discover that one of your house-slaves is behaving in this sort of way?'

'I punish him with the utmost severity until I have made him submit. But look here, Socrates, about these people who are being educated in the art of ruling, which you seem to regard as happiness: how are they any better off than those who suffer through force of circumstances, if they are going to be hungry and thirsty and cold and sleepless and to suffer every other kind of hardship voluntarily? I don't see that there is any difference between having the same skin flogged voluntarily and having it flogged involuntarily, or in general that there is any difference between having the same body harassed by all these trials voluntarily and having it harassed involuntarily, except that anyone who submits to painful experiences deliberately is a fool into the bargain.'

'Come, come, Aristippus,' said Socrates, 'don't you think that voluntary sufferings of this kind are preferable to involuntary ones from this point of view: that the man who is hungry or thirsty of his own free will can eat and drink when he wants to, and similarly in the other cases, whereas the man who suffers through force of circumstances can't stop the suffering when he wants to?[1] And then the man who undergoes hardship voluntarily is encouraged in his efforts by the prospect of success, as, for example, hunters enjoy their exertions because they have a prospect of catching the animals that they are hunting. This sort of reward for effort is trivial; but when people devote their energy to acquiring good friends or worsting their enemies, or becoming physically and mentally efficient and managing their estates well and benefiting their friends and serving their country, surely we must suppose that they find pleasure in working for these ends, and enjoy life, contented with themselves and praised and envied by others. Again, easy tasks and momentary pleasures cannot produce physical fitness, as the experts in physical education remind us, or develop in the mind any knowledge worth mentioning; sustained application, however, enables us to achieve truly good results, as good men tell us. Hesiod says somewhere:[2]

> Evil can be easily found, and freely;
> Smooth is the road, and very near she dwells.
> But sweat the gods have set upon the way
> To goodness: long and steep is the path to it
> And rough at first; but if you reach the summit
> Thereafter it is easy, hard though it was.

'Epicharmus[3] testifies the same in the line "Pain's the price the gods require us to pay for all our benefits", and he also says in another place, "Rascal, do not crave for comfort, lest the lot you have be hard."

1. Compare Plato, *Hippias Minor*, 373c–376b.
2. *Works and Days*, 287–92.
3. Epicharmus of Syracuse (*c.* 530–440) wrote comedies seasoned with apophthegms and maxims. The lines quoted here are Fragments 36 and 37 (Diels-Kranz).

'The same view of moral goodness is also set out by the sophist Prodicus in the story of Heracles, which is one of his most popular displays; it runs like this, as far as I remember.[1] When Heracles was setting out from childhood towards manhood, at the age when the young become independent and show whether they are going to approach life by the path of goodness or by the path of wickedness, he went out to a quiet spot and sat down considering which way he should take. While he was sitting there, he thought he saw two women approach him. Both were tall, but one of them was handsome in appearance with a natural air of distinction, clean-limbed and modest in expression, and soberly dressed in a white robe, while the other was well fed to the point of fleshiness and softness, made up to have a complexion too red and white to be real, and with a carriage more upright than was natural, with a brazen expression, and robed in a way that revealed as much as possible of her charms.[2] She kept on examining herself, and watching to see if anyone was looking at her, and glancing at her own shadow. When they got nearer to Heracles, the first of the two continued to advance in the same way, but the other, wishing to forestall her, ran up to him and said:

'"Heracles, I see that you can't make up your mind which way of life to adopt. If you take me as your friend, I will lead you by the easiest and pleasantest road; you shall not miss the taste of any pleasure, and you shall live out your life without any experience of hardship. In the first place, you will not be concerned with wars or responsibilities; you shall constantly consider[3] what food or drink you can find to suit your taste, and what sight or sound or scent or touch might please you, and which lover's society will

1. Heracles (Hercules) was revered from early times, because of his 'labours', as a benefactor of mankind and a model of courage and endurance; he was later credited with other virtues, such as wisdom and self-control, which are not conspicuous in the stories told about him. Prodicus of Ceos was an eminent contemporary of Socrates and a member of the sophistic movement.
2. Compare *The Estate-manager*, 10.
3. Reading ἀεὶ ἔσῃ with Diels.

gratify you most, and how you can sleep most comfortably, and how you can achieve all these objects with the least trouble. And if there is ever any suspicion of a shortage of any of these benefits, you need not fear that I shall involve you in any physical or mental effort or distress in procuring them; you shall enjoy the fruits of other people's labours, and you shall refrain from nothing from which you can derive any advantage, because I authorize my followers to benefit themselves from all quarters."

'When Heracles heard this, he asked, "What is your name, lady?" She replied, "My friends call me Happiness, but people who don't like me nickname me Vice."

'Meanwhile, the other woman came forward and said, "I too have come to meet you, Heracles, because I know your parents[1] and I have carefully observed your natural qualities in the course of your education, and this knowledge makes me hope that, if you will only take the path that leads to me, you may become a very effective performer of fine and noble deeds, and I may win much greater honour still, and brighter glory for the blessings I bestow. I will not delude you with promises of future pleasure; I shall give you a true account of the facts, exactly as the gods have ordained them. Nothing that is really good and admirable is granted by the gods to men without some effort and application. If you want the gods to be gracious to you, you must worship the gods; if you wish to be loved by your friends, you must be kind to your friends; if you desire to be honoured by a State, you must help that State; if you expect to be admired for your fine qualities by the whole of Greece, you must try to benefit Greece; if you want your land to produce abundant crops, you must look after your land; if you expect to make money from your livestock, you must take care of your livestock; if you have an impulse to extend your influence by war, and want to be able to free your friends and subdue your enemies, you must both learn the actual arts of war from those who understand them, and practise the proper way of applying them; and if you want to be physically efficient, you

1. Zeus and Alcmene.

must train your body to be subject to your reason, and develop it with hard work and sweat."

'Here Vice, as Prodicus tells, broke in. "Do you realize, Heracles," she said, "what a long and difficult road to enjoyment this woman is describing to you? I will put you on a short and easy road to happiness."

'"Impudent creature!" said Virtue. "What good have you to offer, or what do you know of pleasure, you who refuse to do anything with a view to either? You don't even wait for the desire for what is pleasant: you stuff yourself with everything before you want it, eating before you are hungry and drinking before you are thirsty. To make eating enjoyable you invent refinements of cookery, and to make drinking enjoyable, you provide yourself with expensive wines and rush about searching for ice in summer. To make going to sleep pleasant, you provide yourself not only with soft blankets, but also with bases for your beds, for it is not work but boredom that makes you want to go to bed. You force the gratification of your sexual impulses before they ask for it, employing all kinds of devices and treating men as women. That is the sort of training that you give your friends – exciting their passions by night, and putting them to sleep for the best part of the day. Although you are immortal, you have been turned out by the gods, and you are despised by decent men. You are denied the hearing of the sweetest of all sounds – praise of yourself – and you are denied the seeing of the sweetest of all sights, for you have never contemplated any act of yours that was admirable. Who would trust your word? Who would assist you if you needed someone? What sane person would have the face to join your devotees? When they are young, they are feeble in body, and when they get older, they are foolish in mind; they are maintained in their youth in effortless comfort, but pass their old age in laborious squalor, disgraced by their past actions and burdened by their present ones, because in their youth they have run through all that was pleasant, and laid up for their old age what is hard to bear.

'"I associate both with gods and with good men, and no fine

action, human or divine, is done independently of me. I am held in the highest honour both among gods and men who are akin to me. I am a welcome fellow worker to the craftsman, a faithful guardian to the householder, a kindly protector to the servant, an efficient helper in the tasks of peace, a staunch ally in the operations of war, and the best partner in friendship. My friends can enjoy food and drink with pleasure and without effort, because they abstain until they feel a desire for them. Their sleep is sweeter than the sleep of the easy-living, and they neither are vexed when they have to give it up, nor make it an excuse for neglecting their duty. The young enjoy the praise of their elders, and the older people are happy in the respect of the young. They recall their past achievements with pleasure, and rejoice in their present successes, because through me they are dear to the gods, loved by their friends and honoured by their country. And when their appointed end comes, they do not lie forgotten in obscurity, but flourish celebrated in memory for all time.

'"There, Heracles," she said, "child of good parents: if you work hard in the way that I have described, you can possess the most beatific happiness."

'That is roughly how Prodicus describes the education of Heracles by Virtue, except that he actually dressed up the sentiments in language still more splendid than I have used now. At any rate, Aristippus, you had better think this over and try to take some account of the factors that will affect the life that lies in front of you.'

2

Once, when Socrates noticed his eldest son Lamprocles getting angry with his mother,[1] he said, 'Look here, my boy, you know that there are some people who are called ungrateful?'

'Yes, of course,' said the boy.

'Are you clear about what it is that people do to earn this name?'

1. Xanthippe; see also p. 232.

'Yes, I am,' he said. 'People are called ungrateful when they have been well treated and could show gratitude in return, but don't.'

'Then you think that ingratitude is regarded as wrong?'

'Yes, I do.'

'Have you ever considered this question: whether perhaps ingratitude is wrong if it is shown towards friends, but right if it is shown towards enemies, in the same way that it is considered to be wrong to enslave one's friends, but right to enslave one's enemies?'

'Yes, indeed,' he replied, 'and I think that anyone who has received a favour either from a friend or from an enemy and doesn't attempt to show gratitude is morally wrong.'

'Well then, if that is so, ingratitude must be unmitigated injustice.'

Lamprocles agreed.

'Then the greater the favours that a person receives without showing gratitude in return, the more unjust he is?'

He admitted this too.

'Well,' said Socrates, 'whom can we find that enjoy greater benefits than children receive from their parents? Their parents have brought them into existence from non-existence, and have enabled them to see all the beauty and share in all the good things that the gods provide for mankind – privileges which we consider so priceless that anyone would do anything rather than part with them, and States have made death the penalty for the greatest crimes, on the presumption that there could be no stronger deterrent from wrongdoing.

'You don't imagine that people have children just for sexual satisfaction; the streets and brothels are full of potential suppliers of that need. Besides, you can see that we look out for the sort of women who will bear us the best children, and then unite with them to produce children. The husband both supports his partner in child-bearing and provides for the children that are to be born everything that he thinks will be an asset to them in life, and he provides it as fully as he can. The wife conceives and carries this burden, bearing the weight of it, risking her life and giving up a share of her own nourishment; and after all her trouble in carrying it for the full time and bringing it to birth, she feeds and cares for it, although the child has never done her any good and does not know who his benefactor is. He cannot even communicate what he wants; his mother's attempts to supply what will be good for him and give him pleasure depend upon her powers of guessing. And she goes on rearing him for a long time, putting up with drudgery day and night, without knowing whether she will receive any gratitude.

'And it is not merely a matter of rearing children. When they seem to be capable of learning, their parents teach them themselves whatever they can teach that is valuable for life; but if they think that there is anything that is better taught by somebody else, they incur the expense of sending their children to that person. They leave nothing undone in their concern to see that their children's development is as perfect as possible.'

To this the lad replied, 'But really, even if she has done all this and a great deal more besides, nobody could put up with her temper.'

'Which kind of ferocity do you think is harder to bear – a wild beast's or a mother's?'

'A mother's,' he said, 'if she's like mine.'

'Has she ever injured you by biting or kicking, as a good many people have suffered before now from wild animals?'

'Oh no,' he said, 'but she says things that one wouldn't want to hear every day of one's life.'

'And how much trouble,' said Socrates, 'do you think you have given her by your peevish cries and behaviour day and night ever since you were a baby, and how often have you worried her by your illnesses?'

'Well,' said Lamprocles, 'I have never said or done anything to her to make her ashamed of me.'

'Look here,' said Socrates, 'do you think it is harder for you to listen to the things that she says than it is for actors in tragedies when they go all out to abuse one another?'

'Well, they don't imagine that the speaker who accuses them intends to punish them, or that the one who threatens them intends to injure them, so I suppose they take it quite lightly.'

'But *you* get angry, although you know quite well that what your mother says to you is said not only without any unkind intention, but actually out of a desire for your especial benefit? Or do you imagine that your mother is ill-disposed towards you?'

'Oh no,' he said, 'I don't think that.'

'So,' said Socrates, 'although this mother of yours is well-disposed towards you, and does her very best to see to it that you get well when you are ill and that you shan't lack anything that you need; and besides all this, although she is constantly praying to the gods for blessings upon you and paying her vows on your account, you say that she is hard to put up with? In my opinion, if you can't bear a mother like that, you can't bear what is good for you. Tell me, do you think that there is anyone else who claims your respect? Or is there nobody you are prepared to try to please or obey, be he your superior officer or anyone else in authority?'

'Of course that's not the case,' he said.

'Well then,' said Socrates, 'do you want to be pleasant to your neighbour, so that he may give you a light for your fire when you need it, and both contribute to your success and give you prompt and friendly help if you meet with any misfortune?'

'Yes, I do.'

'Take the case of a fellow traveller or fellow voyager, or anyone else you might meet: would it make no difference to you whether he became your friend or your enemy? Do you think that you ought to concern yourself with the goodwill of people like these?'

'I do think so.'

'So you are prepared to concern yourself with these people, and yet see no need to show consideration for your mother, who loves you more than anyone else does? Don't you know that the State cares nothing for any other kind of ingratitude, and prescribes no penalty for it, but turns a blind eye when beneficiaries fail to repay a favour; but if anyone shows no consideration for his parents, the State imposes a penalty upon him and disqualifies him from holding public office, on the presumption that the sacrifices could not be performed on behalf of the State with proper piety if he performed them, nor any other act be well and duly carried out if he were the agent? And what is more, if anyone fails to tend the graves of his dead parents, even this becomes the subject of a State inquiry when candidates for office are having their conduct scrutinized.

'So if you are sensible, my boy, you will beseech the gods to pardon any disregard that you have shown towards your mother in case they count you as ungrateful and refuse to do you good; and at the same time you will take care that your fellow men don't observe you neglecting your parents and all lose respect for you so that you stand revealed as destitute of friends; for if they once got the notion that you were ungrateful to your parents, none would expect gratitude in return for doing you a kindness.'

3

On another occasion, Chaerephon and Chaerecrates, two brothers with whom Socrates was well acquainted, were having a quarrel. Socrates became aware of this and, when he saw Chaerecrates, he said: 'Tell me, Chaerecrates, surely you aren't one of those who think that possessions are more useful than a brother, although they are not endowed with sense and he is, and they need protection whereas he can give it, and, what is more, they are many while he is only one? It is extraordinary, too, that anyone should regard brothers as a liability because he doesn't possess their property as well as his own, and not regard his fellow citizens as a liability on the same ground. Since in the one case people can reason that it is better to have a secure sufficiency and live in a group than to have precarious possession of all their fellow citizens' property and live alone, it is curious that they fail to realize the same fact in the case of their brothers. And they buy house-slaves (if they can afford it) to help them with the work, and they make friends, showing that they feel the need for support; and yet they show no interest in their brothers – as if they expected their fellow citizens to be friendly, but not their brothers. Then again, it's a powerful incentive to affection to have been born of the same parents and brought up together; even animals develop a kind of strong attachment for members of the same litter. Besides, the rest of mankind have a greater respect for those who have brothers, and are less likely to attack them.'

Chaerecrates replied, 'Well, Socrates, if the quarrel weren't a serious one, very likely it would be right to bear with one's brother and not shun him for petty reasons. As you say, a brother is an asset if he behaves as he should; but when he is deficient in every respect and the exact opposite of what he ought to be, why should one attempt the impossible?'

'Tell me, Chaerecrates,' said Socrates, 'is Chaerephon as incapable of getting on with anybody as he is with you, or are there some people with whom he gets on quite well?'

'That's precisely my ground for disliking him, Socrates,' he replied. 'He can be agreeable to other people, but in all his associations with me, in word and in deed, he's more of a liability than an asset.'

'Well,' said Socrates, 'a horse is a liability to a person who tries to manage it without having enough knowledge.[1] Perhaps in the same way a brother is a liability when one tries to manage him without knowledge.'

'How can I not have the knowledge to manage a brother,' said Chaerecrates, 'when I know how to speak and behave civilly to those who are civil to me? But when a man does his best to annoy me by what he says and does, I can't speak or behave civilly to him, and I'm not going to try either.'

'That's a queer thing to say, Chaerecrates,' said Socrates. 'If you had a trained sheep-dog which was friendly to the shepherds, but resented it when you came near, you would pay no attention to its bad temper – you would try to win it over by kindness. You say that your brother would be a great asset to you if he treated you properly; you admit that you know how to behave and speak

1. Compare *The Estate-manager*, 1 (pp. 289–93).

civilly; yet you don't attempt to find a way to make him as well disposed towards you as possible.'

'I'm afraid, Socrates,' said Chaerecrates, 'that I'm not enough of a genius to make Chaerephon behave properly to me.'

'I assure you,' said Socrates, 'so far as I can see, you needn't employ any subtle or novel method on him: I think you could prevail on him to have a high regard for you by using means which you understand yourself.'

'If you have detected that I am the unconscious possessor of some magic formula,' he replied, 'you can't tell me too quickly.'

'Tell me, then,' said Socrates, 'if you wanted to prevail upon one of your acquaintances to invite you to dinner whenever he was holding a celebration, what would you do?'

'Obviously I should begin by inviting him when I was celebrating.'

'And if you wanted to induce one of your friends to take care of your property when you were away from home, what would you do?'

'Obviously I should first try to take care of his when he was away.'

'And if you wanted to make a foreigner give you hospitality when you visited his country, what would you do?'

'Obviously I should first give him hospitality when he came to Athens. And if I wanted him to be eager to achieve the object of my visit for me, obviously I should have first to do the same for him.'

'So you know all the magic spells that influence human conduct, and have kept your knowledge dark all this time! Why do you hesitate to begin? Are you afraid that you will look bad if you treat your brother well before he treats you well? Surely it is considered to be extremely creditable to take the lead in harming one's enemies and benefiting one's friends. If I had thought that Chaerephon was likelier than you to take the lead towards friendliness, I should have tried to persuade him first to try to win you over; but as it is, I think that you are the more likely to take the lead in achieving this result.'

Chaerecrates said, 'It is preposterous, Socrates, and not at all like you, to urge me, the younger brother, to take the lead. Why, the universal practice is just the opposite – that the older should take the lead in everything that is said or done.'

'Surely not,' said Socrates. 'Isn't it customary in all countries for the younger to make way for the older, and to stand up when he approaches, and to show respect for him by giving him the most comfortable seat, and to allow him to speak first? Don't hold back, my dear fellow, but try to pacify him, and he will very soon respond. Don't you see what a noble and generous nature he has? Low types of humanity are most likely to be won over by a gift; but the best way to influence truly good people is by courtesy.'

Chaerecrates said, 'Supposing that I do what you recommend, and he shows no improvement?'

'In that case,' said Socrates, 'you will simply run the risk of demonstrating that you are a good and affectionate brother, and he is a bad one who doesn't deserve to be treated kindly. But I don't suppose that anything of the sort will happen. I think that when he once realizes that you are challenging him to this kind of contest, he will be very keen to outdo you in kindness both spoken and practical. At the moment your attitude towards each other is like this: as if two hands which God created to cooperate with each other were to give up doing this and turn to hindering each other; or as if two feet designed by Providence to help each other were to neglect their duty and get in each other's way. Wouldn't it be great folly and perversity to use for our disadvantage what was intended for our benefit? And yet, so far as I can see, brothers were intended by God to be more helpful to each other than hands or feet or eyes or any other natural pairs with which he has supplied mankind. If the hands are required to perform simultaneously two operations more than six feet apart, they cannot do it; and the feet cannot reach simultaneously two points even six feet apart; and the eyes, which are supposed to have the greatest range, cannot see at the same time two objects at a still lesser distance, if one object is in front and the other behind. But a pair of brothers, if they are on good terms, can carry out two simultaneous operations at a great distance to their mutual advantage.'

4

I once heard Socrates expressing views about friendship which I thought would be extremely helpful to anyone in the acquisition and treatment of friends. He said that although he often heard it stated that a good and sure friend was the best of all possessions, he noticed that most people gave their attention to anything rather than the acquisition of friends. He saw that they took pains to acquire houses and lands and slaves and cattle and furniture, and tried to preserve what they had; but in the case of a friend, who according to them was the greatest blessing, most of them never considered either how to acquire one or how to retain those that they had. Indeed, he noticed, he said, that some people, when their friends and servants were ill, called in the doctor and scrupulously made all the other provisions for the health of their servants, but neglected their friends; and that when friends and servants died, they grieved over their servants and felt a sense of loss, but in the case of their friends considered that they were none the worse; and that they allowed none of their other possessions to lack attention and supervision, but neglected their friends when they needed care.

Further, besides all this, he noticed, he said, that most peopl knew the quantity of their other possessions, even if they were very numerous, but as for their friends, few as they were, they not only did not know how many they had, but when they tried to furnish an inventory in answer to inquiry, they revised their opinion of those whom they had previously reckoned as friends, which showed how much they thought about friends.

Yet, if we compare a good friend with any other possession, it must be obvious that the friend is far superior. What horse or vehicle is as valuable as a staunch friend? What slave is as loyal and trusty? What other possession is so thoroughly useful? A good friend sets himself to supply all his friend's deficiencies, whether of private property or of public service. If it is required to do someone a good turn, he lends vigorous support; if some fear is causing anxiety, he comes to the rescue. As the occasion demands, he shares expense, joins in action, helps to persuade, or uses compulsion; he is equally effective in cheering on the successful and in raising up those who stumble. A friend is just as much a benefactor to a man as are the hands that work for him, the eyes that see for him, the ears that hear for him and the feet that carry him. Often one friend supplies for another something which that other has failed to do or see or hear or carry out himself. And yet although some people try to cultivate trees for the sake of their fruit, most are indolent and negligent in taking care of the most productive of all possessions – what we call a friend.

5

One day I heard another discourse of his which I thought stimulated anyone who heard it to examine himself and see what he was worth to his friends. He saw that one of his associates was neglecting a friend who was distressed by poverty, and he questioned Antisthenes[1] in the presence of the neglectful person and of several others.

'Antisthenes,' he said, 'do friends have values, in the same way that domestic slaves do? For instance, one slave, I suppose, is worth two minae, and another not as much as half a mina, and another five minae and another ten minae; and they say that Nicias[2] the son of Niceratus bought an overseer of his silver mine for a talent.[3] What I am trying to discover is whether friends have their values too, like domestic slaves.'

'Yes, indeed,' replied Antisthenes. 'At any rate, I would rather have A as my friend than two minae, while I wouldn't rate B higher than half a mina; and I would choose C in preference to ten

1. See p. 75, n. 2.
2. A famous moderate politician and over-cautious military commander.
3. The average wage for an artisan at this time was about four minae a year. A talent was sixty minae (or 6,000 drachmae, or 36,000 obols).

minae, and I wouldn't spend any amount of money and effort to obtain the friendship of D.'

'Very well, then,' said Socrates, 'if the facts are as you say, it would be well for a man to examine himself and see what he really is worth to his friends, and to try to be worth as much as possible to them, so that his friends may be less likely to let him down. You see, I have often heard one person say that a friend has let him down, and another say that a man who he thought was his friend has preferred a mina to him; and that is why I am investigating the whole question. Perhaps, just as one offers a bad slave for sale and disposes of him for what he will fetch, in the same way there is a temptation to sell a bad friend when one can get a price greater than his value. But in my experience there is no more question of giving up a good friend than of selling a good slave.'

6

I thought that in the following conversation he was giving instruction about estimating what sort of friends it was worthwhile to make.

'Tell me, Critobulus,' he said, 'if we wanted a good friend, how should we set about our search? Should we first look for a man who can control his desires for food and drink and sex and sleep and idleness? For the man who is a slave to these can't do his duty either to himself or to a friend.'

'No, of course he can't.'

'So you think that one should keep away from people who are governed by their desires?'

'Certainly.'

'Well now,' said Socrates, 'if a man is extravagant and can't meet all his expenses, but is always appealing to his neighbours, and if, when he gets a loan, he can't repay it, and, when he doesn't get one, he bears a grudge against the person who refused it, don't you think that this man too is a difficult sort of friend?'

'Yes, indeed.'

'So one should keep away from him too?'

'Yes, one should.'

'What about the good businessman who is bent on making a great deal of money and consequently drives a hard bargain, and who enjoys receiving money but is reluctant to part with it?'

'In my view,' he said, 'this one is even worse than the last.'

'What about the man who has such a passion for making money that he has no time for anything that won't turn to his own profit?'

'He should be avoided too, in my opinion; he will be no use to anyone who associates with him.'

'What about the trouble-maker who wants to stir up a lot of bad feeling against his friends?'

'He certainly should be given a wide berth too.'

'And supposing that someone, although he has none of these defects, accepts any amount of kindness and never thinks of repaying a good turn?'

'He would be no use either. But tell me, Socrates, what sort of person shall we try to make our friend?'

'Presumably one who has thc opposite qualities – who is self-disciplined with regard to physical pleasures, and who proves to be good at managing his own affairs, reliable in his dealings with others, and eager not to fall short in doing services to his benefactors, so that it is an advantage to associate with him.'

'How can we test these qualities before we commit ourselves, Socrates?'

'We don't judge sculptors on the evidence of their claims,' he said, 'but if we see that a man's earlier works are well executed, we assume that his future works will be of high quality too.'

'Do you mean,' asked Critobulus, 'that anyone who has clearly treated his past friends well will obviously do good to his subsequent friends too?'

'Yes,' said Socrates, 'because, in the case of horses, if I see that someone has treated them well in the past, I assume that he is likely to treat other horses well too.'

'Very good,' he said. 'But when a man seems worthy of one's friendship, how should one set about making friends with him?'

'First of all,' said Socrates, 'you must consider the will of the gods,[1] and see whether they advise you to make friends with him.'

'Well, then, supposing that we decide to make friends with someone and the gods raise no objection, can you tell me how to capture him?'

'Well,' he said, 'certainly not by chasing him, as if he were a hare, nor by snaring him, as if he were a bird, nor by force, as one does one's enemies – it's hard work catching a friend against his will. And it's also difficult to keep him shackled like a slave. That sort of treatment is more likely to make enemies than friends.'

'But how are friends made?' asked Critobulus.

'They say that there are incantations which those who know them can use to win the friendship of anyone that they like; and drugs too, which can be used by those who understand them to make them loved by anyone that they like.'

'Then how can we find out about them?' he asked.

'You have heard from Homer the incantation that the Sirens uttered over Odysseus, which begins something like this:[2] "Come hither, famed Odysseus, great glory of the Greeks."'

'Did the Sirens utter this incantation over all the other victims of their charms, too, to keep them from getting away?' asked Critobulus.

'No, they kept it for those who were eager for recognition of their bravery.'

'What you're saying amounts practically to this: that in each case one should use an incantation designed so that the hearer won't think that he is being praised sarcastically.'

'Yes. You would repel people and incur dislike instead of friendship, if you praised a man by calling him handsome and tall and strong, when he knew that he was short and ugly and weak.'

'Do you know any other incantations?'

'No, but I have heard that Pericles knew a great many, which he used to utter over the State and so won its affection.'

1. By divination.
2. *Odyssey*, 12.184.

'How did Themistocles win its affection?'[1]

'Not by incantations, certainly, but by conferring some benefit upon it.'

'I suppose you mean, Socrates, that if it were our intention to secure a good friend, we ought to make ourselves good both in word and deed.'

'Did you think,' asked Socrates, 'that it was possible for a bad man to acquire good friends?'

'Well, yes,' replied Critobulus, 'because I have seen bad speakers on friendly terms with good orators, and incompetent commanders intimate with men of great military ability.'

'Do you also know,' Socrates asked, 'in the case that we are considering, any persons who can make useful friends although they are useless themselves?'

'No, certainly not,' said he. 'But if it is impossible for a bad man to make truly good friends, there's a question that immediately arises: is it possible for a man who has shown himself truly good to be a friend, by that very fact, to those who are the same as himself?'

'What is bothering you, Critobulus, is that you often see men who act honourably and shun anything discreditable, but instead of being friends, they quarrel and treat one another worse than if they were good for nothing.'

'And it isn't only individuals that do this,' said Critobulus. 'Even States that have the highest regard for honourable dealing and the least tolerance of anything base are often hostile in their attitude towards one another. These considerations make me very despondent about the acquisition of friends. On the one hand, I see that bad people can't be friends with one another – how can you make friends of those who are ungrateful or irresponsible or grasping or untrustworthy or undisciplined? It seems to me that bad men are altogether more naturally inclined to be enemies than

1. Just as Pericles was the outstanding Athenian statesman from *c.* 450 to *c.* 429, so Themistocles was from *c.* 490 to *c.* 470. Between them they bracket the years of Athens' true greatness.

friends to one another. Then again, as you say, it is equally impossible that bad men should be suitable for friendship with men of high character; for how can evil-doers become friends of those who loathe that sort of conduct? And finally, if even those who practise goodness quarrel about pre-eminence in the State, are mutually envious and hate one another, who are there still left to be friends, and in what class of men shall we find trust and goodwill?'[1]

'Well, Critobulus,' said Socrates, 'this is rather a complex problem. By nature human beings have certain tendencies towards friendliness. They need one another, they feel pity, they benefit from cooperation and, realizing this, they are grateful to one another. They also have hostile tendencies. When they have the same opinions about what things are beautiful and pleasant, they fight for their possession, and, falling out, take sides. Rivalry and passion also make for hostility; the desire to overreach is a cause of ill-feeling, and envy arouses hatred. Nevertheless, friendliness finds a way through all these obstacles and unites men who are truly good. Their moral goodness makes them prefer to enjoy moderate possessions and avoid tribulation rather than gain absolute power by means of war, and enables them, when hungry and thirsty, to share their food and drink without a pang, and to control their pleasure in the sexual attraction of beauty in such a way as not to cause improper annoyance to anyone. It enables them not only to suppress greedy instincts and be content with a lawful share of wealth, but even to assist one another. It enables them to settle arguments not only without annoyance, but even to their mutual advantage, and to keep their tempers from rising to a degree that they will later regret. It rids them completely of envy, since they give their own goods into the possession of their friends, and regard their friends' property as their own.

'It must surely follow from this that in the sharing of political privileges too, truly good men not only do not hinder, but

1. Plato's *Lysis* shows Socrates at work on the issues raised in this paragraph, and on other aspects of friendship.

actually help one another. Those who desire political distinction and authority in order that they may have licence to embezzle money, employ force against people and have a good time are likely to be unscrupulous, wicked and incapable of cooperation with others; but if a person wishes for political distinction to protect himself from injustice and to be able to give legitimate help to his friends, and, by holding office, wishes to try to do some good to his country, why shouldn't he be able to cooperate with others like himself? Will he, in company with truly good men, be less able to help his friends? Will he be more incapable of benefiting his country if he has the assistance of such men? Why, even in athletic contests it is obvious that if the strongest were allowed to band together against the weaker, they would win all the events and carry off all the prizes. In athletics, this is not allowed, but in public life, where truly good men have most influence, there is no objection to a man's combining with anyone he likes in order to benefit the State. So surely it is profitable for a man to prepare himself for public life by acquiring the best friends, and to use them as partners and helpers in his activities rather than as opponents.

'Then again, it is obvious that if you are at war with anyone, you will need allies, and you will need more of them if you are opposed by truly good men. Besides, you must benefit those who are prepared to be your allies, so that they may be willing to put their hearts into it; and it is far better to benefit the best, who are few, than the worst, who are many, because bad people demand much more in the way of services than good ones.

'Don't lose heart, Critobulus, but try to make yourself a good man, and when you have succeeded, you can set about hunting for truly good people. Perhaps even I myself might be able to lend you a hand in the search on account of my experience in love. When I take a fancy to anyone, it's extraordinary how completely I throw myself into getting them to reciprocate my friendship, passion or craving for their society, as the case may be.[1] I can see

1. See *Memoirs*, 4.1.2 (p. 177), and pp. 222–3.

that you will feel the same need when you set your heart on making friends with people. Well, don't keep me in the dark about your aspirations; thanks to my efforts to please those who please me, I think I'm not without experience in capturing people.'

'As a matter of fact, Socrates,' said Critobulus, 'I have been anxious for this sort of instruction for a long time, especially if the same technique will help me find both character and physical beauty.'

'Well, Critobulus,' said Socrates, 'my technique doesn't include prevailing upon good-looking people to stay by laying hands upon them. I am convinced that this is why men fled from Scylla – because she laid hands upon them;[1] whereas it is said of the Sirens that because they never laid hands upon anyone, but always sang their enchanting songs from a distance, everyone stayed to hear their singing and was charmed by it.'

'If you've got a good method of making friends, tell me what it is,' said Critobulus. 'I promise I won't lay hands upon them.'

'Then will you also refrain from laying your lips upon their lips?' asked Socrates.

'Don't worry!' said Critobulus. 'I won't even lay my lips upon anyone's lips – unless he is good-looking.'

'There you go, Critobulus!' said Socrates. 'You have said just the opposite of what you ought. Beautiful people[2] don't put up with that sort of thing, whereas ugly ones actually take pleasure in inviting it, and assume that they are called beautiful because of their characters.'

'You can rest assured,' said Critobulus, 'that if I kiss the beautiful, I shall kiss the good even more. Now tell me the art of capturing friends.'

'Well then, Critobulus,' said Socrates, 'when you want to

1. Scylla, a sea-monster, was one of the hazards Odysseus had to face on his return home (Homer, *Odyssey*, 12.85 ff., 235 ff.). As a matter of fact, she laid tentacles on her victims, not hands!
2. That is, morally beautiful people.

become friendly with someone, will you let me inform him that you admire him and are eager to be his friend?'

'Inform away,' said Critobulus. 'Nobody that I know of objects to being complimented.'

'And if I further inform him,' said Socrates, 'that, because of your admiration, you are kindly disposed towards him, you won't consider that I am misrepresenting you?'

'No,' he said. 'I myself feel a kindness towards anyone whom I imagine to be kindly disposed towards me.'

'Very well, then,' said Socrates, 'I shall be allowed to say this about you to any persons whom you wish to make your friends. If you will grant me further permission to say of you that you care about your friends, delight in nothing so much as in good friends, rejoice no less in your friends' good fortune than in your own, never weary in contriving that your friends may have good fortune, and believe that the best quality in a man is to outdo his friends in acts of kindness and his enemies in acts of hostility, then I think I should be a very efficient helper for you in winning good friends.'

'Why do you talk to me like this,' asked Critobulus, 'as if it were not open to you to say whatever you like about me?'

'It certainly is not, for the reason that I once heard Aspasia[1] give. She said that good matchmakers were expert at joining people together in matrimony by giving true reports of their good qualities, but refused to sing their praises falsely, because the victims of such deception hated both each other and the woman who arranged the match. Well, I am convinced that she was right, and so I don't consider that I am entitled, in praising you, to say anything that is not true.'

'I see, Socrates,' said Critobulus. 'You are the sort of friend who will cooperate provided that I myself have some aptitude for the making of friends; otherwise nothing would induce you to fabricate something to say to help me.'

1. An intellectually gifted courtesan who was Pericles' common-law wife for the last fifteen years of his life (after he had divorced his wife). She is also cited as an expert on marriage in *The Estate-manager*, 3.14 (p.300).

'Which do you think would be the better way of helping you, Critobulus,' asked Socrates, 'by praising you falsely or by persuading you to try to be a good person? If the answer isn't clear to you from this point of view, look at it from another. Suppose that I wanted to put you on friendly terms with a shipowner and praised you to him falsely by asserting that you were a good navigator, and suppose that he believed me and entrusted his ship to you, although you knew nothing about navigation: are you optimistic enough to expect that you wouldn't destroy both yourself and the ship? Or suppose that by making a false public declaration, I prevailed upon the State to entrust itself to you, as to a man of military and legal and political ability: what do you think the consequences would be for yourself and the State? Or suppose that I were privately to persuade some of our citizens by false representations to give you charge of their property as an able and scrupulous administrator: when it came to the test, wouldn't you both ruin them and expose yourself to ridicule? No, Critobulus: if you want to be thought good at anything, the shortest, safest and most reputable way is to try to make yourself really good at it. If you consider the virtues that are recognized among human beings, you will find that they are all increased by study and practice. That, Critobulus, is the way in which I think we ought to proceed; but if you incline to some other opinion, tell me what it is.'

'No, Socrates,' said Critobulus, 'I would be ashamed to oppose your point of view; if I did, what I said would be neither honourable nor true.'

7

When his friends had difficulties, if they were due to ignorance, he tried to remedy them by giving advice, and if to deficiency, by teaching them to help one another as much as they could. I will relate what I know about him in this connection too.

One day he saw Aristarchus looking gloomy. 'You look as though you were weighed down by something, Aristarchus,' he said. 'You ought to share the burden with your friends. Perhaps we can even relieve you a little.'

Aristarchus replied, 'Well, Socrates, I am indeed in serious difficulty. Since the civil war broke out, and large numbers withdrew to Piraeus,[1] so many refugee sisters and nieces and female cousins have gathered together under my roof that there are fourteen free persons in the house. We can get nothing from our farm, because it is in the hands of our opponents, and nothing from our house properties, because the town is practically deserted. There is no buyer for one's belongings, and one cannot even raise a loan from anywhere; I think you would sooner find money by looking for it in the streets than get it by borrowing. It is painful, Socrates, to stand by and watch one's family die by degrees; and it is impossible to feed so many in such difficult circumstances.'

When Socrates had heard this story, he said, 'Tell me, how is it that Ceramon,[2] who has to feed a large household, not only is able to provide what is necessary for himself and them, but has so much to spare that he is actually rich, while you in feeding a large household are afraid that you will all die of want?'

'Surely because he is feeding slaves, while I am feeding free people.'

'Do you think that the free people in your house are better than the slaves in Ceramon's?' asked Socrates.

'In my opinion,' he said, 'the free people in my house are the better.'

'Isn't it a shame, then,' said Socrates, 'that he should be well off because he has the worse household, while you who have a much better one are in need?'

'That is doubtless because he is supporting artisans, while I am supporting people who've been raised free.'

'Does "artisans" mean people who know how to make something useful?'

1. The port of Athens, four miles from the city; always a democratic stronghold, it was used by Thrasybulus in 403 as a base for his successful counter-revolution against the Thirty (see p. 78, n. 1).
2. Otherwise unknown (as is Aristarchus, the interlocutor of this dialogue).

'Certainly.'

'Is pearl barley useful?'

'Very.'

'What about bread?'

'No less so.'

'What do you say about men's and women's coats, shirts, cloaks and tunics?'

'They are all very useful too.'

'Well then,' said Socrates, 'don't your guests know how to make any of these things?'

'On the contrary, I imagine that they know how to make all of them.'

'Then don't you know that from one of these trades – making barley into pearl barley – Nausicydes supports not only himself and his servants, but also a large number of pigs and cattle, and has so much to spare that he often carries out public services for the State?[1] And don't you know that from baking Cyrebus both maintains his household in comfort and lives luxuriously, while Demeas of Collytus[2] keeps himself by making cloaks, and Meno by making blankets, and most of the Megarians[3] by making tunics?'

'Yes,' he replied, 'because these people buy and keep foreign slaves so that they can compel them to do whatever work is convenient, but I am dealing with free people and relations.'

'Do you really think,' said Socrates, 'that because they are free and related to you, they ought to do nothing but eat and sleep? What is your view about other free people? Do you find that those who live in this way have a better time, and do you regard them as happier, than those who concern themselves with things that they know are useful to life? Or do you observe that idleness and indifference help people to learn what they ought to know and remember what they have learned, to gain physical health and

1. Nausicydes is also mentioned in passing by Aristophanes (*Ecclesiazousae*, 426); the other individuals mentioned in this paragraph are otherwise unknown.
2. A deme in the north part of the city of Athens.
3. Megara was to the west of Attica on the Corinthian isthmus.

strength, and to acquire and keep what is useful to life, whereas energy and application are no help at all? Did these female relations of yours learn the arts which you say they understand because they regarded them as of no practical use and had no intention of practising them? Wasn't it just the opposite? Didn't they mean to take them seriously and get some benefit from them? Which is the more sensible conduct for a human being – to do no work at all, or to occupy oneself usefully? And which has more integrity – to work, or to ponder about the necessaries of life without working? As things are, I suppose, there is no love lost between you: you feel that they are imposing upon you; they can see that you are annoyed with them; and consequently there is a danger that the ill-feeling will grow and the former goodwill decline. But if you encourage them to work, you will feel friendly towards them, when you see that they are doing something for you, and they will like you when they realize that you are pleased with them; and as you both remember former acts of kindness with greater pleasure, you will increase the gratitude aroused by these acts with the result that the relations between you will become cordial and intimate. Now, if these women were faced with an occupation that was dishonourable, they might fairly choose to die first; but as it is, the kinds of work at which they are competent are apparently those which are considered to be most honourable and appropriate for a woman; and everybody does most easily, quickly, pleasurably and well what he understands. So don't hesitate,' he concluded, 'to suggest to them a course of action that will benefit both you and them. They will probably be glad to comply.'

'Upon my word,' said Aristarchus, 'your advice strikes me as being really good, Socrates. Up until now, I haven't been anxious to borrow, because I knew that, when I had spent what I had, I shouldn't be able to pay it back; but now I feel I can bring myself to do it so as to meet the initial outlay for the work.'

The result of this conversation was that capital was obtained and wool purchased. The women began to work before breakfast, and went on until supper-time; and they were cheerful instead of gloomy. Instead of eyeing each other askance the two parties regarded each other with pleasure: the women felt for Aristarchus the affection due to a guardian, and he grew fond of them for their practical help. In the end he went to Socrates and joyfully told him the whole story, adding that he himself was now criticized as being the only person in the house who did not work for his keep.

'You should tell them the story about the dog,' said Socrates. 'They say that in the days when animals could talk, a sheep said to its master: "I don't understand your conduct. To us, who provide you with wool and lambs and cheese, you give nothing except what we get from the earth; but to the dog, who provides you with nothing of this kind, you give a share of your own food." The dog heard this and said, "Quite right, too: I am the one to whom you owe security from being stolen by men and carried off by wolves. If I didn't watch over you, you wouldn't even be able to graze for fear of being killed." In the light of this argument, the story goes, even the sheep conceded the dog his privileges. So you should tell your women-folk that you take the place of the dog in guarding them and taking care of them; and that it is through you that they are unmolested and can live and work safely and happily.'

8

Seeing another old friend one day after a long time, Socrates said, 'Where did you spring from, Eutherus?'

'At the end of the war, Socrates,' he replied, 'I came back from abroad, but now I live near by. Since we lost our foreign property and my father left me no property in Attica, I have been forced to take up residence here and to earn a living by manual labour. It seems better to do this than to appeal to someone for help, especially as I have no security on which to borrow.'

'And how long do you suppose your constitution is capable of supporting you by working for hire?' asked Socrates.

'Not very long, certainly.'

'Besides,' said Socrates, 'as you get older, obviously your expenses will increase, and no one will be willing to pay you for your manual labour.'

'That's true,' he said.

'Then you had better apply yourself at once to the sort of occupation that will still be suitable for you when you are older. You should approach some owner of a large estate who needs assistance in managing it, so that, by superintending the work, helping to get in the produce and taking care of the property, you may both confer benefit on him and receive it in return.'

'I should find it hard to give up my freedom, Socrates,' he said.

'But in the political sphere the fact that a man holds an official position and manages public affairs makes him regarded not as more servile, but as more free.'

'As a general principle, Socrates,' he said, 'I don't at all like being responsible to anybody.'

'But, Eutherus,' said Socrates, 'it is not at all easy to find an occupation in which one cannot be called to account. It is difficult to do anything faultlessly, and it is difficult, even with a faultless performance, not to incur ill-judged criticism; indeed, even in respect of the work that you say you are now doing, I wonder if you find it easy to get through it without incurring blame. So you must try to avoid censorious people and seek the company of good-natured ones. If a job is within your power, you must put up with it; if it is not, you must avoid it; and whatever you do, you must give it your best and keenest attention. If you take this advice, I think that you will incur the least risk of blame, you will have the best prospect of finding a remedy for your difficulties, and you will live with the least trouble and anxiety, and with the amplest provision for your old age.'

9

I know that he also once heard Crito complain what a difficult thing life in Athens was for a man who wanted to mind his own business. 'At this very moment,' he said, 'some people are bringing an action against me, not because they have any grievance against me, but because they believe that I would rather pay[1] than have trouble.'

Socrates said, 'Tell me, Crito: do you keep dogs to protect your sheep from wolves?'

'Indeed I do,' he replied. 'It is more profitable for me to keep them than not to.'

'Then mightn't you also keep a man who was willing and able to protect you from anyone who tried to do you wrong?'

'I should be glad to,' he said, 'if I weren't afraid that he might turn on *me*.'

'Well,' said Socrates, 'can't you see that it is much more pleasant to benefit by the goodwill of a man like yourself than by incurring his enmity? You may be sure that there are people in this city who would greatly aspire to enjoy your friendship.'

As a result of this conversation, they discovered Archedemus,[2] a person of considerable rhetorical and practical ability, but poor, because he was not the sort to make money indiscriminately; he was a man of strict principles, and he said it was very easy to get money from these sycophants.[3] So whenever Crito was getting in crops of corn, olives, wine, wool or any other useful agricultural produce, he used to set some aside and give it to Archedemus; and, whenever he gave a dinner, he invited him; and he showed him every consideration of this kind. Archedemus regarded Crito's house as a haven of refuge, and treated him with great respect. He very soon found out that the sycophants threatening Crito were far from innocent and had enemies, and he summoned one of them to face a public trial at which it was to be decided what

1. That is, an out-of-court settlement. Socrates' old friend Crito is finding himself almost blackmailed, which a large loophole in the Athenian legal system made feasible (see n. 3 below).
2. Possibly the same Archedemus (see *Hellenica*, 1.7.2) who was a prosecutor of the generals after the battle of Arginusae (see p. 72, n. 2).
3. Under Athenian law any citizen could prosecute any other. If a conviction was gained, the prosecutor might well get a proportion of the fine. Some people, therefore, made a living out of such actions and the out-of-court settlements gained by the threat of them: these people were called 'sycophants'.

punishment or penalty he must suffer. Since the sycophant was conscious of a good many misdeeds, he did everything he could to rid himself of Archedemus; but Archedemus refused to be shaken off until the man abandoned his attack on Crito and gave Archedemus a sum of money.

When Archedemus had carried out this and other similar operations, many of Crito's friends begged him to extend the protection of Archedemus to themselves as well, just as when a shepherd has a good sheep-dog the other shepherds want to station their flocks near him, so that they too might benefit from the dog. Archedemus was pleased to gratify Crito, and not only Crito but his friends too were left in peace. If any of Archedemus' enemies taunted him with toadying to Crito in return for benefits received, he said, 'There are two alternatives. You can either cultivate the friendship of honest men by returning their kindness, which will make bad men your enemies; or you can make truly good men your enemies by trying to do them wrong, and, by collaborating with bad men, try to make *them* your friends and try to get along with them rather than good men. Which of those two alternatives is the more discreditable?' From this time on Archedemus was one of Crito's friends and was highly esteemed by the rest of Crito's friends.

10

I know that Socrates had the following conversation with one of his companions, Diodorus.

'Tell me, Diodorus,' he said, 'if one of your house-slaves runs away, do you see to it that you get him safely back again?'

'Yes, indeed,' he said, 'and I invite the help of others by offering a reward for his recovery.'

'Well,' Socrates went on, 'if one of your house-slaves is ill, do you look after him and call in doctors to guard against his dying?'

'I certainly do.'

'And if one of your acquaintances who is much more useful to you than your house-slaves is in danger of dying of want, don't you think that you should see to it that he is saved? You must surely know that Hermogenes is not insensitive, and that he would feel ashamed if he didn't return your kindness. Also, to have an assistant who is willing, loyal, reliable and able to carry out instructions – and not only that, but capable of independent action, foresight and planning – this is surely worth a good many house-slaves. Now, good estate-managers say that when you can purchase something valuable at a low price, you ought to buy it; and at the present time, owing to circumstances, it is possible to acquire good friends very reasonably.'

Diodorus said, 'You are quite right, Socrates. Tell Hermogenes to come and see me.'

'Certainly not!' said Socrates. 'To my mind it's no more proper for you to summon him than it is to go to him yourself; and it's no more to his advantage to have the business completed than it is to yours.'

So Diodorus went to see Hermogenes, and with a small outlay he acquired a friend who made it his business to look out for every opportunity to help Diodorus and make him happy.

BOOK THREE

I shall now describe how Socrates used to help people with honourable ambitions by making them apply themselves to the objects of those ambitions.

One day he heard that Dionysodorus[1] had come to Athens and was offering to teach the art of military command. So he said to one of his companions, who he knew was eager to attain the position of general in the State, 'You know, my boy, it's a poor thing for one who wants to be a general in the State to neglect the opportunity of instruction when it's available. Such a person would be more justly liable to prosecution than one who undertook to make statues without having learned how to sculpt; for in the perils of war the whole State is entrusted to the care of the general, and the good effects of his success and the bad effects of his failures are likely to be equally far-reaching. So a man who did his best to get himself elected to this position[2] without troubling to learn how to discharge it would surely deserve to be penalized.'

By using arguments like these Socrates persuaded him to go and take lessons. When he came back after completing the course, Socrates began to tease him.

'You know, gentlemen,' he said, 'how Homer describes Agamemnon as "majestic".[3] Don't you think that our friend here seems more majestic now that he has learned how to be a general? A man who has learned to play a musical instrument is a musician even if he is not playing it; and someone who has learned to cure disease is a doctor even if he is not practising. In the same way, from now on our friend will always be a general, even if nobody appoints him; but the untrained person is neither a general nor a

1. One of the two sophist brothers portrayed in Plato's *Euthydemus* (the other gives his name to the dialogue).
2. The command of the military was a political as well as a military job, and was an elected post in Athens.
3. *Iliad*, 3.170.

doctor, even if his appointment is unanimous. However,' he went on, 'in case one of us serves under you as a senior or junior officer, we ought to have a better grasp of military studies; so tell us where he began to teach you the art of military command.'

'At the same point he stopped at,' said the young man. 'He taught me tactics and nothing else.'

'But that is only a fraction of the general's business,' said Socrates. 'A general must be able to get together the resources for making war and provide supplies for his men; he must be inventive, active and attentive, persevering and brilliant, both friendly and harsh, both straightforward and subtle, a good protector and a good thief, lavish and rapacious, generous and grasping, steady and aggressive; and a man must have a great many other qualities, natural and acquired, if he is to be a good general. Still, it is a fine thing to be a tactician. An orderly army is far superior to a disorderly one, just as the materials of a house – bricks and stones, timber and tiles – are no good at all when dumped at random, but when they are arranged as they are combined in a building, with the material which will neither rot nor disintegrate, the stones and tiles, underneath and on top, and with the bricks and timber in between, then the result is a valuable possession – a house.'

'That's a close parallel, Socrates,' said the young man, 'because in war too you should post the best troops in front and in the rear, and the worst in between so that they may be led on by the one lot and pushed forward by the other.'

'That's all right,' said Socrates, 'if the lecturer has taught you how to distinguish the good from the bad; but if he hasn't, what have you gained from your lessons? I mean, if he told you to arrange the finest coinage in front and at the back, and the worst in between, without explaining to you how to tell good money from counterfeit, that would be no use to you either.'

'He certainly didn't teach us that, so we shall have to distinguish good and bad for ourselves.'

'Then why not consider how we can avoid making blunders about them?' asked Socrates.

'I should like to,' said the young man.

'Well then,' said Socrates, 'supposing that we had to carry off some silver, wouldn't it be sound tactics to give the first place to those who were fondest of silver?'

'Yes, I think so.'

'What about facing danger? Should we put the most ardent lovers of glory in the front rank?'

'They are certainly the people who are willing to take risks in order to earn praise. Of course, they aren't hard to identify; they are conspicuous everywhere, and would be easy to pick out.'

'Tell me,' said Socrates, 'did he only teach you how to arrange your troops, or did he also explain how and in what circumstances you should employ each formation?'

'No, not at all,' said he.

'But there are many situations which call for quite different arrangements and movements of troops.'

'He certainly didn't distinguish them clearly.'

'Then surely you ought to go back and ask him more questions,' said Socrates. 'If he knows his subject and has a conscience, he will be ashamed to send you away with gaps in your knowledge after taking your money.'

2

One day Socrates met a man who had just been appointed general, and he asked him: 'Why do you think Homer called Agamemnon "shepherd of the people"?[1] Was it because it is the shepherd's duty to see to it that his sheep are safe and have their food and that the purpose for which they are kept is achieved, and in the same way it is the general's duty to see that his soldiers are safe and have their food and that the purpose for which they are serving is achieved – this purpose being to improve their fortune by defeating the enemy? Or what did he mean by praising Agamemnon as "Both a

1. *Iliad*, 2.243.

good king and a stout warrior"?[1] Was it that he would be a stout warrior not if he alone contended bravely with the enemy, but if he caused the whole army to do so, and a good king not if he merely directed his own life well, but if he also brought happiness to his subjects?[2] For a king is chosen not to take good care of his own interests, but to secure the well-being of those who chose him; and all peoples go to war with one object only, to secure the best possible living conditions for themselves, and they appoint generals for the single purpose of leading them to this goal. So it is the duty of a general to realize the aims of those who appointed him as such; and, in fact, it is not easy to find a nobler purpose than this, or a baser one than its opposite.'

By investigating in this way what is the ideal of a good leader he eliminated all other considerations and left securing the happiness of his followers.

3

I know that he also once had the following conversation with someone who had been appointed to a cavalry command.[3] 'Could you tell us, young man,' he said, 'why you set your heart on becoming a cavalry officer? I presume that it wasn't that you wanted to ride at the head of the cavalry, because that is the privilege of the mounted archers – at least, they ride ahead of even the cavalry commander.'

'That's true,' he said.

'And it wasn't publicity that you wanted either; for even lunatics are recognized by everybody.'

'That's true too.'

'Well then, is it because you think that you might hand back cavalry which you have improved to the State, and that if any

1. *Iliad*, 3.179; the line is also quoted at *The Dinner-party*, 4.6 (p. 240).
2. Compare Plato, *Republic*, 342e, 345c–d, *Euthydemus*, 292a–d.
3. Two cavalry commanders were elected annually. Xenophon devoted a treatise, *Hipparchicus*, to their duties. Some parts of *Hipparchicus* closely resemble our dialogue here.

need for mounted troops should arise you might do our country some service as their commander?'

'Yes, precisely,' he said.

'A very fine thing too,' said Socrates, 'if you can do this. The command for which you have been chosen is, I suppose, over both horses and riders.'

'Yes, it is.'

'Come along, then: first tell us how you propose to improve the horses.'

'But I don't think that is my job,' he said. 'Each man ought to look after his own horse.'

'Well,' said Socrates, 'suppose that you find some of them turning out their horses with such bad feet or legs, or in such poor condition, or so underfed, that they can't keep up with the rest, and you find others coming up with horses which are so fresh that they won't keep their places or are such kickers that you can't get them into position at all – what will be the good of your cavalry? How will you be able to do your country any service if your troopers are mounted like that?'

'You're right,' he said. 'I will do my best to look after the horses.'

'Well, now, what about the horsemen? Won't you try to improve their quality?'

'Yes, I will.'

'Won't you begin by making them better at mounting their horses?'

'I ought to, certainly, because then if one of them fell off, his chances of survival would be improved.'

'And next, if you have to risk an engagement, will you order them to draw the enemy on to the sandy ground where you are accustomed to exercise, or will you try to carry out your training in the sort of country in which campaigns are fought?'

'That would be better, certainly.'

'Next, will you make it a concern of yours that as many of your men as possible can hurl weapons from horseback?'

'That would be a good idea, too.'

'Is it your intention to make your troopers braver warriors by whetting their courage and rousing their anger against the enemy?'

'If it wasn't, I will try to make it so now,' he said.

'Have you given any thought to the question of obedience? For without it there is no use in horses or horsemen, however good and warlike.'

'True,' he said. 'But how can one best direct them towards it, Socrates?'

'You know, I'm sure, that in every situation people are readiest to obey those whom they consider to be best. In illness they pay most attention to the man who they think has most medical knowledge; and on board ship the passengers pay most attention to the man they regard as the most experienced sailor; and in farming most attention is paid to the man who is regarded as the most experienced farmer.'

'Quite so.'

'Then presumably in the case of horsemanship too the man who clearly knows best what ought to be done is most likely to receive the willing obedience of the rest.'

'Then if I am obviously better than any of them, Socrates, will that be enough to make them obey me?'

'Yes, provided that you also let them know that obedience to you will be both more honourable and more salutary for them than disobedience.'

'How shall I teach them that?'

'Much more easily, I assure you, than if you had to teach them that bad conduct is better and more profitable than good conduct.'

'Do you mean,' said he, 'that besides all his other duties a cavalry officer ought to cultivate the ability to speak well?'

'Did you suppose that he had to exercise his command in silence? Haven't you noticed that all the ideals that tradition has taught us – ideals to which we owe our knowledge of how to live – are learned through discourse, and that any other fine accomplishment anyone acquires is acquired by means of discourse; that the best teachers make the most use of discourse, and those who have the profoundest knowledge of the most important subjects are the most brilliant debaters? Now, here's another point: haven't you noticed that when a chorus is chosen to represent this city of ours, like the one which is sent to Delos,[1] no chorus from anywhere else can match it, and no other city can muster a display of manhood like ours?'

'That's true,' he said.

'But it's not so much in quality of voice, or in physical size and strength that Athenians are superior to the rest, as in the love of honour, which is the keenest incentive to noble and honourable actions.'

'That's true too,' he said.

'Then don't you think that if someone made our cavalry his concern, the Athenians would be far superior here too, both in their provision of equipment and horses, and by their discipline and readiness to venture against the enemy, if they thought that by doing so they would win praise and honour?'

'Very likely.'

'Then don't hesitate any longer,' said Socrates, 'but try to induce your men to adopt a course which will benefit both you and, through you, the rest of our people as well.'

'All right,' he said, 'I will certainly try.'

4

One day he saw Nicomachides coming away from the elections, and asked, 'Who have been elected as generals, Nicomachides?'[2]

'Why, naturally, Socrates,' he replied, 'the people of Athens, being what they are, have not elected me, although I am worn out with active service as an officer, and have received all these wounds from the enemy' – as he spoke, he drew back his clothes

1. The 'chorus' would be a company of singers and dancers to compete at the festival which took place on the island of Delos, sacred to Apollo, every five years.
2. Ten generals were elected in Athens each year.

and exhibited the scars – 'but they have chosen Antisthenes,[1] who has never served in the infantry and has won no distinction in the cavalry, and knows nothing except how to pile up money.'

'Surely it's a good thing,' said Socrates, 'if he will be able to provide his men with supplies?'

'Merchants can pile up money too,' said Nicomachides, 'but that doesn't qualify them to be generals.'

'But Antisthenes is set on winning,' replied Socrates, 'which is an appropriate quality for a general. Haven't you noticed that every time he has had to finance a chorus he has always won?'[2]

'Yes,' said Nicomachides, 'but it's one thing to have charge of a chorus, and quite another to have charge of an army.'

'All the same,' said Socrates, 'although Antisthenes had no experience of singing or of training a chorus, he succeeded in finding the best people for his purpose.'

'So in his capacity as general,' said Nicomachides, 'he will find other people to work out his tactics and to do the fighting.'

'Well,' said Socrates, 'if he is as good at searching out and selecting the best agents in his military operations as he is in training his choruses, he will probably be successful in this case too. Besides, he would naturally be prepared to spend more to win a military victory with the whole nation than to win a choral competition with his tribe.'[3]

'Do you mean, Socrates, that a good chorus-trainer would also make a good general?'

'I mean that, when a man is given a post of responsibility, if he knows what is needed and is able to supply it, he can fill that post efficiently, whether it relates to a chorus or an estate or a country or an army.'

'I must say, Socrates,' said Nicomachides, 'I never thought that

1. Not the Socratic philosopher whom we have met before, but an estate-owner, to judge by the following conversation.
2. Rich Athenian citizens were required to provide and train a chorus for the dramatic festivals and for other choral competitions. See also p. 294, n. 2.
3. The citizen population of Athens was divided into ten 'tribes' for various political and social purposes.

I should hear you say that good estate-managers would make good generals.'

'Come along, then,' he said, 'let's consider their respective duties, so that we may see whether they are the same or there is some difference.'

'By all means.'

'Isn't it the duty of both of them to make their subordinates obedient and tractable?'

'Certainly.'

'What about assigning the various tasks to those who are qualified to perform them?'

'That too.'

'Then I suppose it is appropriate for both to punish the bad and give credit to the good.'

'Quite so.'

'And surely it is proper for both to make their subordinates loyal to them?'

'That too.'

'Do you think that it is in the interest of both to win allies and helpers, or not?'

'It certainly is.'

'Shouldn't both be conservative of their possessions?'

'Very much so.'

'Then shouldn't they both be careful and industrious in all their duties?'

'All these qualities are equally applicable to both; but fighting is not.'

'But surely both make enemies?'[1]

'That is so, certainly.'

'Isn't it in the interest of both to get the better of them?'

1. The awkward fact that a military commander needs theoretical knowledge, practical experience and personal qualities not usually available to the civilian is blatantly avoided so that the analogy can be pushed even further. However, since Xenophon picked up most of his experience at command alongside mediocre commanders and inferior troops, it is possible that he thought it was largely a matter of common sense.

'Quite, but you're leaving something out of account: if fighting becomes necessary, what will be the good of estate-management?'

'Surely then it will be more valuable than ever. The good estate-manager, knowing that nothing brings so much profit and gain as defeating one's enemies in battle, and nothing so much loss and ruin as being defeated, will eagerly seek and prepare what is conducive to victory, and will carefully note and guard against what tends towards defeat; and if he sees that his preparations offer hope of victory, he will vigorously fight; and – not least in importance – if he is unprepared, he will avoid an engagement. You mustn't despise estate-managers, Nicomachides. The difference between the care of private and the care of public affairs is only one of degree; in all other respects they are closely similar, especially in that neither can dispense with human agency, and the human agents are the same in both cases. Those who look after public affairs employ just the same agents as in managing their private properties; and if people understand how to use these agents, they carry out their duties successfully, whether public or private, but if they do not, then they come to grief in either case.'

5

One day Socrates was talking to Pericles the son of the famous Pericles.

'You know, Pericles,' he said, 'I have high hopes that if you are appointed as a general, our city will become more efficient and renowned in warfare, and will conquer its enemies.'[1]

Pericles replied, 'I should like it to be as you say, Socrates, but I've no idea how it could happen.'

'Would you like to discuss the subject, then,' said Socrates, 'and try to discover how it could come about?'

1. He was elected in 406, and so was one of the generals executed after the battle of Arginusae (see p. 72, n. 2).

'Yes, please,' he said.

'Very well, then: you know that the Athenians are not inferior in numbers to the Boeotians?'[1]

'Yes, I know that.'

'Do you think that there would be more examples of physical perfection in Boeotia than in Athens?'

'To my mind, we aren't inferior in this respect either.'

'And which people do you suppose is more loyal?'

'I should say the Athenians. A good many of the Boeotians resent the aggressiveness of the Thebans, but I don't see anything of that sort at Athens.'

'Besides, the Athenians have a greater thirst for glory and pride than any other people; and these are no slight incentives to taking risks for the sake of honour and country.'

'In this respect too the Athenians are above criticism.'

'Then again, no people can claim more or greater ancestral exploits than the Athenians; and consequently many of them are inspired by these examples to cultivate virtue and show themselves brave fighters.'

'All this is true, Socrates. But you can see that ever since the disasters suffered by Tolmides and the thousand at Lebadia, and by Hippocrates at Delium,[2] the prestige of Athens has been low in relation to Boeotia, and the confidence of Thebes high in relation to Athens; the result is that the Boeotians, who used not even to dare, in their own territory, to face the Athenians without the support of the Spartans and the other Peloponnesians, are now threatening to invade Attica by themselves; and the Athenians, who used to wreak havoc in Boeotia, are afraid that the Boeotians will ravage Attica.'

'I realize that this is so,' said Socrates, 'but it seems to me that our city is now more amenably disposed towards a good leader.

1. Boeotia, whose chief city was Thebes, lay to the north-west of Attica, and was a long-standing enemy of Athens.
2. The battle of Lebadia took place in 447; the battle of Delium in 424. Both were serious defeats for Athens. Socrates himself was present at Delium (Plato, *Laches*, 181b, *Symposium*, 221a).

Confidence induces carelessness, indifference and disobedience, but fear makes people more inclined to be attentive, obedient and disciplined. You can see an illustration of this in what happens on board ships. When there's nothing to fear, the crew are completely unruly; but so long as they are afraid of storm or enemy, they not only carry out all instructions, but wait for the next order in perfect silence like members of a chorus.'

'Well,' said Pericles, 'assuming that now they are at their most obedient, it would be the right moment to say how we can encourage them to set their hearts again upon their former virtue, renown and happiness.'

'If we wanted them to claim property that was in the possession of others,' said Socrates, 'the best way of inciting them to lay hands upon that property would be by proving to them that it belonged to them by inheritance; and since we want them to make it their object to excel in virtue, we must similarly show them that this has been their special characteristic from of old, and that if they cultivated it seriously, they could be the most powerful nation in the world.'

'How can we teach them this lesson?'

'I suppose by reminding them of the stories they have been told about how excellent their earliest recorded ancestors were.'

'Do you mean the contest of the gods which Cecrops and his advisers were allowed to decide because of their goodness?'[1]

'Yes, and the birth and upbringing of Erechtheus,[2] and the war that broke out in his time against the inhabitants of all the adjoining mainland,[3] and the war against the Peloponnesians in

1. Cecrops was a legendary early king of Athens. The contest was for the post of tutelary deity of the city. Poseidon offered as his gift a spring of water on the Acropolis, but Athena outbid him with an olive tree. In what follows, note that in Socrates' time, history and legend were not always clearly distinguished.
2. I assume that this refers to the legendary early king of Athens who was the son of the gods Hephaestus and Gaia, and was brought up by Athena. However, there seems to be some confusion with another Erechtheus (see next note), but this second Erechtheus' birth and upbringing were not at all remarkable.
3. This probably refers to a war against Eleusis, but this is generally thought to have taken place in the time of a different Erechtheus, the grandson of the first.

the days of the sons of Heracles,[1] and all the campaigns under Theseus,[2] in all of which our ancestors showed themselves plainly to be the best men of their time. Or again there are the feats accomplished later by their descendants not much before our time: those in which they strived unaided against an enemy who was master of the whole of Asia and of Europe as far as Macedonia, and who possessed vaster armies and resources and had carried out greater operations than any previous nation; and those in which they shared the leadership by land and sea with the Peloponnesians. These Athenians too are reputed to have far surpassed the other people of their time.'[3]

'So it is said.'

'And that is why, in spite of the many migrations that have taken place in Greece, they remained in their own country,[4] and often answered appeals for arbitration from those disputing about their rights,[5] and often gave sanctuary to the victims of oppression.'[6]

'I can't understand, Socrates,' said Pericles, 'how it was that our country ever deteriorated.'

Socrates replied, 'You know how athletes sometimes, when they have enjoyed unchallenged superiority, through sheer lack of enterprise become no match for their opponents? My belief is that in the same way the people of Athens were so far supreme that they became negligent, and that their deterioration is due to this.'

1. Eurystheus, the king of Argos in the Peloponnese, made war on Athens for harbouring the children of his old enemy Heracles.
2. Perhaps the most famous of Theseus' wars were against the Amazons and the Centaurs, as depicted on the Parthenon frieze.
3. The Persian Wars of the early fifth century.
4. To be 'autochthonous' was a common Athenian boast.
5. Aeschylus, in his *Eumenides*, shows Orestes being judged in Athens for his matricide. Historically, it is possible that in *c.* 760 the Messenians wanted to refer their quarrel with Sparta to the Athenians.
6. For example (all legendary events), to the sons of Heracles (n. 1 above), to Adrastus and the widows of the Seven against Thebes (Euripides, *Suppliants*), and to Oedipus (Sophocles, *Oedipus Coloneus*).

'Well then,' he said, 'what can they do now to recover their former excellence?'

Socrates replied, 'I don't think that the answer is anything abstruse. If they rediscovered their ancestors' way of life and followed it as well as they did, they would prove to be just as good men as they were. Alternatively, if they took as their model the present leaders of the Greek world[1] and followed their way of life, then with equal application to the same activities they would become no worse than their models, and with greater application they would actually surpass them.'

'You imply,' said Pericles, 'that our country is a long way from true goodness. Are the Athenians ever likely to equal the Spartans in showing respect for their elders, when they despise anyone older than themselves beginning with their fathers, or in developing their bodies, when they not only care nothing for physical fitness themselves but jeer at those who do care about it? Will they ever have as much obedience to authority, when they pride themselves on despising authority? Will they ever have as much unanimity, when, so far from working together for their common interest, they are more envious and abusive towards one another than towards the rest of the world, quarrel more in their meetings, both private and public, than any other people, and bring the greatest number of actions against one another; when they prefer to gain in this way at one another's expense rather than by cooperation, and, while treating public duties as no personal concern of theirs, at the same time fight over them, taking the greatest delight in the qualities that fit them for such quarrelling? As a result of this, a great deal of harm and mischief is developing in our city, and a great deal of mutual enmity and hatred is growing in the hearts of our people; and for this reason I, for my part, am in constant dread that some intolerable disaster will fall upon our city.'

1. The Spartans, for whom admiration was not uncommon among contemporary Athenians, either for the supposed virtues of their disciplined way of life (see Pericles' next speech) or, politically, for their oligarchical system.

'Really, Pericles,' said Socrates, 'you mustn't imagine that the Athenians are suffering from such incurable depravity as that. Don't you see how well-disciplined they are in the navy, and how punctiliously they obey the officials at athletic meetings, and how, when they are members of a chorus, they follow the directions of their trainers as thoroughly as anyone?'

'Yes, that's the strange thing, you know, that people like these should obey their superiors, while the infantry and cavalry, who are supposed to be the pick of the population in general excellence, should be the most unruly.'

Socrates said, 'But what about the Council of the Areopagus, Pericles?[1] Isn't it composed of men of tried character?'

'Yes, indeed.'

'Do you know any other body that tries cases and conducts all its other business better, or more in accordance with law, honour and justice?'

'I have nothing to say against *them*.'

'Then you mustn't despair of the Athenians as being disorderly.'

'But on military service, where there is the greatest need for self-control, discipline and obedience, they give no thought to any of these qualities.'

'Perhaps,' said Socrates, 'that is because in this sphere they have the least expert direction. Don't you see that in the case of musicians and singers and dancers, nobody without expert knowledge attempts to give directions, and similarly with wrestlers and pancratiasts?[2] The authorities on all these subjects can point to the source from which they learned the arts for which they are responsible; but the great majority of military commanders are self-taught. However, I don't imagine that you are that

1. The ancient Council of the Areopagus (a hill in Athens) lost its political power when Athens became fully democratic, retaining only prestige and jurisdiction in cases of homicide. It was recruited from ex-magistrates of proven integrity.
2. Competitors in the pancration, a brutal combination of wrestling and boxing, in which virtually any method of hurting one's opponent was allowed.

sort of person. I expect that you can tell me when you began to learn generalship just as easily as when you began to learn wrestling. I expect that besides keeping a stock of stratagems which you have inherited from your father, you have amassed a great many from every source from which you could learn anything useful for the art of war. And I expect that you are constantly on your guard against inadvertent ignorance of anything that is useful to this end; and that, if you become aware that there is something of this sort which you don't know, you seek out the experts in the subject, grudging neither presents nor favours, in order to learn from them what you don't know and have the help of qualified persons.'

Pericles replied, 'You can't deceive me, Socrates. Your reason for saying all this is certainly not that you think that I *do* take these things seriously; you are trying to show me that one *ought* to take them seriously, if one aspires to be a general. As a matter of fact, I quite agree with you.'

'Have you noted the fact, Pericles, that our frontier is protected by high mountains running down into Boeotia, through which the approaches into our territory are narrow and steep, and that there is a belt of rugged mountains through the middle of Attica?'

'Yes, of course.'

'Well now, have you heard that the Mysians and Pisidians, who occupy extremely rugged country in the territories of the king of Persia,[1] are able, though only lightly armed, not only to preserve their independence, but to do the Persians a good deal of damage by raiding their territory?'

'Yes, I have heard that too.'

'Don't you think that, if the young and active members of the Athenian army were equipped with lighter arms and occupied the mountains that screen our frontiers, they would be able to harass

1. The Mysians, in north-west Asia Minor, and the Pisidians, who occupied what is now south central Turkey, were thorns in the side of the Persian empire (Xenophon, *Anabasis*, 3.2.23).

our enemies and form an effective defence for our people against invasion?'[1]

'I think that all these are useful suggestions,' said Pericles.

'Well then,' said Socrates, 'if you approve of them, give them a trial, my good friend. If you can put any of them into practice, it will be to your credit and the benefit of your country; and if in some respects you can't, you will neither harm your country nor bring discredit upon yourself.'

6

When Glaucon the son of Ariston[2] was trying to become a popular orator, because he was set on being the head of the State although he was not yet twenty years old, none of his friends and intimates could stop him; he was always getting dragged off the public platform and laughed at. The one person who prevailed upon him was Socrates, who was kindly disposed towards him for the sake of two people: Charmides the son of Glaucon,[3] and Plato.[4] Socrates happened to meet him and first won his attention by addressing him in the following way: 'Glaucon,' he said, 'have you made up your mind to become the head of our State?'

'I have, Socrates,' he replied.

'Yes, that is, without a doubt, a fine thing; I don't know that there is any higher human ambition. Clearly, if you succeed in it,

1. Xenophon would have expected his contemporaries to know whether such guerilla tactics were employed by Athens in the Peloponnesian War, and even whether they were instigated by Pericles. There is no extant evidence one way or the other to tell us what was the case; and, anyway, the situation is anachronistic: see p. 54.
2. And Plato's elder brother.
3. This is the elder Glaucon, grandfather of Plato and his brother, and so Charmides is their uncle. Like Critias (see p. 38), he was another of Socrates' associates who had a part in the oligarchic revolution of 404 and died in the democratic counter-revolution of 403.
4. This is Xenophon's sole mention of Plato, and he seems to acknowledge that he was regarded highly by Socrates. Plato never mentions Xenophon, but it is thought that his *Laws*, 694c ff., on Cyrus the Elder of Persia, might be a corrective to Xenophon's eulogistic *Cyropaedia*.

you will have the power to obtain whatever you desire, and be able to help your friends; you will gain distinction for your family and extend the power of your country; and you will win a name for yourself, first in our city, and then in Greece, and perhaps even, like Themistocles, among foreign powers. Wherever you are, every eye will be fixed upon you.'

This description appealed to Glaucon's vanity, and he was glad to linger. Socrates then went on: 'Now, it's obvious, isn't it, Glaucon, that if you want to be held in honour, you must help your country?'

'Certainly.'

'Well then,' he said, 'please don't make a secret of it, but tell us where you will start to benefit your country.'

Glaucon made no reply, as if he were considering for the first time where he should start.

'Surely,' asked Socrates, 'if you wanted to make the family of a friend more important, you would try to make it wealthier. On the same principle I suppose you will try to make your country wealthier, won't you?'

'Yes, of course.'

'Wouldn't it be wealthier if its revenues were increased?'

'Naturally.'

'Tell me, then: what are our country's present revenues derived from, and what do they amount to? No doubt you have looked into this, so that you may make up any of them that are inadequate and supply any that are lacking.'

'Actually,' Glaucon admitted, 'I haven't looked into that.'

'Well,' said Socrates, 'if you have left that aside, tell us what the country's expenditure is. You must be planning to curtail any extravagance.'

'Actually,' said Glaucon, 'I haven't had time for that yet either.'

'Then we will defer the question of making the country wealthier. It is impossible for someone who doesn't know what the expenditure and revenues are to look after them.'

'But, Socrates,' said Glaucon, 'it is possible to enrich one's country from the resources of its enemies.'

'Yes, indeed, perfectly possible,' said Socrates, 'if you are stronger than they are. If you are weaker, you are likely to lose even what you have already.'

'That is true.'

'So before someone starts considering on whom to make war, he ought to know the strength both of his own country and of her opponents, so that, if his country is stronger, he may encourage her to undertake the war, and, if she is weaker, he may persuade her to be cautious.'

'Quite right.'

'Then tell us first what our country's land and sea forces are, and then do the same for the enemy's.'

'Well,' he said, 'I can't, of course, tell you offhand.'

'If you've got the details written down, fetch them; I should very much like to hear the answer.'

'Actually, I haven't got them written down either.'

'Very well, then,' said Socrates, 'we will put off our military discussion too for the time being. Probably, besides your being so newly in office, you haven't yet had time to go carefully into the matter because of its magnitude. But of course I'm sure that you have already given your attention to the defence of our territory, and know how many guard-posts are well placed and how many are not, and how many of the garrisons are adequate and how many are not. And you will recommend the strengthening of those that are well placed and the abolition of those that are superfluous.'

'Actually, I shall recommend abolishing the lot,' said Glaucon, 'because the result of their defence is that our crops get stolen.'

'But if the guard-posts are abolished,' said Socrates, 'don't you think that it will be open to anyone to help himself freely? By the way, have you found this out by personal inspection, or how do you know that the posts are badly manned?'

'I assume it,' he said.

'Shall we wait to discuss this subject too until we have got beyond assumptions and know the facts?'

'Perhaps that would be better,' said Glaucon.

'Then there are the silver mines,'[1] said Socrates. 'I know that you haven't visited them so that you can account for the decline of revenue from them.'

'No, I haven't.'

'As a matter of fact,' said Socrates, 'they say that it's an unhealthy district; so when you have to state your views about it, this excuse will cover you.'

'You're making fun of me,' said Glaucon.

'But there's another problem that I'm sure you haven't neglected: no doubt you've investigated how long the country can be fed on home-produced corn, and how much extra is needed each year. You wouldn't like your country to incur a shortage of this kind without your realizing it; you would wish to be able to advise from personal knowledge about essential supplies, and so give her help and security.'

'That's an enormous task you're suggesting,' said Glaucon, 'if one is to be obliged to look after that sort of thing.'

'But surely,' said Socrates, 'a man could never manage even his own houschold properly unless he knew all its deficiencies and saw to it that they were all supplied. As our city consists of more than ten thousand houses, and it is difficult to look after so many households simultaneously, why don't you first try to look after one, your uncle's? It needs it. And if you can cope with that, you can try your hand at more; but if you can't do any good to one, how can you do good to many? If a man can't carry one talent in weight, surely it's obvious that he shouldn't even try to carry more than one.'

'Well,' said Glaucon, 'I might do something for my uncle's household, if he would follow my advice.'

'So although you can't persuade your uncle,' said Socrates, 'you expect to be able to make the whole population of Athens, including your uncle, follow your advice? Take care, my dear Glaucon, that your craving for distinction doesn't take you in the

1. At Laurium near Cape Sunium at the southern extremity of Attica. They furnished a large proportion of Athens' wealth.

opposite direction. Can't you see how risky it is to say or to do things that one doesn't know about? Among the rest of your acquaintances, consider those whom you know to be the sort of people who obviously say and do things that they don't know about: do you think that they are more admired or despised for this sort of conduct? And then consider the case of those who know what they are saying and what they are doing. In my opinion, you will find in every sphere of action that esteem and admiration are reserved for those who are best informed, while ignominy and contempt are the lot of the most ignorant. So if you want to be esteemed and admired in the State, try to ensure as far as possible that you know about the things that you want to do. If you have this advantage over the rest when you try your hand at politics, I shouldn't be surprised if you realized your ambition quite easily.'

7

When he saw that Charmides the son of Glaucon, though a person of influence and much more capable than the active politicians of that time, was hesitant to enter public life and handle his country's affairs, he said, 'Tell me, Charmides: supposing that there was somebody capable of winning at the major athletic competitions so as to gain honour for himself and enhance his country's reputation in Greece, and supposing that he refused to compete, what sort of man would you think he was?'

'Obviously soft and unenterprising.'

'And supposing that there was somebody who, though capable of handling his country's affairs in such a way as to raise its prestige and win honour himself, was hesitant to do so – wouldn't he reasonably be regarded as unenterprising?'

'Probably; but why do you ask me that?'

'Because I think you are failing to use your administrative ability, and that in a sphere where you are bound as a citizen to take part.'

'What's your evidence for this accusation?' asked Charmides. 'In what kind of activity have you studied my ability?'

'In your relations with politicians. When they consult you, I notice that you give them good advice, and when they make mistakes, your criticism is fair and right.'

'It's not the same thing, Socrates,' he protested, 'to talk to a person privately and to debate in public.'

'All the same,' said Socrates, 'a man who can count counts just as well in public as by himself, and the best private performers of music are also those who are most successful in public.'

'But don't you realize that humility and fear are part of human nature, and that they come out much more in public than in private gatherings?'

'Yes, and I am anxious to show you something. You are neither overawed by the cleverest people nor afraid of the most powerful, and yet you are too modest to speak in front of the silliest and weakest. Whom are you shy of? The fullers or the shoe-makers or the carpenters or the smiths or the farmers or the merchants or the dealers in the agora, whose business it is to buy at a cheaper rate and sell at a dearer one? For all these people go to make up the Assembly. What difference do you think there is between what you are doing and someone who can beat trained athletes and is afraid of amateurs? You converse easily with our leading statesmen, some of whom look down on you, and you are far better qualified than the professional politicians; yet you shrink from speaking in front of people who have never troubled their heads about politics or formed a poor opinion of you – because you are afraid of being laughed at!'

'Well, don't you think,' said Charmides, 'that the members of the Assembly often laugh at those who advocate the right policy?'

'Yes, and so do the others. That's why I am surprised that although you can easily deal with the one class when they behave that way, you imagine that you will be quite incapable of facing the other. My good man, don't be ignorant of yourself, or make the usual mistake. Most people, when they are set upon looking into other people's affairs, never turn to examine themselves.

Don't shirk this responsibility, but make a greater effort to take yourself seriously; and don't neglect public affairs if you can improve them in any way, because, if they are well conducted, it will benefit not only the rest of the citizen body, but your personal friends, and not least yourself.'

8

Aristippus was once trying to argue Socrates down in the same way as he had been argued down by him in the past. Socrates, whose object was to benefit the people listening, answered not like a man who is guarding against getting his argument tangled up, but like one who is fully convinced that he is doing his duty. Aristippus asked him whether he knew anything that was good; his intention was, if Socrates mentioned anything such as food or drink or money or health or strength or courage, to prove that it was sometimes bad.[1] But Socrates knew that if anything annoys us, what we need is something to stop it, and he replied in the most effective way: 'Are you asking if I know something good for fever?'

'Of course not.'

'For ophthalmia?'

'No, not that either.'

'For starvation?'

'No, nor starvation either.'

'Well, if you are asking me whether I know anything that is good for nothing, I don't, and what's more I don't want to.'

Another time, Aristippus asked him whether he knew anything fine.[2]

'Yes indeed, plenty of things.'

'Well then, are they all alike?'

1. Aristippus' question is typically sophistic in that he omits the crucial qualifiers, which Socrates astutely adds ('for fever', etc.).

2. For Socrates on fineness, with parallels to this brief conversation, see Plato, *Hippias Major*. For Aristippus' sophistic approach to the matter, compare Plato, *Euthydemus*, 300c–301c.

'On the contrary, some are as unlike as they can be.'

'How can a thing be fine if it is unlike what is fine?'

'Why, because a man who is a fine runner has another unlike him who is a fine wrestler; and a shield which is fine for defence is totally unlike a spear which is fine for throwing hard and fast.'

'You are giving me just the same sort of answer as when I asked you if you knew anything good.'

'Do you really imagine that goodness and fineness are different? Don't you know that things are always good and fine by the same standards? In the first place, virtue is not good for some things and fine for others; secondly, people are called "fine" and "good" on the same grounds and with the same ends in view; and people's bodies are obviously fine and good in relation to the same end; and everything else that we use is considered to be fine and good in accordance with the same standard – namely, the end for which it is serviceable.'

'Then is a dung-basket fine?'

'Certainly, and a golden shield is contemptible, if the one is finely and the other badly constructed for carrying out its function.'

'Do you mean that the same things are both fine and contemptible?'

'Certainly, and, what's more, both good and bad. Often what is good for starvation is bad for fever, and vice versa; and what is fine for running is contemptible for wrestling, and vice versa. Everything is good and fine in so far as it's well adapted for its purpose, and bad and contemptible in so far as it's ill adapted.'

Similarly, in maintaining that a fine house is one that serves its purpose well, Socrates seemed to me to be teaching the principle that buildings should satisfy practical requirements.[1] He approached the question in this sort of way:

'If a man is to have the sort of house that he needs, ought he to contrive to make it as pleasant and convenient as possible to live in?' When this was admitted: 'Isn't it pleasant to have a house

1. See *The Estate-manager*, 9.2–4 (pp. 321–2).

which is cool in summer and warm in winter?' When they agreed to this too: 'Well, in houses that have a south aspect, in winter the sun shines into the verandas, while in summer it passes over our heads and over the roof and casts a shade. So, if this is the desired effect, one should build the south side higher so as not to shut off the winter sun, and the north side lower so as to avoid exposure to the cold winds. In short, the most pleasant and fine residence is likely to be that which offers at all seasons the most agreeable retreat for the owner and the safest repository for his possessions. Frescos and decorations deprive us of more amenities than they supply.' As for temples and altars, he said that the most suitable site for them was one that was at once conspicuous and off the beaten track: it was pleasant for passers-by to say their prayers upon seeing a shrine, but it was also pleasant to approach it in a reverent frame of mind.

9

On another occasion he was asked whether courage was a matter of teaching or a natural gift.[1] 'I think,' he said, 'that just as one body is born with more strength than another for doing work, so one mind is naturally endowed with greater fortitude than another for facing danger; for I observe that people who are brought up under the same laws and customs differ greatly in courage. But I think that every natural disposition can be developed in the direction of fortitude by instruction and application. It's obvious that the Scythians and Thracians would never dare to take shields and spears and fight it out with the Spartans; and it is evident that the Spartans would refuse to join mortal combat either with light shields and javelins against the Thracians or with bows and arrows against the Scythians. My personal experience is that similarly in all other cases people both differ in

1. This was a common debating topic, where any of the virtues is concerned, or virtue as a whole: see especially Plato, *Protagoras* and *Meno*. The debate is also reflected on pp. 231, 332, 359 and elsewhere. Compare Plato's *Laches* for Socrates on courage.

natural capacity and improve greatly by the help of application. From this it clearly follows that everyone, whether his natural ability is above or below the average, ought to study and exercise any qualities for which he wishes to earn recognition.'

He did not distinguish wisdom from prudence, but judged that the man who recognizes and puts into practice what is truly good, and the man who knows and guards against what is disgraceful, are both wise and prudent. When somebody asked him if he thought that those who understood what they ought to do, but did the opposite, were wise and weak, he replied, 'No more than I think them both unwise and weak. I presume that everyone acts by choosing from the courses open to him the one which he supposes to be most expedient. So I think that those who act wrongly are neither wise nor prudent.'[1]

He used to say that not only justice, but all the other moral virtues were wisdom.[2] Just actions and any others proceeding from a virtuous motive were truly good; those who knew how to do them would choose to do nothing else, and those who did not understand them could not do them, and, if they tried to, failed. Thus it was the wise who performed truly good actions: those who were not wise could not, and, if they tried to, failed. So, since just actions and all other good and honourable deeds were all done from a virtuous motive, obviously both justice and all the other moral virtues were wisdom.

He also said that madness was contrary to wisdom; yet he did not think that mere lack of knowledge was madness, but to be ignorant of oneself, and to form opinions about and think that one comprehends what one does not know – this in his view was very near to madness. He said that most people did not consider that those who blundered about things that were generally unknown were crazy, but they called those crazy who were mistaken about things that were generally known. If a man thinks that he is so tall

1. That is, all errors of conduct are errors of judgement. Compare Plato, *Protagoras*, 352a–357e; and see pp. 12, 14–15.
2. 'Virtue is wisdom' is the first so-called Socratic paradox; the second is 'No one does wrong deliberately'.

that he stoops as he goes out through the city gates, or so strong that he tries to pick up houses or attempts any other feat which is quite obviously impossible, he is called crazy, but those who are only a little mistaken are not generally considered to be crazy. Just as it is only a strong desire that is called love, so it is only a serious abnormality that is called madness.

Considering the nature of envy,[1] he concluded that it was a species of distress, but not the sort that arises over the misfortunes of friends or the good fortune of enemies; he said that only those people were envious who were distressed at the success of their friends. When some people expressed surprise that anyone who cared for a person should be vexed at his success, he reminded them that many people are so disposed towards certain others that they cannot ignore their troubles, but go to their help when they are unfortunate, and yet are annoyed when they are fortunate. This, he said, could not indeed happen to a sensible person, but was the constant experience of the foolish.

Considering the nature of leisure, he said that he found that most people occupied themselves in some way, because even playing draughts or making jokes was a kind of occupation; but all such people were, he said, 'at leisure', in the sense that it was possible for them to go on to do something better. But nobody had 'leisure' to go from better to worse; and if anyone did so, that person, he said, had no leisure and was occupying himself wrongly.

He said that it was not those who held the sceptre who were kings and rulers, nor those who were chosen by unauthorized persons, nor those who were appointed by lot, nor those who had gained their position by force or fraud, but those who knew how to rule. When anyone agreed that it was for the ruler to lay down what ought to be done and for the subject to obey, he used to point out that in a ship it is the man who knows that takes command and the owner and everybody else on board obeys the man who knows; that in farming those who possess land, in

1. See Plato, *Philebus*, 48b ff.

illness those who are ill, in physical training those who are exercising their bodies, and all other persons who have anything that needs attention, if they think that they have the necessary knowledge, look after themselves; but otherwise they not only follow the advice of experts, if they are on the spot, but call in their help if they are not, so that, by taking their advice, they may follow the right course. And he pointed out that in the case of wool-spinning, women actually exercise control over men, because they know how to do the work and the men do not. If anyone objected that a despot can disregard good advice, he used to reply, 'How can he, when there is a penalty for disregarding it? For in any case where a person disregards good advice he will presumably go wrong, and in going wrong he will pay the penalty.' And if anyone objected that a despot has the power even to put the wise man to death,[1] he said, 'Do you suppose that the man who puts to death his most effective allies goes unpunished or pays only a trivial penalty? Which do you think that a person who acts in this way would be more likely to do: find safety or precipitate his ruin?'

When he was asked what he thought was the best occupation for a man, he replied, 'Effective action.' And when he was further asked whether he considered good luck to be an occupation, he replied, 'I regard luck and action as totally opposed to each other. I consider that coming upon something that you need without looking for it is good luck, but to do a thing well after learning and practising how to do it is, I think, effective action; and it is those who make a practice of this who seem to me to be effective.'[2]

He used to say that in every sphere of action those people were best and most favoured by the gods who did their work effectively – whether in farming or in medicine or in politics; while the man who did nothing effectively was neither good for anything nor favoured by the gods.

1. See Plato, *Gorgias*, 466b ff.
2. Compare Plato, *Euthydemus*, 279c–280a for Socrates on luck, and see p. 22.

10

Again, whenever he talked to those craftsmen who practise their craft professionally, he was helpful to them too. When one day he paid a call on the painter Parrhasius, he asked him: 'Would you say, Parrhasius, that painting is representing things that one sees? You painters represent with your pigments and copy hollows and heights, darkness and light, hard and soft, rough and smooth, young bodies and old ones.'

'That's true.'

'Also, when you are painting beautiful figures, as it isn't easy to come across one single human being who is beyond criticism in every detail, you combine the best features of a number of people, and so convey the appearance of bodies which are entirely beautiful.'

'Yes, that is what we do.'

'Well now, do you represent the mind's character, which is the most attractive and pleasing and appealing and desirable and lovable part of us? Or is it not a subject for representation at all?'

'How could it be, Socrates, when it has neither shape nor colour nor any of the other qualities that you mentioned just now, and is not even visible at all?'

'Tell me, then, can a person look at other people in a friendly or unfriendly manner?'

'I would say so.'

'Then can this be represented in their expressions?'

'Certainly.'

'Do you think that those who care about their friends' good and bad fortune wear the same expressions on their faces as those who don't?'

'No, indeed: they look glad at their friends' good fortune and dejected at their misfortune.'

'Is it possible to depict this too?'

'Certainly.'

'Then again, dignity and freedom, meanness and slavishness, discipline and discretion, insolence and vulgarity – all show themselves both in the face and in the gestures of still and moving subjects.'

'True.'

'Can one represent these too?'

'Certainly.'

'Do you think it's more pleasant to see people who exhibit fine, good and admirable characters, or those who exhibit base, bad and odious ones?'[1]

'There's really no comparison, Socrates.'

On another day he called on Clito the sculptor and got into conversation with him. 'I can see and appreciate, Clito, the beauty you produce in your runners, wrestlers, boxers and pancratiasts;[2] but the quality of seeming alive – how do you produce this in your statues?'

Clito didn't reply at once, because he didn't know what to say.

'Perhaps,' said Socrates, 'you make your statues more lifelike by reproducing the appearance of living models.'

'Yes, indeed.'

'Do you make the various parts of the body seem more lifelike and convincing by representing them as concave or convex, compressed or expanded, tautened or relaxed, according to the posture?'

'Certainly.'

'But doesn't it in fact afford some pleasure also to see represented the feelings of people in action?'

'I suppose so.'

'So you should represent the expression of warriors as threatening, and the faces of victors should be made to look joyful?'

'Definitely.'

'In that case,' concluded Socrates, 'the sculptor ought to make his works correspond to the type of character represented.'

He called on Pistias the armourer, and on being shown some

1. The implication, of course, is that painters should depict characters which are pleasanter and more profitable to contemplate. Plato notoriously condemns artists of all kinds for failing to provide this sort of wholesome art.

2. See p. 150, n. 2.

well-made corselets, he said: 'It is most emphatically a splendid idea, Pistias, that the corselet should protect the parts of a man's body that need protection without preventing him from using his hands. But tell me, Pistias, why is it that you charge a higher price than other makers for your corselets, although they are no stronger and cost no more to make?'

'Because mine are better proportioned, Socrates.'

'And do you put a higher price on your corselets because their proportion is demonstrable by their measurements or their weight? I presume that you don't make them all in the same or even in similar proportions, if you make them to fit.'

'Oh, yes I do,' he said. 'A corselet is no good without proportion.'

'Surely some people's bodies are well proportioned and some badly.'

'Quite so.'

'Then how do you make a corselet that fits a badly proportioned body well proportioned?'

'In the same way as I make it to fit. A corselet that fits *is* well proportioned.'

'It seems to me,' said Socrates, 'that you are using the term "well proportioned" not absolutely, but in relation to the wearer, as you might say that a shield or a cloak is well proportioned for anyone that it fits; and the same, apparently, applies to everything else by your account. But perhaps fitting implies another important advantage.'

'Tell me, Socrates, what's your point?'

'A corselet that fits irks one less by its weight than an equally heavy one that doesn't fit. A badly fitting corselet either hangs entirely from the shoulders or presses severely on some other part of the body, and that makes it clumsy and uncomfortable. A well-fitting one has its weight distributed both over the collar-bone and shoulder-blades and over the shoulders, chest, back and abdomen, so that it seems almost more like an appendage than something to carry.'

'That's exactly why I think my products give the best value.

Some people, though, prefer to buy decorated and gilded corselets.'

'All the same,' said Socrates, 'if the consequence is that they buy misfits, it seems to me that they pay dearly for their decoration and gilding. But here's another point. The body doesn't always stay the same: sometimes it's bent and sometimes upright. How can precisely shaped corselets always fit?'

'They can't possibly.'

'When you talk of fitting, you mean not what is precisely shaped, but what is not uncomfortable to use.'

'You take the words out of my mouth, Socrates, and your grasp of the point is quite correct.'

11

At one time there was in the city a beautiful woman called Theodote, who was of the sort to consort with anyone persuasive. One of the company had mentioned her, and remarked that her beauty was beyond description; he added that artists visited her to paint her picture, and that she let them see as much of her as was proper. 'We ought to go and see her,' said Socrates. 'We can't form a clear idea about what is beyond description from hearsay.'

'The sooner you all come with me, the better,' said the informant.

So they went off to Theodote, found her posing for a painter, and took a good look at her. When the painter had finished, Socrates said: 'Gentlemen, ought we to be more grateful to Theodote for letting us see her beauty, or she to us for looking at her? I suggest that, if the display has been more to her advantage, she ought to be grateful to us, and if the sight has been more to ours, we ought to be grateful to her.'

Somebody said, 'That's right.'

'Well then,' he went on, 'she is already enjoying the tribute of our admiration, and when we have spread our report, she will benefit still further. On the other hand, we are now desirous of touching what we have seen; we shall go away with our emotions titillated; and when we have gone, we shall feel an unsatisfied longing. The natural inference from this is that we are performing the service and she is receiving it.'

'I must say,' said Theodote, 'if that's how it is, I should have to be grateful to you for looking at me.'

Socrates could see that she was expensively got up, and that she had her mother with her, dressed and arrayed in no casual manner, and several pretty maids in attendance, who similarly showed no signs of neglect; and that the house was lavishly appointed in all other respects. So he now said, 'Tell me, Theodote, have you got a farm?'

'Not I,' she said.

'Well then, a house that brings in money?'

'Nor a house.'

'Perhaps you have some slaves who work at a craft?'

'No, none.'

'Then how do you support yourself?'

'If anyone gets friendly with me and wants to be generous, that's how I get my living.'

'Good heavens, Theodote,' said Socrates, 'it's a splendid asset to have a flock of friends – much better than having a flock of sheep and goats and cattle. But tell me, do you leave it to chance whether a friend wings his way towards you, like a fly, or do you devise something yourself?'

'How could I find a device to bring that about?' she asked.

'You could do it much more naturally than a spider. You know how spiders hunt to support themselves: they spin fine webs and feed on anything that flies into them.'

'Are you advising me to weave some kind of snare too?' she asked.

'No, you mustn't expect to hunt friends, who are the most valuable prey of all, as simply as that. Don't you see that even in hunting common game like hares, people use various methods? In the first place, hares feed by night, so the hunters provide themselves with hounds trained for night work, and hunt them with these. Then, because hares run away from their feeding-grounds when day comes, they acquire other hounds which find them by picking up the scent from the trail that they leave from the feeding-grounds to their forms. Then, because they are swift-footed, so that they can escape by running even when sighted, the hunters further supply themselves with swift hounds to run them down. And because some of the hares escape even from these, nets are set up in their escape paths, so that the hares may run into them and get entangled.'

'Well,' said Theodote, 'what method like that might I use to catch friends?'

'Surely by providing yourself with a human hound, who will track down men of wealth and good taste, and, after finding them, devise a means of driving them into your nets.'

'Nets!' said she. 'What nets have I got?'

'One, certainly,' said Socrates , 'which is very close-enfolding: your body. And in it is your mind, which teaches you how to look charming and talk gaily, and tells you that you must give a warm welcome to an attentive lover, but bolt the door against a selfish one; that, if a lover falls ill, you must look after him devotedly; that, if he has a stroke of luck, you must share his pleasure enthusiastically; and that, if he cares for you deeply, you must gratify him wholeheartedly. As for loving, I am sure that you know how to love not only passively, but with real affection; and you convince your lovers that you are fond of them, I know, not by words but by deeds.'

'Honestly,' said Theodote, 'I don't use any of these methods.'

'Then again,' said Socrates, 'it's much better to keep one's human relationships natural and right. You can't capture or keep a friend by force; but by showing the creature kindness and giving it pleasure, you can both catch it and keep it by you.'

'That's true,' she said.

'So in the first place,' said Socrates, 'when people care for you, you should make only such demands of them as they can satisfy with a minimum of trouble. Then, you should repay their favours in kind. In this way they are likely to become most attached to you, to go on loving you for the longest time, and to be most generous to you. And you are likely to give them most pleasure if you bestow what you have to give only when they ask for it. You can see that even the most delightful dishes seem disagreeable if they are served before the appetite is ready, and if one is satiated, they actually cause disgust; but even inferior food seems quite attractive if it is served after hunger has been aroused.'

'Very well,' said she, 'how am I to arouse hunger for what I have to give?'

'Why, surely,' said Socrates, 'if, when your admirers are satiated, you neither offer nor hint at your favours, until the satisfaction has passed and they feel the want again; and next, when they most feel the want, if you drop hints by a combination of the most modest behaviour and obviously wanting[1] to gratify them, and by obviously holding back until their need is as great as possible – for the same favours are much better then than before the desire for them is aroused.'

Theodote said, 'Why don't you help me in my hunt for friends, Socrates?'

'I will, believe me,' said Socrates, 'if you persuade me.'

'How can I persuade you?'

'You'll look to that yourself,' he said, 'and you'll find a way, if you need any help from me.'

'Then come and see me often,' she said.

'Well, Theodote,' replied Socrates, poking fun at his own avoidance of public life, 'it's not very easy for me to find the time for it. I have a great deal of private and public business that keeps me occupied; and I have some girlfriends[2] too, who will never let me leave them by day or night, because they are learning from me about love-charms and spells.'

'Do you really know about them too, Socrates?' she asked.

'Why do you suppose that Apollodorus here and Antisthenes never leave me? And that Cebes and Simmias come to visit me

1. Omitting μή as the manuscripts do.
2. He is, of course, using an ironical metaphor: he means the male companions he is trying to instruct.

from Thebes? You may be sure that these things don't happen without a lot of love-charms and spells and magic wheels.'[1]

'Lend me your magic wheel, then, so that I may spin it first for you.'

'Certainly not,' he said. 'I don't want to be drawn to you; I want you to come to me.'

'Very well, I will,' she declared. 'Only mind you let me in.'

'Yes, I'll let you in,' said Socrates, 'unless I have someone with me that I like better.'

12

Seeing that Epigenes, one of his companions, was in poor physical condition for a young man, he said, 'You're out of training, Epigenes.'

'I don't do physical training, Socrates,' he replied.

'But you ought to, just as much as a prospective competitor at the Olympian games. Or do you think that the mortal struggle against her enemies in which Athens will sooner or later involve you doesn't matter? And yet in the hazards of war, it's not uncommon for people to lose their lives through lack of fitness, or to save it only ignominiously. For the same reason, many are captured alive, and once captured either spend the rest of their lives, perhaps, in the bitterest servitude, or, after being subjected to the most cruel duress and paying in some cases a ransom greater than the sum of their possessions, live out their lives in want and misery. Many too win a bad reputation because their physical debility makes them seem to shirk danger. Perhaps you don't take these penalties of unfitness seriously, and assume that you can easily put up with that sort of thing? In my view, at any rate, the prospects that await a man who cares about his physical fitness are much easier and more pleasant. Or perhaps you think that unfitness is both healthier and in general more good for you than

1. According to Pindar, *Pythians*, 4.214, the magic wheel was invented by Aphrodite to make Medea fall in love with Jason.

fitness, or are scornful of the results that fitness brings? In point of fact, the consequences of keeping oneself fit are entirely contrary to those of failing to do so.

'In the first place, those who keep themselves fit are healthy and strong; and this means that many of them come through the conflicts of war with honour, and escape from all its dangers; many help their friends and do service to their country, and so earn gratitude and win great glory and achieve the most splendid honours, and consequently live out their lives with greater pleasure and distinction, and leave behind them a better start in life for their children. The fact that our country does not conduct military training at public expense is no reason for individuals to neglect it; they should regard it no less seriously. You can take it from me that there is no other feat of endurance either – in fact there is no activity of any kind – in which you will be at a disadvantage from having your body better prepared. The body is valuable for all human activities, and in all its uses it is very important that it should be as fit as possible. Even in the act of thinking, which is supposed to require least assistance from the body, everyone knows that serious mistakes often happen through physical ill-health. Many people's minds are often so invaded by forgetfulness, despondency, irritability and insanity because of their poor physical condition that their knowledge is actually driven out of them. On the other hand, those who are in good physical condition have ample cause for confidence and run no risk of any such misfortune through debility. Their physical fitness is likely to contribute towards results that are contrary to those of unfitness – results which a sane man would surely endure any hardships to secure. Besides, it is a shame to let yourself grow old through neglect before seeing how you can develop the maximum beauty and strength of body; and you can't have this experience if you are negligent, because these things don't normally happen by themselves.'

13

Once, when somebody was angry because another person did not return his greeting, Socrates said, 'It's funny that, although you wouldn't have been angry if you had met a person in a rather poor physical state, it upsets you to come across one in a rather rude state of mind.'

Somebody else said that he took no pleasure in eating. 'Acumenus[1] can tell you a good cure for that,' said Socrates.

'What sort of cure?' asked the other.

'To give up eating. Once you've done that, you'll find life not only more pleasant, but cheaper and healthier.'

On another occasion, somebody else complained that the drinking-water at his house was warm.

'Then whenever you want a warm bath, it'll be ready for you.'

'But it's too cold to wash in.'

'Do your slaves object to drinking it and washing in it too?'

'Not at all,' said the man. 'In fact, I've been surprised to see how contentedly they use it for both purposes.'

'Which is warmer to drink, the water in your house or the water in the temple of Asclepius?'[2]

'The water in the temple of Asclepius.'

'And which is the colder for bathing, yours or the water at the shrine of Amphiaraus?'[3]

'The water at the shrine of Amphiaraus.'

'You should reflect, then,' said Socrates, 'that you look like being more fussy than a slave or an invalid.'[4]

1. A medical friend of Socrates, who is also mentioned in Plato's *Phaedrus* (227a, 268a).
2. The god of healing. The centre of his worship was at Epidaurus, but he had a shrine with a warm spring at Athens.
3. A legendary hero and seer who perished in the expedition of the Seven against Thebes. He had a shrine at Oropus near the east end of the Attic-Boeotian frontier.
4. At both Asclepius' and Amphiaraus' shrines, invalids bathed before sleeping; priests then interpreted their dreams in terms of possible cures.

A man had punished his retainer severely, and Socrates asked why he was angry with his servant.

'Because he's as lazy as he is greedy, and as shy of work as he is fond of money,' replied the man.

'Have you ever considered which of you needs the bigger thrashing – you or your servant?'

Somebody was afraid of travelling to Olympia. 'Why are you afraid of the journey?' asked Socrates. 'Don't you spend nearly the whole day walking when you're at home? On your way to Olympia, you will walk for a while and then have lunch; then walk for another while, have dinner and go to bed. Don't you realize that if you joined together, end to end, the walks that you take in five or six days, you would easily cover the distance from Athens to Olympia?[1] Besides, it is pleasanter to start a day too soon than to arrive too late, because it is awkward to be forced to lengthen the stages of your journey too much; but to increase the time of the journey by one day makes for considerable ease. So it's better to hurry over the start than on the journey.'

When someone else said that he was exhausted after making a long journey, Socrates asked him whether he was carrying baggage too. 'Good heavens, no,' he said, 'only my coat.'

'Were you travelling alone,' asked Socrates, 'or did you have a servant with you?'

'Yes, I had.'

'Was he empty-handed or carrying something?'

'Carrying my bedding, naturally, and my other belongings.'

'And how did he get through the journey?'

'Better than I did, I should say.'

'Well, now,' said Socrates, 'if you had had to carry his luggage, what sort of state do you think you would have been in?'

'Very poor – or rather, I couldn't have brought it at all.'

'Do you really think it's natural for a fit man to be so much less capable of effort than a boy servant?'

1. Even by the shortest route (which involves some stiff climbing) this is about 150 miles.

14

When there was a communal dinner and some of the party brought more food than others, Socrates used to tell his servant either to pool the smaller contributions or to distribute them in equal shares. The result was that those who brought a large quantity felt ashamed to refuse a share of the pooled food and also felt ashamed to keep their food to themselves; so they put their food into the pool too. And since they got no more than those who brought a small quantity, they gave up spending large sums on food.

On one occasion, Socrates noticed that one of the company at dinner had stopped eating bread and was eating the savouries by themselves.[1] As the conversation was about the proper application of names to occupations, Socrates said: 'Can we say, gentlemen, what sort of conduct gets a man called a savoury-eater?[2] Of course, everybody eats savouries with his bread if he's got any, but I presume that this is not enough to earn the name of savoury-eater.'

'No, indeed,' said one of the company.

'Well, now,' he went on, 'if somebody eats savouries by themselves, without bread, not with a view to training but for pleasure, do you think he is a savoury-eater or not?'

'There could hardly be a better claim to the title.'

Another member of the company said, 'What about a man who eats a great deal of savouries with a little bread?'

'In my view,' said Socrates, 'it would be fair to call him a savoury-eater too. And when everyone else is praying to the gods for plentiful crops, I suppose he would pray for plentiful savouries!'

1. Greek diet consisted (broadly speaking) of two elements: some sort of bread and something to give it taste – especially cheese, fish or vegetables. The latter were collectively called *opson*, translated here as 'savoury'. Good manners required you to take a little savoury with each bit of bread.
2. The word, though rare, was in (largely comic) usage, meaning a gourmet, or perhaps a fussy eater.

When Socrates said this, the young man realized that the discussion had been aimed at him and, although he did not stop eating the savouries, he took bread with them. Observing this, Socrates said, 'I want you who are sitting near him to watch and see whether he will treat the bread as savoury or the savouries as bread.'

He once saw another of his dinner-companions sampling several kinds of savoury with one piece of bread. 'Could there be,' he asked, 'a form of gastronomy more extravagant or more ruinous of good food than is practised by a person who eats several dishes at once and puts all kinds of flavours into his mouth at the same time? By combining more ingredients than his cooks use he is acting rather extravagantly, and since he combines what they refuse to combine, as being incompatible, then, if they are right, he is wrong, and is desecrating their art. And yet it is surely absurd for a man to engage the most expert cooks and then interfere with their menus when he doesn't even profess the art in question. Besides, there's another thing that happens to a man who has made a habit of eating several kinds of food at once. If he hasn't got several kinds, he is likely to feel discontented through missing what he is accustomed to. On the other hand, a man who had made a habit of helping down one piece of bread with one kind of savoury could be content with one kind if more were not available.'

He also used to say that in the Athenian dialect 'good living' was synonymous with 'eating', and that the qualification 'good' referred to eating foods which were innocuous to both mind and body, and not difficult to procure. Thus he regarded even good living as the privilege of those whose lives are well ordered.

BOOK FOUR

Socrates was so helpful in every activity and in every way that anyone who considers the matter and estimates it fairly must see that nothing was more profitable than associating with Socrates and spending one's time with him in any place or circumstances. Indeed, even to recall him now that he is gone is no small help to those who were his habitual companions and who accept his views.

His influence on his companions was just as salutary in his lighter moments as when he was serious. He would often say that he loved somebody; but anyone could see that he was drawn not towards those endowed with physical attractiveness, but towards those endowed with mental virtue. He inferred that they had natural talent from their learning quickly anything to which they applied their minds, and remembering what they had learned; and from their eagerness for any kind of instruction that enables one to manage an estate or a community efficiently, and in general to be successful in one's dealings with people and in one's management of human affairs. He thought that people of this sort, when trained, would not only be happy themselves and manage their estates well, but would be able to make other persons and communities happy too.

He did not approach everyone in the same way. If people thought that they were naturally talented and were scornful of instruction, he explained to them that the natures which are regarded as the best have the greatest need of training. He pointed out that the best-bred horses are spirited and impetuous, and that if they are broken in when they are quite young, they become more manageable and better than any others; but if they grow up unbroken, they are very difficult to control and worse than any others. Again, pedigree puppies, which are tireless and eager to attack their prey, become very good hounds and most serviceable for hunting, if they are properly trained; but if they grow up untrained, they become wild and erratic and very difficult to control. In the same way, the best types of men, people with exceptional strength of mind and ability to carry through whatever they undertake, if they are educated and learn to do their duty, become excellent and most useful people, because they perform a great many important services; but if they grow up uneducated and ignorant, they turn out worse and cause more harm than anybody. Not knowing how to decide where their duty lies, they often set their hands to wicked deeds; and since they are proud and impetuous, they are difficult to restrain or divert from their course, and consequently they commit a great many serious crimes.

As for those who were proud of their wealth and thought that they had no need of education as well, but assumed that their riches would be quite enough to secure for them any result that they wanted and to win the esteem of their fellow men, he tried to put sense into them by saying that a man was a fool if he expected to be able to distinguish beneficial and harmful activities without learning how to do so; and a fool if, unable to draw this distinction, but using his wealth to procure whatever he wanted, he nevertheless thought that he would be able to act to his own advantage. And if he could not act to his own advantage, it was stupid to think that he was fortunate and well or adequately equipped for life, and also stupid to think that he would be considered good for anything because of his wealth if he had no knowledge, or that he would enjoy popularity if he was considered good for nothing.

2

I shall next describe what his attitude was towards those who thought that they had received the best education and prided themselves on their wisdom.

He discovered that the handsome Euthydemus[1] had collected a

1. The Euthydemus who figures in several dialogues in this fourth book of the *Memoirs* is a pupil of Socrates, not the sophist mentioned on p. 136, n. 1.

great many writings of the best-known poets and sages, and that consequently he now considered himself to be more enlightened than anyone of his age-group, and entertained high hopes of becoming unrivalled in eloquence and administrative ability. So first of all, realizing that because of his youth Euthydemus did not yet go into the agora if he wanted to conduct any business, but took up his position in a saddler's shop close by, Socrates went to the shop himself with some of his friends. Someone opened the conversation by inquiring whether it was through association with one of the sages or by natural talent that Themistocles rose so far above his fellow citizens that the State looked to him whenever it needed a man of action. Socrates wanted to stir up Euthydemus, so he replied that it was silly to imagine that, although the lesser arts were not practised seriously without the help of competent teachers, the art of public administration, which was the greatest accomplishment of all, came to people of its own accord.

On another occasion when Euthydemus was present, Socrates noticed that he was withdrawing from the group and taking care not to seem impressed by Socrates' wisdom. 'Gentlemen,' he said, 'it is easy to see from the way in which our friend Euthydemus spends his time that, when he is old enough, he won't refrain from advising the State on any political issue that comes up. And it seems to me that by carefully avoiding the appearance of learning anything from anybody, he has provided himself with a splendid preface to his public speeches. Evidently, when he begins to speak, he will introduce what he has to say like this: "Gentlemen of Athens, I have never learned anything from anybody, nor have I sought the company of any person whose abilities in speech and action I had heard of, nor have I troubled to acquire a teacher from among those who understand these matters. On the contrary, I have consistently avoided not only learning anything from anybody, but even giving the impression of doing so. However, I shall offer you whatever advice occurs to me of its own accord." Such an introduction would be appropriate for candidates applying for a public medical post. They could suitably begin their speech in this way: "Gentlemen of Athens, I have never learned medicine from anyone, nor have I tried to secure any doctor as a teacher. I have consistently avoided not only learning anything from medical men, but even giving the impression of having learned this art. However, I ask you to give me this medical post. I shall try to learn by experimenting on you."'

This introduction made everyone present laugh. It was now obvious that Euthydemus was paying attention to what Socrates was saying, although he was still careful not to say anything himself, thinking by his silence to invest himself with an air of discretion. Socrates wanted to stop him behaving like this, and said: 'You know how people who want to be competent performers on a stringed or wind instrument, or on horseback, or in any other similar skill, try to practise the desired accomplishment as continuously as possible, not only by themselves but under the supervision of acknowledged experts, and go to all lengths and put up with anything, just so long as these experts approve of all they do, because they feel that they cannot otherwise become worthwhile practitioners of their art. I find it astonishing that, on the other hand, some of those who wish to become proficient in public speaking and administration expect to be able suddenly to do this of their own accord without preparation or application. Yet political proficiency seems to be harder to achieve than the other kinds, inasmuch as more people pursue political ends and fewer achieve them. So obviously political ambition calls for more and closer application than other kinds.'

Socrates began by making observations of this sort in the hearing of Euthydemus. When he noticed that Euthydemus was putting up with his comments more readily and listening with greater interest, he went alone to the saddler's shop, and, when Euthydemus sat down near him, said, 'Tell me, Euthydemus, is it true what I hear, that you have collected a large number of books by reputed experts?'

'Indeed it is, Socrates,' replied Euthydemus, 'and I'm still adding to the collection, until I've got as many as I can.'

'I really do admire you for preferring to stockpile wisdom

rather than silver and gold,' said Socrates. 'Evidently you think that silver and gold make people no better, whereas the maxims of the wise enrich their possessors with moral goodness.'

Euthydemus cheered up as he heard this, thinking that Socrates approved of his method of pursuing wisdom; but when Socrates noted that he was pleased at this commendation, he said, 'What exactly is it that you want to become good at, Euthydemus, by collecting these books?'

When Euthydemus remained silent, wondering what he should reply, Socrates went on: 'Can it be medicine? There are a great many treatises written by doctors.'

'That's not my idea at all,' said Euthydemus.

'Perhaps you want to become an architect? That's another profession that calls for a skilled mind.'

'No, I don't want to become an architect.'

'Perhaps you are keen to become a good geometrician, like Theodorus?'[1]

'Not that either,' he said.

'Perhaps you want to be an astronomer?' When he denied this too, Socrates asked, 'Perhaps a rhapsode?[2] They say that you have got all the poems of Homer.'

'Certainly not,' he said. 'I know that rhapsodes are word-perfect, but they have very little intelligence themselves.'

At this Socrates said, 'You don't mean to tell me, Euthydemus, that you are aiming at the kind of proficiency that makes people politicians and administrators and capable of governing, and helpful both to others and themselves?'

'I am very anxious to acquire this kind of proficiency,' replied Euthydemus.

'Good heavens!' said Socrates. 'It's a most splendid and important art that you have set your heart on. It's the province of kings, and is called the art of kingship. But have you satisfied yourself

1. Of Cyrene, a famous mathematician who is one of the characters in Plato's *Theaetetus*.
2. A professional reciter of epic poetry: see Plato's *Ion*.

whether it is possible to become good at these things without being morally good?'

'Certainly I have,' he said, 'and it's impossible to become even a good citizen without moral goodness.'

'Well,' said Socrates, 'have you achieved this?'

'I think, Socrates, that I should prove to be as moral a man as anyone.'

'Well then, do moral men have products in the same way that carpenters do?'

'Yes, they have.'

'Carpenters can display their products – can moral men give an account of theirs too?'

'Are you suggesting,' said Euthydemus, 'that I can't give an account of the products of morality? I assure you that I can do it for the products of immorality too! There are plenty of them to be seen and heard every day.'

'Look here,' said Socrates, 'shall we write an R here and a W there, and then put down whatever we think is a right thing to do under R and whatever we think is wrong under W?'

'If you think there's any point, do it.'

Socrates wrote the letters as he had suggested, and then said, 'Is there such a thing in human life as telling lies?'

'Yes, there is.'

'On which side shall we put that?'

'Obviously under Wrong.'

'Is there such a thing as deception?'

'Certainly.'

'On which side shall we put that?'

'Obviously that too under Wrong.'

'What about doing harm?'

'That too.'

'And enslaving?'

'That too.'

'And shall we list none of these under Right, Euthydemus?'

'No, that would be shocking.'

'Well now, suppose that a man who has been appointed to a

military command reduces a wicked and hostile city to slavery, shall we say that he is acting wrongly?'

'Of course not.'

'Shall we not say that he is acting rightly?'

'Certainly.'

'And supposing that he deceives them in fighting against them?'

'That is right too.'

'And if he steals and plunders their possessions, will he not be acting rightly?'

'Certainly,' he said. 'I thought at first that you were asking about these actions only in relation to friends.'

'So perhaps all the things that we have put under Wrong ought to be put under Right too.'

'It looks like it.'

'Now that we have settled that, shall we revise our definition and say that it is right to do this sort of thing to enemies, but wrong to do it to friends, and that to the latter one should be as straightforward as possible. Is that what you wish?'

'Very much so,' said Euthydemus.

'Well then,' said Socrates, 'supposing that a general sees that his force is downhearted and issues a false statement that help is approaching, and by this falsehood restores the morale of his men: on which side shall we put this deceit?'

'I think under Right.'

'And supposing that someone has a son who needs medical treatment and refuses to take his medicine: if the father surreptitiously gives him the medicine in his food and by this artifice restores him to health, where should we put this example of deceit?'

'I think in the same category.'

'Well now, supposing that someone has a friend who is in a state of depression, and is afraid that he will do away with himself; and supposing that he covertly or openly removes a sword or some other weapon from him – in which column should we put this?'

'Surely this ought to go under Right too.'

'Do you mean that we ought not *always* to deal straightforwardly even with our friends?'

'Of course we shouldn't,' he said. 'I am revising my earlier statement, if that's all right.'

'Well, that's much better than putting things in the wrong categories,' said Socrates. 'But take the case of those who deceive their friends to their detriment (so as not to leave even this aspect unconsidered): which is the worse morally, to do it voluntarily or involuntarily?'[1]

'Well, Socrates, I've lost confidence in my answers. Everything that I said before seems to be different now from what I thought then. However, take it that I say that voluntary is worse than involuntary deception.'

'Do you think that one can learn and understand morality as one can the alphabet?'

'Yes, I do.'

'Who do you consider to be more literate, the man who deliberately reads or writes wrongly, or the man who does it involuntarily?'

'The former, I think, because he could do the same thing correctly if he wanted to.'

'So the man who deliberately writes incorrectly would be literate, and the one who does it involuntarily would be illiterate?'

'Of course.'

'Who knows what is right – the man who lies and deceives voluntarily or the one who does so involuntarily?'

'The former, obviously.'

'You hold that the man who knows his alphabet is more literate than the one who doesn't?'

'Yes.'

'And that the man who knows what is right is morally better than the one who doesn't?'

'Obviously. I think that is, in a sense, implied in what I said.'

1. See the discussion of voluntary and involuntary error in Plato's *Hippias Minor*.

'Well now, take the man who wants to tell the truth, but never says the same about the same things: in describing the same route, he calls it sometimes eastward and sometimes westward and, in totalling up an account, he makes the same total now bigger and now smaller – what do you think of him?'

'His is a clear case of not knowing what he thought he knew.'

'You know that there are people whom we call slavish?'

'Yes.'

'Because of their wisdom or because of their ignorance?'

'Obviously because of their ignorance.'

'Is it because they are ignorant of metalwork that they get their description?'

'Of course not.'

'Ignorant of carpentry, then?'

'Not that either.'

'Well, of cobbling?'

'None of those reasons; just the opposite. Most of the people who understand these crafts are slavish.'

'Then does this name apply to those who don't know what is honourable and good and right?'

'So I believe.'

'In that case, we ought to make every effort to avoid being slavish.'

'I swear, Socrates,' said Euthydemus, 'I really thought that I was following a philosophy of life which would give me the right sort of education for one whose object is true goodness. But now you can't think how depressed I feel when I see that my past efforts have left me unable to answer questions even about the most important subjects, and with no other course available by which I can make myself better.'

Socrates said, 'Tell me, Euthydemus: have you ever been to Delphi?'

'Yes indeed, twice.'

'Did you notice the inscription "Know yourself" somewhere near the shrine?'

'Yes, I did.'

'Did you ignore the inscription, or did you pay attention to it and try to examine what sort of person you were?'

'Good heavens!' he said. 'No, I didn't. You see, that was one thing I thought I did know. I could hardly have known anything else if I hadn't even been acquainted with myself.'

'Who do you think knows himself – the man who merely knows his own name, or the one who behaves like people buying a horse? They don't consider that they know a horse in which they are interested until they have satisfied themselves whether it's obedient or disobedient, strong or weak, swift or slow, and how it stands with respect to all the other qualities which make a horse desirable or undesirable as regards its usefulness; and the man I am thinking of has in the same way ascertained his own ability by examining his own qualifications in respect of human relationships.'

'To my mind, the man who doesn't know his own ability is ignorant of himself.'

'And isn't this obvious,' said Socrates, 'that people derive most of their benefits from knowing themselves, and most of their misfortunes from being self-deceived? Those who know themselves know what is appropriate for them and can distinguish what they can and cannot do; and, by doing what they understand, they both supply their needs and enjoy success, while, by refraining from doing things that they don't understand, they avoid making mistakes and escape misfortune. Self-knowledge also enables them to assess others; and it is through their relations with others that they provide themselves with what is good and guard against what is bad for them. Those who do *not* know themselves and are totally deceived about their own abilities are in the same position whether they are dealing with other people or any other aspect of human affairs. They don't know what they want or what they are doing or what means they are using; and, through making gross mistakes about all these, they miss the good things and get into trouble. People who know what they are doing succeed in their activities and become famous and respected. Those who are like them gladly associate with them, while those who are unsuccessful in their affairs are anxious for these men to make decisions for them and to represent their interests, and pin to them their hopes of prosperity, and for all these reasons regard them with special affection. But those who don't know what they are doing make bad choices and fail in whatever they attempt, and so not only suffer loss and retribution in respect of these actions, but damage their reputation in consequence, get themselves laughed at, and live despised and unhonoured. You can see, too, that any States which have gone to war with stronger ones through not knowing their own capability either lose their territory or exchange freedom for slavery.'

Euthydemus said, 'You can take it from me, Socrates, that I quite recognize the importance of knowing oneself. But I am looking to you in the hope that you may be willing to explain to me at what point one should begin self-examination.'

'You are quite clear in your mind, I suppose,' said Socrates, 'what things are good and what are bad?'

'Certainly,' he said. 'If I don't even know that, I should be worse off than slavish people.'

'Come on, then, and expound them to me.'

'Well, that's not difficult. In the first place, I think that health is a good thing in itself, and sickness an evil. Then, the things conducive to each of these – drinks and foods and occupations that promote health – are good, and those that cause illness are bad.'

'So even health and illness may be good things when they have a good result and bad when they have a bad one.'

'When could health have a bad result and disease a good one?'

'Why, to be sure,' said Socrates, 'in the case of a shameful expedition or a disastrous voyage or many other such events, when those who have taken part because they were able-bodied have perished, while those who have been excluded by infirmity have escaped.'[1]

1. This seems rather specious: the misfortune is not a *direct* result of good health. It also contradicts *Memoirs*, 3.12 (pp. 171–2); but then, as Xenophon says (p. 177), Socrates tailored his conversations to suit the audience.

'True. But you see that in the case of beneficial activities too some people participate through fitness and others are excluded by infirmity.'

'Then, if these things are sometimes beneficial and sometimes harmful, are they any more good than bad?'

'Not a bit, it seems, according to your argument. But surely wisdom, Socrates, is beyond all question a good thing. What action is there that a person would not perform better if he were wise than if he were ignorant?'

'Why, haven't you heard of Daedalus,' said Socrates, 'how he was captured by Minos because of his skill and compelled to serve him, and was deprived at the same time of his country and of his liberty; and how, when he tried to escape with his son, he both lost the boy and didn't even reach safety himself, but was carried away into a foreign country and there became a slave again?'[1]

'That is certainly the story.'

'And haven't you heard of the fate of Palamedes? All the poets sing of how he fell a victim to Odysseus' jealousy because of his cleverness.'[2]

'That again is the story.'

'And how many other people do you think owe it to their cleverness that they have been carried off to the king of Persia, and served there as slaves?'[3]

'It looks as if the most unquestionable good is happiness, Socrates.'

'Provided that it isn't composed of questionable goods, Euthydemus.'

'Why, what constituent of happiness could be questionable?'

1. The usual tale of Daedalus, the legendary craftsman, is that, although his son Icarus was lost, he himself reached Sicily safely, and lived and worked there. Socrates is adding a twist, perhaps by assuming that, since Daedalus was an Athenian and Sicily a foreign country, Daedalus must have been forced to stay there.
2. See p. 47, n. 1.
3. The Persian king had a habit of gathering experts around him, by force if he could not do so otherwise.

'None – unless we include in it beauty or strength or wealth or fame or something else of that kind.'

'But we certainly shall include them. How could anyone be happy without them?'

'Then I assure you that we shall be including constituents from which many unpleasant consequences follow for mankind. Beauty often brings disaster through the excitement aroused by physical attraction; strength is often the cause of no small downfall by inducing people to attempt tasks which are too much for them; wealth often causes ruin through self-indulgence or the covetousness of others; fame and political power often lead to great calamities.'

'Really,' said Euthydemus, 'if I'm not right in praising happiness either, I must admit that I don't even know what to pray to the gods for.'

'Well,' said Socrates, 'probably you haven't so much as considered the question, because you were so confident in your knowledge. But since you are proposing to be a leader in a city with a democratic government, obviously you know what a democratic government is.'

'Perfectly, of course.'

'Do you think it's possible to know democratic government without knowing the people?'

'No, indeed I don't.'

'So you know what the people is?'

'I believe so.'

'And what do you think the people is?'

'The poor among the citizens.'

'So you know the poor also?'

'Of course.'

'Then do you know the rich too?'

'No less well than the poor.'

'What sorts of persons do you call poor and rich?'

'I suppose I call poor those who have not got enough to pay for what they need, and rich those who have more than enough.'

'Have you noticed that some of those who have very little not only find it enough, but actually save out of it, and that for some a great many possessions are not enough?'[1]

'Yes, indeed,' said Euthydemus, 'you are quite right to remind me; I know even some despots who are driven to do wrong because they haven't enough, just like the neediest classes.'

'Well then,' said Socrates, 'granted that this is so, we shall class the despots among the people, and those who have few possessions among the rich, if they are good managers of their property.'

Euthydemus said, 'I'm forced to admit that too. Evidently the fault lies with my own incompetence; and I am considering whether it may be best to keep my mouth shut. It looks as though I know absolutely nothing.'

He went away very much dejected, because he had come to despise himself and felt that he really was slavish.

Many of those who were treated in this way by Socrates stopped going to see him; these he considered to lack resolution. But Euthydemus decided that he would never become a person of any importance unless he associated with Socrates as much as possible; and from that time onwards, he never left him unless he was obliged to, and he even copied some of Socrates' practices. When Socrates realized that Euthydemus was in this frame of mind, he stopped teasing him and explained as simply and precisely as he could what he thought it was necessary for Euthydemus to know, and what lines of action were best for him to follow.[2]

3

He was in no hurry for his associates to become eloquent or capable or inventive; he thought that they ought first to acquire a sense of responsibility, because he considered that without this the possession of those other faculties made them more unscrupulous and more capable of doing wrong.

1. See also pp. 87, 95–6, 245–6, 293–4.
2. This final sentence marks a clear Xenophontic shift from the early-Platonic mood of the rest of the dialogue.

In the first place, then, he tried to make his associates think sensibly about religion.[1] Different people were present at different discourses of his on this subject, and have tried to describe them; I was present when he was having the following discussion with Euthydemus.

'Tell me, Euthydemus,' he said, 'has it ever occurred to you to reflect how carefully the gods have supplied all human needs?'

'No, as a matter of fact it hasn't,' he replied.

'Well, do you realize that in the first place we need light, which the gods supply us?'

'Certainly; without it we should be no better than blind for all the good our eyes could do us.'

'Then we also need rest; and they provide us with night as the best possible time for it.'

'We ought to be very grateful for that too.'

'And since the sun is bright and enables us to distinguish the times of the day, as well as everything else, while the night because of its darkness is more obscure, they have made stars shine in the night which inform us how the time is passing and so enable us to do many of the things that we need to do. Isn't that so?'

'Yes, it is.'

'Then the moon marks for us the divisions not only of the night, but also of the month.'

'Quite so.'

'There is also the fact that we need food, and the gods produce this from the earth, providing for the purpose appropriate seasons, which supply us not only with all kinds of things we need but also those things in which we find enjoyment.'[2]

'That is very kind of them too.'

'And then there is the fact that they give us water, which is so precious that it helps the earth and the seasons to germinate and grow everything that is useful to us, and helps also to feed us ourselves, and by combining with all the things that feed us makes

1. Compare also *Memoirs*, 1.4.
2. See p. 305.

them more digestible and beneficial and agreeable; and because we need a great deal of it, they supply it in the greatest possible abundance.'

'This too shows their forethought.'

'And what about their providing us with fire as an ally against cold and darkness, and as a partner in every art and in all the things that people prepare for their own convenience? To put it briefly, of all the aids for living with which people equip themselves not one of any importance is independent of fire.'

'That is another outstanding example of kindness.'

'And the fact that after the winter solstice the sun comes nearer, ripening some things and drying up others which have passed their prime; and that, after finishing this task, it comes no closer, but turns back for fear of injuring us by too much heat. And then when, as it recedes again, it reaches the point where even we can see that, if it recedes any further, we shall be frozen stiff by the cold, it turns again and approaches, so that it traverses just that part of the heavens in which it can do us most good. What about all this?'

'Yes, indeed,' he said, 'this too gives a very strong impression of happening for the benefit of mankind.'

'And then, since it is also plain that we could not endure either the heat or the cold if it came on suddenly, what about the fact that the sun approaches and recedes so gradually that we don't notice that we are passing into either extreme of temperature?'

'I am wondering now,' said Euthydemus, 'whether the gods have any function other than looking after men. My only difficulty is that the animals share these benefits as well.'

'Naturally,' said Socrates, 'because it's obvious, isn't it, that animals too are born and reared for the benefit of mankind? What other creature enjoys so many benefits as man does from goats, sheep, cattle, horses and donkeys? More, it seems to me, than from plants. At any rate, people obtain food and profit from the former no less than from the latter; and there are many tribes which don't use the produce of the earth for food, but support themselves on the milk, cheese and flesh of their herds; and all nations tame and domesticate useful animals and employ their help for war and for many other purposes.'

'I agree with you about that too. I observe that even those animals which are much stronger than ourselves are brought so far under human control that people use them just as they like.'

'And what of the fact that they have equipped us with senses appropriate to the different kinds of beautiful and beneficial objects that surround us, so that by means of these senses we can enjoy all good things? And the fact that they have implanted in us reason, which enables us to think about and remember our sensations, and so discover the beneficial effects of each class of objects and devise various means for enjoying what is good and avoiding what is bad for us? Then there is their gift of communication, which enables us through instruction to share reciprocally with others everything that is good, and to enact laws and live in organized communities.'

'There is every reason to suppose, Socrates, that the gods show great concern for human beings.'

'Then there is their direct assistance in a sphere in which we are incompetent – that is, in foreseeing our future interests. By means of divination they reveal to those who consult them what is going to happen, and explain how it can be turned to the best advantage.'

'And they seem to be on even friendlier terms with you than with others, Socrates, if it is true that they forewarn you what to do and what not to do without even being asked.'[1]

'You will discover for yourself that what I say is true if, instead of waiting until you see the gods in physical form, you are content to worship and honour them on the evidence of their works. You should reflect that the gods intimate as much themselves. Other deities give us good gifts, but never reveal themselves in any act of giving; and in particular he who controls and regulates the whole universe, with all its good and beautiful contents, which he ceaselessly supplies for our use, fresh and healthy and unmarred

1. He is referring to Socrates' inner voice: see pp. 34–5.

by age, obeying his commands unfailingly and faster than thought – he can be seen to be carrying out the greatest works, but in the detailed administration he is invisible to our eyes. Reflect that the sun, which is supposed to be manifest to all, does not permit human beings to regard him directly; anyone who attempts to observe him without due respect is deprived of sight. Even the agents of the gods, you will find, are invisible. The thunderbolt is obviously discharged from above and overcomes everything that it meets; but neither in its approach nor at the moment of impact nor in its withdrawal can it be seen. Winds are themselves invisible, but their effects are plain to us, and we can perceive their approach. Moreover, there is the human mind, which partakes of divinity if anything else human does; that it is the ruling part of us is evident, but even it cannot be seen. You should take this to heart, and not despise things that are unseen, but appreciate their power from their effects, and honour the divine.'

'Speaking for myself, Socrates,' said Euthydemus, 'I am quite sure that I shall not disregard the divine even to a small degree. But what depresses me is that it seems to me that no human being could ever repay the goodness of the gods towards us by adequate gratitude.'

'Don't feel depressed about that, Euthydemus,' said Socrates. 'You can see that the god at Delphi, when he is asked how one can show gratitude to the gods, replies: "By the law of the State." And I presume that it is the law everywhere to please the gods to the best of one's power by sacrificial offerings. Well then, how can we honour them better and more devoutly than by doing as they themselves direct? But one must not fall short of one's capacity; when a man does this, it is surely obvious that he is not honouring the gods. So if he consistently honours the gods to the best of his power, he may feel confident and expect the greatest blessings. It wouldn't be sensible to expect greater ones from any other source than from those who can grant the greatest benefits, or on any other ground than that of pleasing them. And how can one please them better than by the greatest possible obedience?'

By enunciating such principles as these and by putting them into practice himself, he made his associates more devout and responsible.

4

As for his views about what is right, so far from concealing them, he demonstrated them by his actions. In all his personal relationships he was law-abiding and helpful; in public life he obeyed the authorities in respect of their lawful requirements, both in civil affairs and on military service, so punctiliously that he was conspicuous for exceptional obedience. When he was appointed president in the Assembly,[1] he did not permit the people to pass an illegal motion, but in support of the law he resisted a popular outburst which no other man, in my opinion, could have withstood. He disobeyed the illegal orders of the Thirty: first, when they forbade him to converse with the young,[2] and second, when they instructed him, with some others, to arrest a citizen[3] for execution, he alone disobeyed on the ground that what he was ordered to do was illegal. When he was facing prosecution by Meletus, he rejected as illegal the usual practice in courts of law. All other accused persons used to address the jury ingratiatingly and flatter them and appeal to them illegally, and many of them by this sort of behaviour often secured an acquittal.[4] But although Socrates might easily have been acquitted if he had made even a moderate concession to common practice, he chose to abide by the law and die, rather than break it and live.[5]

He actually expressed these convictions on many occasions to others; and in particular, I know that one day he had the following

1. See p. 72, n. 1.
2. See *Memoirs*, 1.2.32–38 (pp. 78–80).
3. Leon of Salamis: see *Hellenica*, 2.3.39; Plato, *Apology*, 32c–d.
4. This behaviour was not actually made illegal in Athens until later. Xenophon is expressing his (and/or Socrates') opinion. See also p. 42, n. 1.
5. See Plato, *Apology*, 38d–e.

discussion about right conduct with Hippias of Elis.[1] Hippias had arrived at Athens after a long absence and joined Socrates just as he was saying to some of his friends how remarkable it was that if one wanted to have somebody taught cobbling or joinery or metalwork or horsemanship, there was no difficulty about knowing where to send him for this purpose, but if one wanted to learn oneself what is right, or to have a son or a slave taught this knowledge, one did not know where to go in order to get it. When Hippias heard this, he said playfully, 'Dear me, Socrates, are you still saying the same things I heard you say all that time ago?'

Socrates replied, 'Yes, and what is even stranger, Hippias, I'm not only saying the same things but saying them about the same subjects. You, no doubt, because of your wide learning, never say the same thing about the same subject.'

'Of course,' he said. 'I always try to say something new.'

'Even about facts that you know? I mean, if somebody asks you how many letters there are in "Socrates", and what they are, do you try to say something different now from what you said before? Or if you are asked about numbers, whether twice five is ten, don't you give the same answer now as before?'

'About things like these, Socrates, I always make the same statements, just as you do; but about what is right, I am quite confident that I have something to say that neither you nor anyone else could contradict.'[2]

'Good heavens!' said Socrates. 'This is certainly a valuable discovery you claim to have made, if it will stop jurymen from disagreeing over their verdicts, and ordinary citizens from arguing and litigating and rioting about their rights, and stop States from disputing and going to war about theirs. For my part, I don't know how I can tear myself away from you before hearing about this priceless discovery from the man who made it.'

1. A prominent sophist and polymath.
2. Hippias is not after absolute truth, just approbation. This is just one similarity between the dialogue here and Plato's *Hippias Major* and *Hippias Minor*.

'No, no,' said Hippias, 'you shan't hear about it until you have told us your view about what is right. You content yourself with making fun of other people by questioning and testing them all, while you won't state your own case or disclose your own opinions to anyone about anything.'[1]

'Why, Hippias,' he said, 'aren't you aware that I never stop revealing what I think is right?'

'I should like to know what this account of yours is.'

'If I don't reveal my views in a formal account, I do so by my conduct. Don't you think that actions are more reliable evidence than words?'

'Much more, of course. People often say what is right and do what is wrong; but nobody can be in the wrong if he is doing what is right.'

'Well then, have you ever known me give false evidence or be a sycophant or stir up trouble between friends or in the State, or do anything else that is wrong?'[2]

'No, I haven't,' he said.

'And refraining from what is wrong is right, don't you think?'

'I can see, Socrates, that you are still trying to avoid explaining what you think "right" means. You are describing not what right-minded people do, but what they don't do.'

'Well,' said Socrates, 'I should have thought that to refuse to do wrong was a sufficient demonstration of moral rectitude. But if you don't agree, see whether you like this better. I say that what is lawful is right.'

'Do you mean that "lawful" and "right" are the same, Socrates?'

'Yes, I do.'

'I ask because I don't grasp what you mean by "lawful" and "right".'

1. This statement rings far more true of Plato's Socrates than Xenophon's: Xenophon is borrowing from Plato's earlier works.
2. See *Defence*, 3–5 (pp. 41–2) and *Memoirs*, 4.8.4–6 (p. 215); on sycophants, see p. 133, n. 3.

'You know what is meant by a country's laws?' asked Socrates.

'Yes.'

'And what do you think they are?'

'What the citizens have recorded after agreement about what they ought to do and what they ought to refrain from.'

'So a law-abiding person would be one who orders his life in the community in accordance with these, and a lawless person one who transgresses them?'

'Certainly.'

'So a person who obeyed them would be doing what is right, and one who disobeyed them what is wrong?'

'Certainly.'

'So the person who did what was right would be right, and the one who did wrong would be wrong?'

'Of course.'

'Then a law-abiding person is right, and a lawless one wrong.'

Hippias objected, 'How can one regard laws or obedience to them as a serious thing when the very same people who enacted them often repudiate and alter them?'[1]

'Yes,' said Socrates, 'and States often undertake a war and then make peace.'

'Very true.'

'Do you think there is any difference,' he said, 'between your belittling obedience to the laws on the ground that the laws may be repealed, and criticizing good discipline in time of war because peace may be made? Or do you actually find fault with those who help their country wholeheartedly in time of war?'

'No, I certainly don't,' he said.

'Are you aware,' said Socrates, 'that Lycurgus[2] the Lacedaemonian would have made Sparta no better than any other city if he had not inculcated in it the greatest obedience to the laws?

1. A good example of the critical attitude adopted by many sophists towards accepted beliefs. As the subsequent conversation shows, Hippias probably set up an ideal of natural, unbreakable law, as distinct from man-made conventions.

2. See p. 44, n. 3.

Don't you know that the best leaders are those who are most efficient in making the people obey the laws, and that a city in which the people are most obedient to the laws has the best life in time of peace and is irresistible in war? Moreover, concord is accepted to be the greatest blessing in a State, and very commonly in a State the senate[1] and aristocracy call upon the citizens to agree; and everywhere in Greece there is a law laid down that the citizens take an oath to agree, and everywhere this oath is taken. I presume that the purpose of this is not that the citizens may come to the same decision about plays, or praise the same musicians, or choose the same poets, or take pleasure in the same things, but that they may obey the laws; for it is when the inhabitants abide by these that countries become strongest and happiest, but without agreement a State cannot be well organized nor an estate well managed.

'And in private life, how can anyone incur less punishment or more honour from the State than by obeying the laws? How could he be less likely to lose or more likely to win in the courts? To whom would one more confidently entrust one's money or one's sons and daughters? Whom would the State as a whole consider more dependable than the law-abiding man? From whom would parents, relations, servants, friends, fellow countrymen or foreigners be more likely to obtain their rights? To whom would an enemy more readily entrust the making of truces or treaties or terms of peace? To whom would people be more willing to ally themselves than to the law-abiding man? To whom would allies more readily entrust supreme command or the defence of a fortress or the protection of cities? From whom would a benefactor expect to receive more gratitude than from a law-abiding man? Whom would one be more inclined to benefit than a person from whom one anticipates a return of favour? Whom would one wish more to have for a friend, or less to have for an enemy? Whom would one be less likely to fight than the

1. The Greek word (*gerousia*) is the name of one of the main administrative bodies in Sparta.

man whom one would wish most to be one's friend and least to be one's enemy, and to whom the largest number wished to be friends and allies, and the smallest number enemies and foes? Personally, Hippias, I express the view that lawful and right are the same. If you hold the opposite view, please explain it to me.'

'No, really, Socrates,' said Hippias, 'I don't think I do hold the opposite view to yours about what is right.'

'Do you know what is meant by "unwritten laws", Hippias?' he asked.

'Yes, those which are observed in every country with respect to the same circumstances.'

'Can you assert that it was men who laid them down?'

'How could it be, considering that they couldn't all meet together and don't speak the same language?'

'Then who do you think are the authors of these laws?'

'I suppose that these laws were ordained for men by gods. At any rate, among all peoples the first established custom is to worship gods.'

'Isn't it a custom everywhere to honour parents?'

'Yes, that too.'

'And that parents should not copulate with their children or children with their parents?'

'I don't think that this is a god-given law like the others, Socrates.'

'Why not?'

'Because I observe that some people break it.'

'In point of fact they break a good many other laws. But those who transgress the laws laid down by the gods pay a penalty which no man can escape in the way that some transgressors of man-made laws escape paying the penalty, either by escaping detection or by the use of force.'

'What penalty, Socrates, cannot be escaped by parents who copulate with their children or children who copulate with their parents?'

'The greatest of all, I can tell you. What greater misfortune could happen to human beings in the procreation of their children than to procreate badly?'

'Why should they procreate badly,' asked Hippias, 'seeing that there is no reason why the fathers should not be good themselves and beget children by good mothers?'

'Because surely the partners in procreation ought not only to be good, but at their physical prime. Or do you suppose that the seed of those who are in their prime is no different from that of those who have not yet reached it or who have already passed it?'

'No, indeed,' he said, 'they're not likely to be the same.'

'Which is the better, then?'

'Obviously the seed of those who are in their prime.'

'So that of others is not of high quality.'

'It is certainly not likely to be.'

'Then one ought not to procreate under these conditions.'

'No, indeed.'

'So those who do so are procreating as they ought not.'

'So it seems to me.'

'What else could be bad procreation, then, if theirs isn't?'

'I accept your view about this too.'

'Well now, isn't it customary everywhere to repay benefits?'

'Yes, it is, but this is transgressed too.'

'Don't those who transgress it pay a penalty as well, by being deprived of good friends and being compelled to pursue the company of people who dislike them? Isn't it a fact that those who do good to their associates are good friends, whereas those who don't repay their debts are disliked for their ingratitude, but still try with all their might to form such associations because of the profit to be gained from them?'

'Certainly, Socrates,' he said, 'all this looks like the work of the gods. That the laws themselves should entail penalties for their transgressors seems to me to imply a law-giver of more than human excellence.'

'Well then, Hippias, do you think that the gods' legislation is right or not?'

'It must be right: it's hard to see how anyone else could lay down what is right if a god couldn't.'

'So it follows, Hippias, that the gods are satisfied that "right" and "lawful" mean the same.'

By this sort of conversation and conduct, he made those who came into contact with him better men.

5

I shall now tell how he made his associates more efficient. Believing that self-discipline was a good thing for anyone to have who intended to achieve a creditable result, in the first place he let his companions see clearly that he himself kept the strictest training that anyone could; and in the second place, in his conversation he used to urge his companions on to self-discipline above all. He was constantly mindful himself, and was always reminding his companions, of the things that are conducive to moral goodness; and I know that he once had a discussion about self-discipline with Euthydemus to the following effect.

'Tell me, Euthydemus,' he said, 'do you think that liberty is a fine and splendid possession both for an individual and for a State?'

'Yes, beyond the slightest shadow of a doubt.'

'If a man is governed by the pleasures of the body and because of them cannot act as is best, do you think that he is a free man?'

'Far from it.'

'Presumably you say that because you think it is the mark of a free man to act in the best way; and consequently to have masters who prevent you from so acting is slavish.'

'Absolutely.'

'So it seems to you that those who have no self-discipline are absolutely slavish.'

'It does indeed, naturally.'

'Do you think that these people are merely prevented from acting in the best way, or that they are actually forced to do the most disgraceful things?'

'In my opinion, they are just as much compelled to do the one as they are prevented from doing the other.'

'And what sort of masters do you think those are who prevent the best actions and compel the worst?'

'Surely the worst possible.'

'And what do you consider to be the worst form of slavery?'

'I think it is slavery under the worst masters.'

'So self-indulgent people endure the worst form of slavery?'

'That is my opinion.'

'Don't you think that self-indulgence debars people from wisdom, which is the greatest good, and drives them into the opposite state? Don't you think that, by dragging them off in pursuit of pleasure, it prevents them from studying and apprehending their real interests; and that it often confuses their perception of good and bad and makes them choose the worse instead of the better?'

'That does happen.'

'And who, Euthydemus, can we say has less concern with self-discipline than the self-indulgent man? For surely the effects of self-discipline and self-indulgence are directly opposed.'

'I admit that too.'

'Do you think that anything is more likely to hinder one from devoting oneself to the proper objects than self-indulgence?'

'No, I don't.'

'Do you think there is anything worse for a man than that which makes him choose what is bad for him instead of what is good, and persuades him to cultivate the former and disregard the latter, and compels him to behave in the opposite way to that which is adopted by disciplined people?'

'No, nothing.'

'Isn't it likely that self-discipline brings results for those who practise it, which are opposite to those of self-indulgence?'

'Certainly.'

'Isn't it also likely that the cause of these opposite results is supremely good?'

'Yes, it is.'

'So doesn't it look as if self-discipline were the best thing for a man?'

'Very likely, Socrates,' he said.

'Have you ever reflected on this, Euthydemus?'

'On what?'

'The fact that although self-indulgence is supposed to be the sole guide to pleasure, it cannot even take us there itself; it is self-discipline, above all, which causes pleasure.'

'How so?'

'Self-indulgence doesn't allow us to endure hunger or thirst or sexual desire or sleeplessness, which are the only things that make eating and drinking and sexual intercourse pleasurable, and likewise rest and sleep. It doesn't permit us to hold out and wait for the moment of maximum enjoyment; and consequently it prevents us from getting any appreciable pleasure from the most necessary and regularly recurrent acts.[1] On the other hand, self-discipline, which is the only thing that gives us endurance in the cases I have described, is also the only thing that in these cases gives us any pleasure worth mentioning.'

'What you say is absolutely true.'

'Then again, there is the process of learning something really good, and taking an interest in one of those activities by means of which a man can govern his body well and manage his estate efficiently and make himself useful to his friends and to the State, and get the better of his enemies – activities which offer not only the greatest benefits, but also the greatest pleasures. The self-disciplined practise these activities and enjoy them, but the self-indulgent have no part in any of them. Whom could we call worse qualified for such activities than the man who is least capable of performing them, obsessed as he is by his eagerness for the pleasures that are nearest to hand?'

'It seems to me, Socrates,' replied Euthydemus, 'that you are saying that a man who can't resist physical pleasure is quite incapable of any goodness at all.'

1. See *Memoirs*, 2.1.30 (p. 108).

'Yes, Euthydemus, because how can a man without self-discipline be any better than the most ignorant beast? If a person doesn't consider what is best, but tries by every means to do what is most pleasant, how can he be any better than the most senseless animals? Only the self-disciplined have the capacity to consider what are the best objects of action and, by both theoretically and practically categorizing good and bad, to choose the former and abstain from the latter.'

This was the way, he said, in which people became best and happiest, and also most capable of philosophical discussion. He said that discussion was so called because, when people join together for deliberation, they divide their subject-matter into categories.[1] Hence one should try to prepare oneself as fully as possible for this activity, and apply oneself to it above all; for it was through it that people developed the highest qualities of character and leadership, as well as becoming excellent philosophers.

6

I shall now try to describe how Socrates made his associates better at philosophical discussion. He believed that those who understood the nature of any given thing would be able to explain it to others as well, whereas it was no wonder, he said, if those who did not understand made mistakes themselves and misled others. Consequently, he never stopped investigating with the help of his companions the meaning of every single term. It would be a laborious task to describe fully all the distinctions that he drew; I shall mention only a few examples, which I think will serve to illustrate his method of inquiry.

First of all, he examined the meaning of piety in some such way as this. 'Tell me, Euthydemus,' he said, 'what sort of thing do you think religiousness is?'[2]

1. The root of the Greek verb meaning 'discuss' (*dialegesthai*) means to 'pick and sort out'.
2. Notice how by now 'Euthydemus' has become a cipher for 'a typical Socratic interlocutor'. See also Plato's *Euthyphro* for Socrates on religiousness.

'A very fine thing, to be sure.'

'Can you say what sort of person a religious man is?'

'I think he is a man who worships the gods.'

'Can one worship the gods in any way one likes?'

'No, there are laws which must be observed in worshipping.'

'Then a person who knows these laws would know how one ought to worship the gods.'

'That is my opinion.'

'Does a man who knows how one ought to worship the gods think that one ought not to worship them in a different way from the way that he knows?'

'Surely.'

'Does anyone worship the gods in a different way from that in which he thinks he ought to worship?'

'I imagine not.'

'So the man who knows what is lawful with regard to the gods is likely to worship them lawfully.'

'Certainly.'

'Does the man who worships lawfully worship as he ought?'

'Of course.'

'And the man who worships as he ought is religious?'

'Certainly.'

'So we may take it that the man who knows what is lawful with regard to the gods would be correctly defined as religious.'

'That is how it seems to me.'

'What about people? Is one allowed to treat them just as one likes?'

'No, here again there are points of law in accordance with which people have to be treated.'

'Do people who treat one another in accordance with these treat one another as they ought?'

'Of course.'

'Do those who treat people as they ought treat them well?'

'Certainly,' he said.

'Do those who treat people well conduct their human affairs well?'

'Presumably,' he said.

'Do those who obey the laws do what is right?'

'Certainly.'

'Do you know what is meant by "right"?'

'What the law commands.'[1]

'So those who do what the law commands do what is right and what they ought to do?'

'Of course.'

'Are those who do what is right moral?'

'I presume so.'

'Do you think that any people obey the laws without knowing what the laws command?'

'No, I don't.'

'Do you think that any people who know what they ought to do think that they ought not to do it?'

'I imagine not.'

'Do you know of any people who do things other than what they think they ought?'[2]

'No, I don't.'

'So those who know what is lawful with regard to men do what is right?'

'Certainly.'

'Are those who do what is right moral?'

'Yes, who else could be?'

'So we should be correct if we defined moral people as those who know what is lawful with regard to men.'

'I think so.'

'And how can we define wisdom? Tell me, do you think that a wise man is wise in relation to what he knows, or are some people wise in relation to what they don't know?'[3]

'Obviously they are wise in relation to what they know,' he

1. See pp. 197–202.
2. This apparent paradox is the basis, in Plato's *Protagoras*, of Socrates' denial of 'weakness of will': no one is swayed to act wrongly by desires, say, because everyone does what he *thinks* is best for him. See also pp. 12, 14–15.
3. Compare the sophistic paradox at Plato, *Euthydemus*, 275d–276c.

replied. 'How could anyone be wise in relation to what he doesn't know?'

'Then are the wise wise because of their knowledge?'

'What else could make one wise if not knowledge?'

'And do you think that wisdom is anything other than what makes people wise?'

'No, I don't.'

'So wisdom is knowledge.'

'So it seems to me.'

'Do you think that it is possible for a human being to know everything that there is?'

'No, indeed, not even the minutest portion of it.'

'So it isn't possible for a human being to be wise in respect of everything?'

'No, certainly not.'

'Then every man is wise only in respect of that which he knows.'

'So it seems to me.'

'So shall we also investigate goodness, Euthydemus, starting as follows?'[1]

'How?' he asked.

'Do you think that the same thing is beneficial to everyone?'

'No, I don't.'

'Don't you think, in fact, that what is beneficial to one person is sometimes harmful to another?'

'I do indeed.'

'Would you say that "good" is different from "beneficial"?'

'No.'

'So what is beneficial is good for anyone to whom it is beneficial?'

'I think so.'

'Can we give any different account of fineness? Can you name a fine body or article or anything else which you know to be fine for all purposes?'

1. See also pp. 158–9.

'No, indeed I can't,' he said.

'Is it proper to use everything for the purpose for which it is useful?'

'Certainly.'

'Is a thing fine for any purpose other than that for which it is proper to use it?'

'No, in relation to nothing else.'

'So what is useful is fine for the purpose for which it is useful?'

'So it seems to me.'

'Next, courage, Euthydemus: do you think that it is a fine thing?'[1]

'I should say that it is a very fine thing.'

'You don't consider, then, that courage is useful for the most trivial things?'

'On the contrary,' he said, 'for the most important things.'

'Does it seem to you that it is useful in relation to dangers and perils to be unaware of them?'

'Not at all.'

'So those who are not afraid of such things because they don't know what they are are not brave?'

'No, indeed. On that basis a great many lunatics and cowards would be brave.'

'What about those who fear even what is not dangerous?'

'Surely, they are even less brave.'

'Then do you consider that those who are good in relation to perils and dangers are brave, and those who are bad in relation to them are cowardly?'

'Certainly.'

'Do you think that anyone is good at these things apart from those who can deal with them well?'

'No, only those.'

'And the bad are those who are of the kind to deal with them badly?'

'Yes, who else?'

1. Compare Plato's *Laches* and *Protagoras* for Socrates on courage.

'Do both types deal with them as they think they should?'

'Yes, how else?'

'Do those who can't deal with them well know how they ought to deal with them?'

'Of course not.'

'So those who know how they ought to deal with them also have the ability to deal with them?'

'Yes, and they are the only ones who have.'

'Well now, do those who are not completely mistaken deal with these situations badly?'

'I think not,' he said.

'So it is those who deal with them badly that are completely mistaken?'

'Presumably.'

'So those who know how to deal well with dreadful and dangerous situations are brave, and those who are completely mistaken are cowardly?'

'So it seems to me,' he said.

Socrates considered that kingship and despotism were both forms of authority, but differed from each other. He thought that authority with the consent of the people and in accordance with the laws of the State was kingship, whereas authority without consent and in accordance not with the laws but with the whim of the ruler was despotism. Where offices were filled by men who satisfied the legal requirements, he considered the constitution to be an aristocracy; where they were filled in accordance with a property qualification, a plutocracy; and where they were filled by anybody, a democracy.

If anyone was arguing with him about something and had nothing definite to say, but claimed, without proof, that the person he was talking about was the wiser or more statesmanlike or more courageous or superior in some other such quality, Socrates used to refer the whole argument back to first principles in this sort of way: 'Do you maintain that the person you are praising is a better citizen than mine?'

'Yes, I do.'

'Then hadn't we better first consider what is the function of a good citizen?'

'Let's do that.'

'If it were a matter of financial administration, wouldn't the better man be the one who increased the public revenue?'

'Certainly.'

'And in war he would be the one who gave his country the upper hand over its opponents?'

'Of course.'

'And in diplomacy the man who makes friends instead of enemies?'

'Naturally.'

'Then in politics he is the one who stops civil strife and creates a spirit of unity?'

'So it seems to me.'

When the argument was referred back to first principles in this way, the truth became apparent to his opponents too. And when he himself was setting out a detailed argument, he used to proceed by such stages as were generally agreed, because he thought that this was the infallible method of argument. Consequently, when he was talking, he used to win the agreement of his audience more than anyone else that I have known. He used to say that Homer himself attributed to Odysseus the quality of being an infallible speaker,[1] because he could base his arguments on the accepted beliefs of his hearers.

7

It is obvious, I think, from the foregoing account, that Socrates used to reveal his opinions candidly to his companions. I shall now show that he also tried to ensure that they should be self-sufficient in their appropriate activities.

Of all the people that I have known, he was the most concerned to know the extent of any of his associates' special knowledge,

1. The reference seems to be to *Odyssey*, 8.165 ff.

and the most enthusiastic to teach, so far as he was competent, the subjects which a truly good man should know; and where he himself was not well qualified, he put them in touch with experts.

He also instructed them how far a properly educated person should be informed about each subject. For example, he thought that geometry should be learned so far as to enable one, if the occasion arose, to receive or convey or apportion land accurately in point of measurement,[1] or to carry out a task. This, he said, was so easy to learn that a man who applied his mind to the calculation could at one and the same moment know the extent of the ground and carry away the knowledge of how it was measured. But he deprecated taking the learning of geometry as far as figures which are difficult to comprehend. He said that he didn't see the use of them – although he was not unacquainted with them – and he said that these studies were capable of wasting a man's life and keeping him from learning many other useful things.

He told them to become acquainted also with astronomy, but here again only so far as to be able to recognize the time of night or month or year, so that by distinguishing their phases they might have evidence to use for a journey or a voyage or guard-duty, or for any other business that is carried out during a night or month or year. This too, he said, was easy to learn from night hunters and pilots and many others whose business it was to know such things. But to learn astronomy to the extent of even acquiring a knowledge of bodies moving in different orbits, such as the planets and other irregularly moving bodies, and to wear oneself out with trying to discover their distances from the earth and their paths and the causes of these – from this he vigorously tried to dissuade them. He said that in these studies too he saw no utility (although he was not uninstructed in them either);[2] and they too, he said, could waste a man's life and keep him from much that was profitable.

In general, he dissuaded them from concerning themselves

1. The literal meaning of 'geometry' is 'land-measurement'.
2. Compare Plato, *Phaedo*, 96a ff.

with the way in which God regulates the various heavenly bodies;[1] he thought that these facts were not discoverable by human beings, and he did not consider that a man would please the gods if he pried into things that they had chosen not to reveal. He said that a person who bothered about these things would run the risk of going just as crazy as Anaxagoras,[2] who prided himself enormously on his exposition of the workings of the gods. When Anaxagoras said that fire and the sun were identical, he was failing to take into account the fact that men can easily look at fire, but cannot fix their gaze upon the sun; and that exposure to the sun makes their skins darker, but exposure to fire does not. He failed also to take into account the fact that no plant can grow properly without sunlight, whereas all plants die when they are heated by fire. And when he said that the sun was a red-hot stone, he also failed to appreciate the fact that, if a stone is placed in a fire, it neither shines nor persists for any length of time, whereas the sun remains all the time the brightest of all things.

Socrates recommended the study of arithmetic; but here too, just as in the case of the other subjects, he told his companions to guard against purposeless research; and he himself helped them in their investigations and explanations only so far as was useful.

He also strongly encouraged his companions to be careful about their health, and not only to learn all that they could about it from those who knew, but also to study their own constitutions throughout life to see what food or drink or what kind of exercise was good for them individually, and by what use of these they could live the healthiest lives. He said that anyone who observed himself in this way would find it hard to discover a doctor who could recognize what was good for his health better than he could himself.[3]

If anyone wanted help beyond the resources of human wisdom, he advised him to take up divination. A man who knew the means

1. Compare *Memoirs*, 1.1.11–15 (pp. 70–71).
2. An eminent fifth-century philosopher and scientist.
3. This was doubtless true given the crude state of medical science at the time.

by which the gods communicated to men about events, he said, was never in lack of divine counsel.

8

If anyone thinks that Socrates was convicted of making a false claim about the divine because he was condemned to death by the jury even although he claimed that the divine communicated to him in advance what he ought and ought not to do,[1] let him reflect, first, that Socrates was already so far advanced in age that he would soon have reached the end of his life, even if he had not done so then; and second, that he escaped the most disagreeable part of life, in which everybody's intellect deteriorates, and instead of this displayed his strength of mind and won distinction by pleading his cause with unparalleled veracity, dignity and integrity, and by facing the death-sentence with the utmost serenity and fortitude.

It is generally agreed that no one in the memory of man has ever met his death more nobly. He had to live on for thirty days after his trial, because the festival of Delos[2] fell in that month, and the law does not permit any publicly sanctioned execution until the mission has returned from Delos. It was evident to his intimate friends that during this time he did not deviate at all from his former way of life – and he had previously been remarkable above all men for the cheerfulness and equanimity of his life. How could anyone die more nobly than this? What death could be nobler than a death most nobly accepted? What death could be more happy than the noblest? And who could be more beloved of the gods than the happiest?

I shall relate also what I heard about him from Hermogenes the

1. See pp. 34–5. Both Plato's *Apology of Socrates* and especially Xenophon's (pp. 41–9), of which there are verbal echoes, are worth comparing with this chapter.

2. See p. 142, n. 1. As a matter of fact, however, it was the return of the *annual* Athenian mission to Delos which delayed his death, not the *quinquennial* festival, as Xenophon here suggests. See also Plato, *Crito*, 43c–d, *Phaedo*, 58a–c.

son of Hipponicus. He said that, after Meletus had already laid his indictment, he heard Socrates discussing anything rather than the trial and told him that he ought to be considering his defence. At first Socrates said, 'Don't you think that my whole life has been a preparation for it?' And when Hermogenes asked him how, he replied that he had spent all his time in studying nothing but questions of right and wrong, doing what was right and refraining from what was wrong; and he considered that this was the finest preparation for a defence. Then Hermogenes tried another tack: 'Don't you see, Socrates, that the jurors at Athens have often before now been prevailed upon by argument to put innocent men to death and to acquit guilty ones?'

'Yes, but as a matter of fact, Hermogenes,' he said, 'when I was trying to consider my defence before the jury, the divine opposed me straight away.'

'That's remarkable,' said Hermogenes.

Socrates answered, 'Do you think it's remarkable that God should decide that it is better for me to end my life now? Don't you realize that up to now I would not have conceded to anyone that he had lived a better or more pleasant life than I? For I believe that the best life is lived by those who take the best care to make themselves as good as possible, and the pleasantest life by those who are most conscious that they are becoming better. Up to the present time I have felt that this was happening to me, and, in my contacts with other people and in comparing myself with others, I have invariably come to this conclusion about myself. And not only I, but my friends have always come to this conclusion, not because they love me (because if that were all, everyone who is fond of someone else would come to the same conclusion about his friends), but because they believe that they are likely to improve most by associating with me. But if I go on living, I shall probably have to pay the penalties of old age: my vision, hearing and intelligence will become impaired; I shall become in consequence slower to learn and more forgetful, and inferior to those to whom I used to be superior. Now, even if one were unconscious of this, life would not be worth living; and when one is conscious of it, surely it must make one's life worse and more disagreeable. Then again, if I am wrongly executed, this may be discreditable to those who wrongly put me to death, because if it is shameful to do wrong, it is surely shameful to do *anything* wrongly; but what disgrace is it to me if other people fail to decide or act rightly with regard to me? I see also that the reputation left to posterity by the dead is not the same for the doers as for the sufferers of wrong. I know that, even if I die now, people will regard me and those who put me to death in different lights; for I know that it will always be testified of me that I never wronged anybody or made anybody a worse person, but always tried to make my associates better people.'

This was what he said in conversation with Hermogenes and the rest. Of those who knew what Socrates was like, all who have virtue as their goal continue still to miss him more than anything, because they feel that he was their greatest help in the cultivation of virtue.

In my experience, Socrates was, as I have described him, so devout that he never did anything without the sanction of the gods; so upright that he never did the slightest harm to anybody, but conferred the greatest benefits upon those who associated with him; so self-disciplined that he never chose the more pleasant course instead of the better; so wise that he never made a mistake in deciding between better and worse, and needed no advice, but was self-sufficient for such decisions; he was capable of explaining and defining such matters, and capable moreover of both assessing and refuting errors and encouraging people towards virtue and true goodness. In view of these qualities, he seemed to me to be the perfect example of goodness and happiness.

If anyone disapproves of this assessment, let him compare other people's characters with these qualities, and then make his own decision.

THE DINNER-PARTY

TRANSLATED BY HUGH TREDENNICK
TRANSLATION REVISED AND INTRODUCED
BY ROBIN WATERFIELD

INTRODUCTION

Apart from apparently being a stock setting for writers of *Sokratikoi logoi* (see p. 11), the dinner-party was a regular feature of upper-class Athenian life. The Greek word *sumposion* more literally means 'drinks-party', but since the connotations of that phrase in English are likely to be misleading (the Greeks did not stand around at symposia sipping cocktails), I have preferred the translation 'dinner-party'. A typical Athenian symposium – and Xenophon's is in many ways typical, or, rather, an important source for our knowledge of symposia – might have the following features. The guests are likely to be men, who, garlanded and perfumed, meet for dinner. After dinner religious libations are poured and a paean is sung. There then follows an extended period of drinking – the symposium proper. The drink would be wine diluted with water in the Greek custom and, unless or until things got out of hand, the proportion of water and the quantity of alcohol consumed would be regulated by a president. During the drinking, the host would provide entertainment, if he could afford to, in the form of hired female pipe-players, and/or dancers, acrobats and mimes. Occasionally, the drinking session would get out of hand, especially if the host had thoughtfully laid on prostitutes as well; more often, the guests would intersperse the hired entertainment with telling one another jokes, riddles and stories, reciting verse and singing hymns and *skolia* (drinking-songs), and playing games such as *kottabos*, in which the guests, while reclining on their couches, had to flick the last drops of wine from their cups into a bowl set in the middle of the couches: the purpose was either simply not to spill a drop, or to fill saucers floating on water in the bowl with wine until they sank.[1]

We can fix the dramatic date of Xenophon's *The Dinner-party*. The party is occasioned by Autolycus' victory in the pancration at a Great Panathenaea (see p. 227). These festivals occurred every four years at known intervals. The comic playwright Eupolis mocked Autolycus' recent victory in a play produced in 421; therefore Autolycus' victory occurred in 422, and that is the supposed date of the party. None the less, there are plenty of anachronisms: the homosexual 'Sacred Band' of Theban soldiers, for instance, which is referred to in chapter 8, was not formed until *c.* 378 BC.

The date of composition is less easy to fix, but we can provide an upper terminus. There are several general points of similarity between Xenophon's *Symposium* and Plato's (for instance, both parties are occasioned by a victory),[2] but where the two coincide in detail (see pp. 242, n. 1; 242, n. 3; 263, n. 2), it is extremely likely that Xenophon is dependent on Plato rather than the other way round. The arguments for this are complex and historical, and I can only refer the reader to an article by K. J. Dover.[3] Dover also argues convincingly that Plato's work was written between 384 and 378, and that the upper terminus for Xenophon's work is not before 378 (the formation of the Sacred Band).

The Dinner-party is undoubtedly Xenophon's best and most polished Socratic work. Its tone is light, but there are more serious themes under the surface. What makes it better than the other works in this volume, however, is that the serious themes rarely obtrude – the piece can be read and enjoyed almost entirely

1. This sketch of a typical symposium (see also Webster, pp. 54–7) is drawn from many sources. Apart from Plato's *Symposium*, the only other extended source likely to be accessible to readers of this introduction is the comic version of a symposium in Aristophanes, *Wasps*, 1208–64.
2. For a thorough comparison of the two works, see H. G. Dakyns (trans.), *The Works of Xenophon*, vol. 3, part 1 (Macmillan, 1897), pp. lx–lxvii.
3. 'The Date of Plato's *Symposium*', *Phronesis*, 10 (1965), pp. 2–20.

as a piece of light drama. Our pleasure is also greatly enhanced by a far higher degree of scene-setting and characterization than Xenophon has allowed himself elsewhere.

However, these lighter aspects are self-evident; from this point of view, in order to introduce the work, I need say only: read and enjoy! So it is my intention in this introduction to bring out the underlying serious issues, which we can do satisfactorily by reviewing the work from a standpoint which Xenophon himself asks us to take. At the very beginning of the work he says that the tale is concerned with true goodness (on 'true goodness', see also pp. 59–62); and close to the end (p. 265) he has Lycon get up to leave the party, but turn back to Socrates and say: 'I swear, Socrates, it does seem to me that you are a truly good man.'[1] These statements, bracketing the work, require us to look through it and try to see what Socrates has said or done to earn this comment.

The chief unifying theme is that of love. Socrates speaks at length on love; we hear about Callias' love for Autolycus, the Syracusan's for his boy, Critobulus' for Clinias; at the beginning of chapter 8 we are told that all the guests present are in love with someone; finally even the entertainment which closes the evening depicts a blatantly erotic scene between Dionysus and Ariadne.

The way in which we can expect Socrates' true goodness to emerge from the book, therefore, is through what he himself says about love, and how this contrasts with the other examples of love that are given.

*

1. Incidentally (see p. 37), I think it is unlikely that our Lycon is the Lycon who was one of Socrates' prosecutors at his trial. If he was, however, then Xenophon's attribution to him of this comment on Socrates would be highly poignant, equivalent to the centurion at the foot of the cross saying of Jesus, 'Truly, this was the Son of God' (Matthew 27.54). Those who believe that he is Socrates' prosecutor sometimes offer the following scenario: Lycon was not initially hostile towards Socrates, but the death of his son Autolycus at the hands of the Thirty in 404, for insulting a Spartan, aroused such hostility because of Socrates' alleged pro-Spartan and oligarchic leanings (see pp. 6, 37–8). Autolycus' noble death became almost legendary; the story is told in Plutarch, *Life of Lysander*, 15.4.

The main contrast is between pure and impure (that is, physical) homosexuality. In his speech Socrates is made to condemn physically consummated homosexuality as 'debauchery' (8.32), and his comments on the Syracusan's relations with his boy are extremely derisive (4.54). Critobulus is said to be obsessed with Clinias, but gradually improving as a result of his association with Socrates (4.12–26). Only Callias is commended for the non-physical nature of his relationship with Autolycus (8.11) – but then this praise turns out to be double-edged and ironic, since Hermogenes comments that Socrates is telling Callias what he *ought* to do, as much as or rather than praising what he actually does.

Nevertheless, in Xenophon as in Plato, there is no attempt to disguise the fact that Socrates was attracted towards his young male followers, as they were towards him. That he never physically consummated these relationships is most memorably shown by Alcibiades' story of how Socrates spurned his advances, told in Plato's *Symposium*. But we constantly hear in both Plato and Xenophon that the attraction Socrates felt for his followers is one of love (in Xenophon, see especially *The Dinner-party*, 8.2; and *Memoirs*, 2.6.28, 3.11.16, and 4.1.2), and one of the few things Socrates claims expertise in, even in Plato (which is the more remarkable, given the Platonic Socrates' constant disavowal of knowledge), is 'erotics'.

There are elements of play in these literary accounts, but they should not obscure the serious points. Socrates' friends, for instance, playfully tease him for being in love with his followers: in Plato, he is teased for being in love with Alcibiades (*Protagoras*, 309a), and in Xenophon for being in love with Critobulus (*The Dinner-party*, 4.27–28).

It is possible to diminish the serious or perhaps distasteful aspects of Socrates' relationship with his followers by arguing that their attraction for him is simply the attraction anyone is likely to feel for a person as charismatic as Socrates (despite his ugliness, on which see pp. 252–3). While this is true, it seems to me less plausible to claim that this attraction is describable as erotic love.

In short, the fact that Socrates did feel attracted towards his followers cannot be explained away. To refer again to the story of Alcibiades and Socrates, as G. M. A. Grube has remarked: 'The story loses all point if we refuse to admit that Socrates was tempted. It is his self-control, not his indifference, that is being extolled.'[1] Whether or not there was such a physical attraction, however, it is also clear from both Plato's and Xenophon's accounts that Socrates used the erotic nature of the relationship to enhance his followers' desire for moral goodness. This is the serious element underlying the erotic themes. The attraction of his followers towards Socrates is attraction towards realized goodness, and the attraction of Socrates towards his followers is attraction towards potential goodness.[2] It is never far from the surface in all this that the literal meaning of *philosophia* is '*love* of wisdom', and this is portrayed by Greek philosophers as passionate, not insipid, love. The master–pupil relationship in philosophical training is therefore erotic (see also 4.62–64) inasmuch as the master embodies the wisdom the pupil wants. Despite their different concepts of wisdom, it is clear that for both Plato and Xenophon, Socrates was such a master. I say this not to try to explain away Socrates' bisexuality (he was married), but to stress that the pictures we are given of Socrates insist that he exploited homosexual attraction for philosophical purposes.[3]

This brings us to the rest of Socrates' speech on love in *The Dinner-party*, 8. The basis is the distinction, which was recognized in Greek religion, between a Celestial and a Common Aphrodite. This distinction is soon assimilated to the difference between 'love for the mind' and 'physical love'. The argument that follows is supposed to show that the former kind of love is 'better' than the latter. So it is argued that while love for the mind is no less

1. G. M. A. Grube, *Plato's Thought* (Methuen, 1935), p. 90. Socrates himself is made to profess love for Alcibiades in Plato at *Gorgias*, 481d, and *Alcibiades I*, 103a ff., and in Aeschines, Fragment 11c.
2. See *Memoirs*, 4.1.2, for this explanation of Socrates' attraction towards his followers, and *Memoirs*, 3.11.16 – in context – for the attraction of his followers towards him.
3. On the whole topic see K. J. Dover, *Greek Homosexuality* (Duckworth, 1978).

passionate than physical love, it is longer-lasting, more likely to be reciprocated and less concerned with trivia such as physical appearance. The crux of the matter, however, turns out to be that both parties who love each other for their minds are simultaneously master and pupil to each other: they teach each other to 'say and do what they ought' (8.23) and inculcate 'true goodness' in each other (8.26–27) – though this teaching role is also implied to be chiefly the older partner's responsibility. Socrates then supports his argument with doubtful mythological and historical precedents and specious etymology (8.28–8.35). Finally (8.39–8.41), he exhorts Callias to make sure that his affair with Autolycus is of the kind where Autolycus loves him for his goodness (which in his case is realizable especially in politics). Again, given the emphasis on Callias' potential, we recognize that Socrates is telling him what he ought to do with Autolycus, rather than commenting on how he actually conducts himself.[1]

The parallels with Socrates himself are obvious. In his love-affairs with his followers he is a devotee of the Celestial Aphrodite, a lover of their minds rather than their bodies, a truly good man who can, by his example and teaching, lead the recipients of his love on to the same goal.

As I have said, since love is the main theme of the work, this is the chief means by which Socrates' true goodness is brought out. Apart from his speech in chapter 8, there are at least three other aspects, still concerned with love, which corroborate Socrates' true goodness.

The first is purely artistic. The party is introduced with a statement (1.8–10) about the calming effects of 'pure love': it

1. I have read Lycon's affirmation of Socrates' goodness as relevant to the whole book (p. 221), but it also has a particular point in its immediate context. It follows directly on from Socrates' speech about love and his urging Callias to avoid physical relations with Autolycus. Although homosexuality was common in Athens, it was not altogether approved of, and we know from Plato (*Symposium*, 183c) that fathers tried to protect their sons from it. Thus Lycon's comment refers directly to Socrates' recommendation that Callias should not have sex with his son Autolycus.

makes people kind, gentle and civil. At first, all the company are affected in this way by the presence of love at the party, and they dine in silence. But as the party progresses, nearly all the guests lose this civility: Antisthenes becomes rather aggressive (4.2, 6.5), Critobulus' thoughts turn to his physical longing for Clinias (4.12 ff.), Hermogenes becomes sullen and antisocial (6.1–4), the Syracusan becomes rude (6.6–8), and Philippus is in danger of being equally negative (6.8–10). Throughout all this, Socrates remains cool, calm and collected; his tone is a sober bass note sustained through the symphony of the story. Even when he professes to be somewhat influenced by the wine (8.24), he is only being inspired to champion the pure love of which he is a devotee.

The second is the light-hearted beauty competition between himself and Critobulus, promised in 4.19–20 and fulfilled in chapter 5. Underneath the joking, as Socrates claims to be physically more attractive than Critobulus, is, of course, the more serious point that physical beauty is not important, a point confirmed by Socrates' later speech on love.

Finally, what should we make of Socrates' claim to be a pimp (3.10, 4.56–64)? Socrates argues that the best pimp is the one who is able to make his clients attractive to as many people as possible – even to the whole city. We only have to substitute 'his pupils' for 'his clients' to see that the meaning is that Socrates can make his *pupils* attractive to large numbers of people – even to the whole city. If we recall that part of true goodness is the ability to make good friends and do them good, and to do this in a political context if necessary (p. 60), then the point is plain: Socrates teaches his pupils to be truly good.

One could argue that Socrates is implicitly contrasted with all the major characters in the book. The Syracusan, like Socrates, is a teacher – but of trivial entertainment, which Socrates belittles (3.2, 7.1–5).[1] Philippus' humour is frenetic and superficial,

1. The Syracusan's contribution to the theme of love follows as a direct contrast to Socrates' speech: his mime on the subject of Dionysus and Ariadne is physically erotic and encourages others to be the same.

whereas Socrates' is calm and serious (but no less amusing, we are supposed to think). Hermogenes claims to have the gods for his friends, but still allows moodiness to get the better of him; Antisthenes reflects the ascetic side of Socrates, but is uncivil, as we have seen; Critobulus is obsessed with physical beauty, and in Xenophon's works Socrates often says that infatuation is slavish; Charmides reflects the Socratic principle that detachment from worldly goods is freedom, but turns out still to want material benefits (4.33); Niceratus can see no deeper than the traditional morality and wisdom of Homer.

But throughout, the main opposing character is Callias, because he is, in Xenophon's economical portrait, the type of the 'truly good' man in the usual sense of the word (p. 60). Born *c.* 455 BC, he inherited from his father Hipponicus shortly before the dramatic date of *The Dinner-party* (422) not only a vast fortune, but also important civic duties (8.40–41). His higher education, however, has been sophistic (1.5–6) and he asserts the standard sophistic claim to 'make people better', which is identified with teaching them true goodness (3.4). When we learn that he attempts to fulfil this claim by giving people money, we are, of course, meant to contrast the confusion of this notion with the valid teaching offered by Socrates.

Nevertheless, Xenophon has Socrates imply that Callias does have the potential for truc goodness in the Socratic (or rather, Xenophontic) sense of the phrase (8.7–8, 8.37–40). What would Xenophon's readers have made of this? It is uncertain when Callias died, but he was still alive in the late 370s – that is, after the possible date of publication of *The Dinner-party*. What Xenophon's readers would particularly know about him is that throughout his life he was held up by comic playwrights and orators as a model, not of true goodness on anyone's understanding of the phrase, but of profligacy and intellectual dilettantism. Xenophon's message in this respect is that Callias may have had the potential in his youth for true goodness, but he failed to attach himself to Socrates, and so failed to realize that potential. Socrates remains the only case of the realized ideal.

THE DINNER-PARTY

It seems to me that in writing about the deeds of truly good men, it is proper to record not only their serious activities, but their diversions too.[1] I should like to describe something I witnessed[2] which led me to this conclusion.

There was a horse-race at the Great Panathenaic festival.[3] Callias the son of Hipponicus happened to be strongly attracted to a boy called Autolycus and had brought him along to watch, fresh from his victory in the pancration.[4] When the race had finished, Callias set off to his house in Piraeus,[5] taking Autolycus and his father with him. He was accompanied also by Niceratus. Seeing a group consisting of Socrates, Critobulus, Hermogenes, Antisthenes and Charmides, Callias arranged for someone to show the way to Autolycus and his party, while he himself went up to Socrates and the others and said, 'This is an opportune meeting. I'm having Autolycus and his father to dinner. I'm sure that my establishment would seem much more stately if my dining-room were graced by persons with purity of mind, like yourselves, than if my guests were generals or cavalry-commanders or ambitious politicians.'

1. This became a standard biographer's sentiment: compare, for instance, Plutarch, *Life of Alexander*, 1.
2. On this claim, see pp. 21, 58.
3. The Panathenaea was an annual festival in honour of Athena. Every fourth year it was held on a grander scale and was called the Great Panathenaea.
4. See p. 150, n. 2; Autolycus had presumably just won the boys' competition. Homosexuality was an accepted fact of life, especially among upper-class Athenians.
5. See p. 128, n. 1.

'You're always teasing us,' said Socrates. 'You turn up your nose at us because you've paid a great deal of money to Protagoras, Gorgias, Prodicus[1] and a lot of others for expert instruction, and you can see that we are, so to speak, self-taught philosophers.'

'Well,' said Callias, 'up till now I've kept you in the dark about my powers of fluent and witty conversation, but now, if you'll visit me, I'll show you that I deserve your very serious attention.'

Naturally, Socrates and his friends began by thanking Callias for his invitation but excusing themselves from dining with him; but when it became clear that he really would be annoyed if they didn't come too, they joined the party. In due course they presented themselves, some rubbed down with oil after their exercise, others freshly bathed as well. Autolycus sat down beside his father and the others, as you would expect, reclined.[2] An observer of the scene would at once have reflected that beauty has something naturally regal about it, especially if it is combined with modesty and self-discipline in the possessor, as it was then in Autolycus. In the first place, his good looks drew everyone's attention to him, as surely as a light draws all eyes towards it in the dark; and secondly, there was not a man there whose feelings were not moved at the sight of him. Some became more silent, and the behaviour of others underwent a sort of transformation. Possession by a god always seems to have a remarkable effect. Those who are influenced by other gods tend to become more intimidating in their appearance, more truculent in their speech and more aggressive in their conduct; but those who are inspired by discreet Love wear a kindlier expression, speak in a gentler tone and behave in a way more befitting a free man. Such was the effect that Love had upon Callias on this occasion, as was duly noted by those who were initiates of this god. So they proceeded

1. Well-known sophists. Plato's *Protagoras* portrays Callias' house as a hostel for sophists when they visited Athens.
2. Women and minors sat rather than reclined. The name of Autolycus' father, we soon hear, was Lycon; but it is unlikely that he is the Lycon who was one of the prosecutors of Socrates at his trial (p. 37).

to dine in silence, as if they had been ordered by some superior to do so.

At this point Philippus the joker knocked at the front door, and told the servant who answered it to announce who he was and why he wanted to be let in. He said that he came fully equipped with everything he needed for dining at another person's house, and added that his servant was quite exhausted because he had nothing to carry and hadn't eaten.

When Callias heard this, he said, 'Well, gentlemen, it would be a shame to grudge him shelter at any rate. Let him come in.' As he spoke, he glanced at Autolycus, evidently looking to see how the jest had appealed to him.

Philippus paused in the doorway of the dining-room and said, 'You all know that I'm a joker. I've come here on purpose, because I thought it was more of a joke to come to dinner without an invitation than with one.'

'Sit down, then,' said Callias. 'The company are full of seriousness, as you see, but perhaps a little short of humour.'

They went on with the meal, and Philippus at once tried to make a joke to fulfil the usual purpose for which he was invited to dinner-parties. When he didn't get a laugh,[1] he was obviously hurt. A little later he ventured another joke; and, when they still failed to laugh at him, he suddenly stopped in the middle of eating, covered his head[2] and lay down.

'What's the matter, Philippus?' asked Callias. 'Have you got a pain?'

Philippus uttered a loud groan. 'I certainly have, Callias, a violent one. If laughter has gone from the world, my occupation's ruined. Up till now I have been invited to dinner-parties to entertain the company by making them laugh; but now what reason will anyone have for inviting me? I can no more be serious than I could make myself immortal; and no one will invite me in

1. Presumably because people were still 'possessed by love' for Autolycus rather than because Philippus' jokes were bad.
2. With his cloak – a conventional sign of distress.

the hope of being invited back, because everyone knows that it's quite without precedent for a dinner to be held at my house.'

As he spoke, he blew his nose, and his voice showed unmistakably that he was crying. So everybody assured him that they would laugh next time, and told him to eat his dinner; and Critobulus actually guffawed at his pitiful complaint. When Philippus heard him laugh, he uncovered his head and telling his heart to take courage,[1] because there would still be engagements,[2] he went on with his dinner.

2

When the table had been removed and they had poured libations and sung a paean, a Syracusan came in to provide entertainment. He had with him a girl who was an expert pipe-player, another who was an acrobatic dancer, and a very attractive boy who both played the lyre and danced extremely well. The man made a living by exhibiting these turns as a novelty. When the girl had played her pipes for them and the boy his lyre, and both performances seemed to give a very satisfactory amount of pleasure, Socrates said, 'You are indeed a perfect host, Callias. You have not only served us an irreproachable dinner; you are providing us with most delightful sights and sounds.'

Callias said, 'What about having some perfume brought in, so that our party may proceed fragrantly too?'[3]

'No, please don't,' said Socrates. 'You know that one kind of clothing looks well on a woman and another on a man: in the same way the smells that suit men and women are different. No man, surely, daubs himself with scent for the benefit of another man. And as for women, especially if they're newly married, like the

1. In the epic manner; so Odysseus, for instance, addresses his heart at Homer, *Odyssey*, 20.17–18.
2. There is a pun here (which also gives 'taking courage' a double meaning): the word can mean either 'conflicts' or 'parties'.
3. Perfume and scented oil were very popular among Greek men, especially at parties. For Socrates' attitude, compare *The Estate-manager*, 10.2–9 (pp. 324–6).

wives of Niceratus here and Critobulus – why should they need extra perfume, when they smell of it themselves? The smell of oil in the gymnasia gives more pleasure by its presence than perfume gives to women, and excites more longing by its absence. A daub of scent automatically makes everyone, slave or free, smell alike; but the smells that come from the efforts of free men in sport call above all for strict training over a long period, if they are to be pleasing and worthy of a free man.'

'That may be so for the young,' said Lycon, 'but what about us who are too old for the gymnasia – what ought we to smell of?'

'True goodness, of course,' said Socrates.

'And where can one get this lotion?'

'Not at a perfumery, certainly.'

'Well, where then?'

'Where Theognis told us:

> 'Good company will edify you: bad
> Will rob you even of the wits you had.'[1]

'Hear that, son?' said Lycon.

'Of course he does,' said Socrates, 'and he acts upon it. At any rate when he wanted to win the pancration, he looked about with your help [for the best trainer, until he found him, and] now he will attach himself to the person who seems best qualified to give him this other kind of training.'[2]

Here several people spoke at once. One said, 'Where will he find a teacher of this subject?' Another said that goodness wasn't a thing that could be taught at all; and someone else that, if anything was learnable, that was. But Socrates said, 'As this is a controversial subject,[3] let's defer it to another occasion. For now, let's finish the matter before us. I see that this dancer here has taken up her position, and somebody is bringing her some hoops.'

At this moment the other girl began to play for her on the pipes,

1. Theognis 35–6; see p. 76.
2. There is a gap in the text which must have contained some such words as those in brackets. Callias turns out (p. 264) to be the possible moral tutor.
3. See p. 160, n. 1.

and a man standing by the dancer handed her hoops until she had twelve. She took them and threw them spinning up into the air as she danced, judging how high to throw them so as to catch them in time with the music.

Socrates said, 'It's evident from this girl's display, gentlemen, as well as on many other grounds, that women have no less natural ability than men; they only lack judgement and physical strength. So any one of you who has a wife can teach her with confidence any skill that he would like her to acquire and practise.'

'If that's your view, Socrates,' said Antisthenes, 'why don't you train Xanthippe instead of having a wife who is of all living women – and I believe of all that ever have been or will be – the most difficult to get on with?'

'Because I notice that people who want to become good horsemen keep not the most docile horses but ones that are high-spirited, because they think that if they can control these, they will easily manage any other horses. In the same way, since I wish to deal and associate with people, I have provided myself with this wife, because I'm quite sure that, if I can put up with her, I shall find it easy to get on with any other human being.' This explanation was felt to be not far off the mark.

Next a circular frame was brought in, closely set around with upright sword-blades, and the dancer turned somersaults into this and out again over the blades,[1] so that the spectators were afraid that she would hurt herself; but she went through her performance confidently and safely. Socrates hailed Antisthenes and said, 'I don't imagine that the witnesses of this act will continue to deny that courage is a thing that can be taught, when this girl in spite of her sex throws herself so daringly over the swords.'

Antisthenes replied, 'Don't you think that this Syracusan had better exhibit his dancing-girl to the State, and say that, if the Athenians pay him a fee, he will make all of them bold enough to charge on to spears?'

'Yes, indeed,' said Philippus. 'Speaking for myself, I should

1. See *Memoirs*, 1.3.9 (p. 88); Plato, *Euthydemus*, 294e.

love to see that tub-thumper Pisander[1] learning how to tumble on to the swords; as it is, he won't serve in the army at all, because he can't look a spear in the face.'

After this the boy performed a dance, and Socrates said, 'Did you see how, beautiful as the boy is, he nevertheless looks even more beautiful in the figures of the dance than when he is keeping still?'

'You seem to be congratulating his dancing-master,' said Charmides.

'I certainly am,' said Socrates. 'I've noticed something else too, that in the dance no part of his body was idle: neck, legs and arms were exercised together. It was just the sort of dancing to develop suppleness of the body. Personally, I should very much like you, my Syracusan friend, to teach me the figures.'

'What will you do with them?' asked the man.

'I shall dance, of course.'

This raised a general laugh. Socrates went on, with a perfectly straight face, 'Are you laughing at me? Is it at the idea of my wanting to take exercise to improve my health or to enjoy my food and sleep better? Or is it because I'm bent on this kind of exercise, not wanting to develop my legs at the expense of my arms like a long-distance runner, nor my arms at the expense of my legs like a boxer, but by working hard with my whole body to make it evenly proportioned all over? Or are you laughing because I shan't have to find myself a training-partner or undress in public at my advanced age, because a seven-couch dining-room will be large enough for me to work up a sweat in, just as this room served for our young friend here, and because in cold weather I shall exercise under cover, and in a heat-wave beneath the shade? Or is *this* why you're laughing, because my stomach is larger than it should be and I want to reduce it to a more normal size? Don't you know that the other day Charmides here caught me dancing at daybreak?'

1. A prominent activist in the oligarchic revolution of 411 – and a notorious coward (Aristophanes, *Birds*, 1556 ff.).

'Yes, indeed I did,' said Charmides, 'and at first I was astonished and afraid that you were out of your mind, but, when I heard you explain it to me in the way that you are doing now, I went home myself and – well, I didn't dance, because I've never learned how, but I waved my arms about, because I knew how to do that!'

'Quite so,' said Philippus, 'and as a result you seem to have your legs so evenly matched with your arms that I believe if the market police made you weigh the lower items against the upper ones, like the loaves on a stall, they wouldn't be able to fine you.'[1]

Callias added, 'Call me in, Socrates, when you start to take dancing-lessons, so that I can act as your partner and learn along with you.'

'Come on, now,' said Philippus, 'let the girl pipe for me, so that I may dance too.' He stood up and went through a parody of the two dances, the boy's and the girl's. First, because they had praised the boy for looking even more beautiful as he danced the figures, Philippus on the contrary made every part of his body as he moved it look funnier than normal; and because the girl had formed the shape of a hoop by bending over backwards, he tried to produce the same effect by bending himself forward. Finally, because they had praised the boy for exercising the whole of his body in the dance, Philippus told the girl to speed up the tempo on her pipes, and he let fly legs, arms and head all together.

When he was exhausted, he said, as he lay down again, 'Here's proof, gentlemen, that my dances too provide good exercise: I, at any rate, am thirsty, and I should like the servant to fill up the large bowl for me.'[2]

'No, no,' said Callias, 'we'll share it, because we're thirsty too, from laughing at you.'

1. The practice of putting the biggest loaves on top of the display was punishable by a fine. Philippus means, of course, that Charmides' legs and arms are equally puny.
2. The large bowl was usually passed around all the diners (Plato, *Symposium*, 223c) rather than being reserved for a single person.

But Socrates said, 'Well, gentlemen, drinking gets my approval, in so far as it's a fact that wine refreshes the heart, and both allays worry like a sedative and feeds the flame of good cheer like oil. But it seems to me that the human body is affected in just the same way as plants are. When God gives plants too much to drink at a time, they can't stand up or breathe in fresh air; but when they drink only as much as is pleasant, they grow up quite straight and flourish and reach the fruiting stage. In the same way, if we imbibe all the drink at once, both our bodies and our minds will quickly let us down, and we shan't be able to breathe, much less speak. But if the servants drop for us frequent dew in goblets small, to put it as Gorgias would have,[1] then, instead of being forced into intoxication by the wine, we shall reach a more playful mood through gentle persuasion.'[2]

This proposal was immediately adopted, Philippus adding a rider to the effect that the wine-servants should follow the example of skilled charioteers and drive the cups round with increasing speed; and the wine-servants did so.

3

The boy now tuned his lyre to the pipe and sang while playing the lyre. At this everybody applauded, and Charmides further remarked, 'It seems to me, gentlemen, just as Socrates said about the wine, that this combination of youthful beauty and music allays one's cares and awakens thoughts of love.'

Socrates now interposed again. 'These people, gentlemen, show that they are capable of entertaining us, but I'm sure that we believe ourselves to be much better than they are. Won't it be a

1. Gorgias of Leontini in Sicily was famous for his metaphors and poetic diction. In talking of 'force' and 'persuasion', Socrates continues his parody of Gorgias, who in his famous *Helen* talked of speech being a 'persuasive force', though elsewhere he seems to have distinguished the gentle persuasion of speech from brute force (see Plato, *Philebus*, 58a–b).
2. Socrates is taking on the role of president of the drinking: see p. 219.

disgrace if, while we are together here, we don't even try to improve or amuse one another?'[1]

At this several people said, 'Well, you tell us how we are most likely to succeed: what sort of subject should we discuss?'

'What I should like best,' he replied, 'is to take up Callias' offer. He said, I believe, that if we would dine with him, he would give us a display of his expertise.'

'And so I will,' said Callias, 'if each one of you too will inform the company what beneficial thing he is expert in.'

'Well,' said Socrates, 'nobody objects to the proposal that each of us should state what he *thinks* is his most valuable area of expertise.'

'Very well, then,' said Callias, 'let me tell you what I am most proud of: I believe that I can make people better.'[2]

'By teaching them what,' asked Antisthenes, 'some manual skill, or true goodness?'

'The latter – if true goodness means morality.'

'Of course it does,' said Antisthenes, 'most unquestionably. Courage and cleverness are admitted to be sometimes injurious both to one's friends and to one's country, but moral goodness has no connection at all with wickedness.'

'Well, when each of you has told us what benefit is his to confer, I won't object to telling you the art by which I produce this effect. It's your turn, Niceratus: tell us what accomplishment you're proud of.'

Niceratus said, 'My father, because he was concerned to make me a good man, made me learn the whole works of Homer; and I could now repeat by heart the entire *Iliad* and *Odyssey*.'[3]

'Has it escaped you,' asked Antisthenes, 'that the rhapsodes[4] all know these poems?'

1. Similarly, in Plato, *Protagoras*, 347c–e, Socrates insists that 'truly good' people should be able to entertain one another at parties.
2. This was a standard, if vague, sophistic claim.
3. Despite the fact that the world had changed considerably since Homer's time, he was still taken to be the fount of all wisdom, and any educated person would have been able to quote at least parts of the poems.
4. See p. 181, n. 2.

'How could it,' he replied, 'when I listen to them almost every day?'

'Well, do you know any class of people sillier than they are?'

'No, indeed,' said Niceratus, 'I don't think I do.'

'No,' said Socrates, 'because they obviously don't understand the underlying ideas.[1] But you have paid a lot of money to Stesimbrotus, Anaximander and many others,[2] and so none of the important points has escaped you. What about you, Critobulus? What do you pride yourself on most?'

'On my good looks,' he replied.

'Will you really be able to claim that you can make us better by your good looks?'

'If I can't, I obviously shan't look very good!'

'What about you, Antisthenes?' asked Socrates. 'What are you proud of?'

'My wealth,' said he.

Hermogenes asked him if he had a great deal of money, and he swore that he hadn't so much as an obol.

'Well, do you own a lot of land?'

'It might be just enough to serve as a dust-bath for Autolycus here.'[3]

'We shall have to hear from you too. What about you, Charmides? What are you proud of?'

'For my part,' he said, 'I'm proud of my poverty.'[4]

'Certainly a gratifying asset,' said Socrates. 'Nothing could provoke less jealousy or rivalry; it remains safe without protection, and neglect improves it.'

'You now,' said Callias. 'What are you proud of, Socrates?'

He lengthened his face into a very serious expression and said,

1. See especially Plato's *Ion*.
2. Stesimbrotus was a biographer from Thasos who also wrote on Homer; Anaximander is not the famous Milesian philosopher, but the author of a book on Greek heroes.
3. Wrestlers powdered themselves with fine sand to afford a better grip and to cool themselves down.
4. Charmides' poverty, if not pure fiction, is probably a result of the inaccessibility of his estates due to the war.

'My skill as a pimp.'[1] They laughed at him. 'You can laugh,' he said, 'but I know that I could make a great deal of money if I chose to follow the profession.'

'In your case, anyhow,' said Lycon to Philippus, 'it's obvious that you pride yourself on raising laughs.'

'And with better reason, I fancy,' he said, 'than the actor Callippides,[2] who gives himself extraordinary airs because he can set vast audiences weeping.'

'Won't you tell us, Lycon,' said Antisthenes, 'what you are proud of?'

He answered, 'Why, surely you all know that it's this son of mine.'

'And he,' said somebody, 'is obviously proud of being a champion.'

'Certainly not!' said Autolycus, blushing.

Everyone looked towards him, pleased to hear him speak, and someone asked him, 'Well, what *are* you proud of?'

'My father,' he said, leaning up against him as he spoke.

When Callias saw this, he said, 'Do you know, Lycon, that you're the richest man alive?'

'No, that I certainly don't.'

'Don't you realize that you wouldn't accept all the wealth of the Great King[3] in exchange for your son?'

'It seems to be a clear case against me,' he said. 'I'm the richest man in the world.'

'You, Hermogenes,' said Niceratus, 'what do you delight in most?'

'The goodness and influence of my friends,' he said, 'and the fact that, having these qualities, they care for me.'

This turned all eyes towards him, and several people at the same time asked if they too might be introduced to his friends. He said that he wouldn't object.

1. Compare Plato, *Theaetetus*, 151b (and see pp. 225, 249–51).
2. A famous tragic actor who, however, was criticized even in his own time for overacting.
3. The king of Persia, who was to a Greek the personification of prosperity.

4

Socrates now said, 'I suppose it remains for each of us to demonstrate the value of what he claimed to possess.'

'You can hear my statement first,' said Callias. 'While I listen to you all puzzle about what moral goodness is, I spend the time making people morally better.'

'How, my good friend?' asked Socrates.

'By giving them money, of course!'

Antisthenes got up and stood over him and questioned him very critically: 'Callias, do you think that people keep morality in their minds or in their pockets?'

'In their minds.'

'Then do you make their minds morally better by putting money in their pockets?'

'Certainly.'

'How?'

'Because when they know they've got something with which to buy what they need, they don't want to risk committing crimes.'

'Do they repay all that they get from you?'

'Dear me, no!' he said. 'Indeed they don't.'

'Well then, do they do you favours in return for your money?'

'Oh no,' he said, 'they don't do that either; some of them are even more hostile than they were before.'

'It's a curious thing,' said Antisthenes, looking at him as if he had cornered him, 'if you can make them act morally towards everyone else, but not towards you.'

'What is there curious about that?' asked Callias. 'Don't you realize that there are plenty of carpenters and builders who make houses for large numbers of other people but can't do it for themselves, and live in rented homes? You really must accept that you're confuted, professor!'

'He must indeed,' said Socrates. 'Prophets too, as you know, are supposed not to foresee what is coming to themselves, although they foretell the future for others.'

That was the end of that topic. Next Niceratus said, 'You can now hear from me how you will be improved if you associate with me. You know, I presume, that within the poems of that greatest of sages, Homer, is information about practically every aspect of human affairs; so if any one of you wants to become a good estate-manager or politician or general, or wants to become like Achilles or Ajax or Nestor or Odysseus, let him give his attention to me, because I have all this knowledge.'[1]

'Do you know how to be a king too,' said Antisthenes, 'just because you are aware that Homer praised Agamemnon as "both a good king and a stout warrior"?'[2]

'Indeed I do,' he said, 'and that when one is driving a chariot one must turn close to the post

> and oneself lean out of the polished car
> to the left, but goad the right-hand horse,
> cheering him on, and slacken off his reins.[3]

And besides this I know something else, which you can try at this very moment. Homer said somewhere, "And onion as a savoury for their drink".[4] So if someone provides an onion, you can have this benefit, at least, immediately: you will enjoy your drinking more.'

'Gentlemen,' said Charmides, 'Niceratus is set on going home smelling of onions, so as to convince his wife that nobody would even have thought of kissing him!'[5]

'No doubt,' said Socrates, 'but I think there's a risk of our creating another ridiculous impression too. Onion does really seem to be a kind of savoury, because it adds pleasure not only to food but to drink too. So if we munch it after dinner as well, we must be careful that someone doesn't say that we went to Callias' house and indulged in pleasures.'

1. In Plato's *Ion*, the rhapsode of that name makes a similar claim, which is swiftly refuted.
2. *Iliad*, 3.179, also quoted at *Memoirs*, 3.2.2.
3. *Iliad*, 23.335–7.
4. *Iliad*, 11.630.
5. Compare Aristophanes, *Thesmophoriazousae*, 493–6.

'That would never do,' was the reply. 'It's all right for a soldier going into action to munch an onion first, just as some people feed their cocks on garlic before they set them on to fight, but we are presumably planning to give someone a kiss[1] rather than start a battle.'

That was more or less how this topic came to an end.

'Now *I*'ll tell you,' said Critobulus, 'why I'm proud of my good looks.'

'Go on,' they said.

'Well then, if I am not good-looking, as I think I am, you could properly be sued for fraud, because you're always, of your own free wills, swearing that I am good-looking. What's more, I believe you, because I regard you as truly good men. But if I really am good-looking, and if you feel just the same towards me as I feel towards the person who seems beautiful to me, I swear by all the gods that I wouldn't choose the throne of Persia in preference to being good-looking. As things are, I get more pleasure from looking at Clinias[2] than from all the beauty in the world; and I would rather be blind to everything else than to this one person, Clinias. Night and sleep exasperate me, because then I can't see him; but I overflow with gratitude to the day and the sun, because they show me Clinias.

'There is another reason why we who are good-looking are entitled to be proud: a strong man has to exert himself to gain his ends, and a brave man to run risks, and a clever man to speak; but a handsome man can achieve all his effects without moving a muscle. For my part, although I know that it's a pleasant thing to have money, it would please me better to give all that I have to Clinias than to receive as much from somebody else; and it would please me better to be a slave than to be free, if Clinias would be my master. Working for him would be easier than resting, and to

1. Autolycus, probably, especially if Callias is the speaker (which is not clear).
2. Son of Axiochus and cousin of Alcibiades; he appears as a handsome youth in Plato's *Euthydemus*.

face danger for him would be more pleasant than a life of security.[1]

'So if you, Callias, pride yourself on the ability to make people more upright, I have a better claim than you to lead them on to goodness of every kind. The inspiration that we good-looking people give to our admirers makes them less slavish with regard to money, and, in danger, gives them a greater zeal for effort and a greater thirst for glory; it also makes them more modest and self-controlled, because they feel reverence for what they most desire.

'It is madness, too, not to choose good-looking people as military leaders. Personally, I would go through fire in Clinias' company, and I know that all of you would do the same in mine. So you needn't wonder any more, Socrates, whether my good looks will do people good.

'There is no reason, either, for disparaging beauty on the ground that it quickly passes its prime; as we find a beauty of childhood, so we do of adolescence, of maturity and of old age. Here is the evidence: they choose good-looking old men to carry the olive-shoots in honour of Athena,[2] which shows that beauty is the accompaniment of every age. And if it is a pleasant thing to have one's wishes granted willingly, I am sure that at this very minute, without saying a word, I could persuade this boy and girl here to kiss me more quickly than you could, Socrates, even if you spouted wisdom.'

'What's this?' said Socrates. 'You're bragging as if you were more beautiful than I am.'

'Of course,' said Critobulus, 'otherwise I should be uglier than any Silenus in the satyr-plays.'[3]

1. See Plato, *Symposium*, 184b ff., *Euthydemus*, 282a–b on being a slave to love.
2. In the Panathenaic festival (see p. 227, n. 3); however, for the festival, it was probably 'noble' rather than 'good-looking' old men who were required – Critobulus is making a pun (see p. 59 and p. 252, n. 2).
3. Satyr-plays were burlesque versions of Greek myths, which invariably managed to introduce Silenus and his company of satyrs – vulgar followers of Dionysus. On Socrates' resemblance to the standard portrait of Silenus, see Plato, *Symposium*, 215a–216e, and p. 253.

'All right, then,' said Socrates, 'mind that you remember to settle the question of our beauty when the topics that we have tabled have gone all round. Our judge shall be not Alexander the son of Priam,[1] but these very persons who you think are eager to kiss you.'

'Couldn't you leave it to Clinias, Socrates?' he asked.

'No. I wish you'd stop thinking of Clinias!'

'Do you suppose I think of him any the less if I don't mention his name? Don't you know that I have such a clear picture of him in my mind that if I were a sculptor or a painter, I could execute a portrait of him just as well from that picture as by looking at him?'

'Well then,' Socrates retorted, 'if you've got such an accurate picture of him, why do you plague me by dragging me about to places where you can see him?'

'Because, Socrates, the sight of Clinias himself has the effect of making me happy, but the picture in my mind gives me no pleasure – it only fills me with longing.'

Hermogenes said, 'Look here, Socrates, I don't think it's at all like you to let Critobulus get so infatuated.'

'Do you imagine,' said Socrates, 'that he got into this state after he came under my influence?'

'Well, when *did* it happen?'

'Don't you see that soft hair is just creeping down by his ears, whereas on Clinias it's now climbing up towards his back?[2] Well, Critobulus was fired with a violent passion for him while they were going to the same school; so when his father[3] noticed it, he handed him over to me to see if I could do anything to help him. And he is really much better now. Before, he used to gaze at Clinias with a fixed stare, as though he were looking at a

1. Alexander, better known as Paris, judged the beauty contest between Athena, Hera and Aphrodite, which in turn led to the Trojan War.
2. The Greeks used hair-growth as an indication of age. Clinias is younger than Critobulus.
3. Socrates' constant companion Crito.

Gorgon,[1] and never left his side; but now I've seen him actually blink! All the same, I do assure you, gentlemen, that it seems to me, just between ourselves, that he has even kissed Clinias, and nothing is a fiercer incitement to love than that. It's an insatiable thing, and it produces a kind of delicious anticipation. That's why I say that anyone who wants to be able to behave responsibly ought to refrain from kissing the young and attractive.'[2]

'Come, come, Socrates,' said Charmides. 'What do you mean by trying like this to scare us, your friends, away from good-looking people, although I've seen you yourself, I swear, with my own eyes, when you were both in the school-room searching for something in the same book, touching Critobulus' head with your head and his bare arm with yours?'

'Dear me!' said Socrates. 'So that's why I had a sore arm for more than five days, as if some wild beast had bitten me, and felt a sort of ache in my heart. Well, I now give you warning, Critobulus, before all these witnesses, not to touch me until your chin is as hairy as your scalp!'

In this way they combined joking with seriousness.

Callias now said, 'It's your turn, Charmides, to tell us why you are proud of your poverty.'

'It's an admitted fact,' he said, 'that it's better to be confident than to be frightened, and to be free than to be a slave, and to be courted than to court others, and to be trusted by one's country than to be distrusted. Well, in the days when I was a rich man in this city, in the first place I used to be afraid that somebody would break into my house, take my goods and even do me myself some injury. Then, I used to make myself agreeable to the sycophants,[3] knowing that I was more vulnerable than they were. Besides this, the State was always ordering me to finance something,[4] and I was never able to leave the city. But now that I'm deprived of my

1. Monstrous females (Medusa is the most famous) whose gaze could turn one to stone.
2. See *Memoirs*, 1.3.8–13.
3. See p. 133, n. 3.
4. See p. 294, n. 2.

properties abroad, and get nothing out of these that I have here, and the contents of my house are sold,[1] I sleep happily and fully relaxed, I have won the confidence of my country, I am no longer threatened but now threaten others, and I am free to leave or stay in the city. Rich men now give up their seats to me and make way for me in the street. Now I am like a dictator, but then I was clearly a slave; then I used to hand over money regularly to the people, but now the State supports me out of its revenue.[2] They even denounced me for associating with Socrates when I was rich; but now that I've become poor, it doesn't matter any more to anybody. Besides, when I had many possessions, I was always losing something thanks to the State or to fortune; but now I lose nothing (because I haven't got anything), but I'm always expecting to get something.'

'So you actually pray,' said Callias, 'never to be rich; and if you dream of any stroke of luck, you sacrifice to the gods who protect us from harm?'

'Good heavens, no!' he said. 'I don't do that. I stand my ground very heroically if I expect to get anything from anywhere!'

'Well, come along now, Antisthenes,' said Socrates. 'You tell us how it is that you pride yourself on your wealth, although you have such limited means.'

'Because, gentlemen, I believe that it's not in their estates that people have wealth or poverty, but in their minds. I see many private persons who, although they have very great wealth, consider themselves so poor that they submit to any hardship and any hazard with a view to increasing their possessions; and I know cases too of brothers who have inherited equal shares and, although one of them has more than enough to cover his expenditure, the other is altogether indigent. And I observe some despots too who are so hungry for wealth that they commit far more dreadful crimes than the desperately poor.[3] It is need, no doubt,

1. Presumably all as a result of the war.
2. He means that he now gets remuneration from public funds for minor services such as attendance in the Assembly or the courts.
3. See pp. 87, 95–6, 189–90, 293–4.

that makes the latter steal and break into houses and kidnap; but there are some despots who destroy whole houses, commit mass murders, and often sell whole populations away into slavery for the sake of money.

'Personally, I feel very sorry for these people in their most distressing disease: it seems to me that they are in much the same state as a man with ample provisions who eats heavily and is never satisfied. The quantity of my possessions is such that I myself can hardly discover them; but still I have quite enough to satisfy my hunger when I eat, to quench my thirst when I drink, and to clothe myself so that out of doors I am no colder than Callias here for all his great wealth. And when I get home, the walls of my house seem to me like a really warm tunic, and the roof like a really thick cloak, and my bedclothes are so adequate that it's hard work even to wake me up! If my body ever feels the need for sexual intercourse, I am so content with what is available that any women I approach welcome me with open arms, because nobody else will go near them. And, mark you, I find such pleasure in all these things that my prayer would be to enjoy doing each of them not more, but less; I have such a feeling that some of them give me more pleasure than is good for me.

'But I reckon that the most precious possession in my fortune is this: that if I were robbed even of what I now possess, I can imagine no kind of work so mean that it couldn't provide me with enough to live on. For instance, when I want to have a good time, I don't buy luxuries in the market – it costs too much; I supply myself from my own mind.[1] And it gives me far greater pleasure when I wait until I feel the need before I refresh myself, than when I enjoy some luxury – just as now I am drinking this Thasian wine[2] not because I am thirsty, but because the opportunity presented itself.

'Besides, those who are more concerned with thrift than with

1. See *Defence*, 18 (p. 45), and there are many other echoes of Socrates by Antisthenes.
2. Thasian was, after Chian, the best Greek wine.

extravagance are likely to be far more moral in their conduct, because those who are most content with what they have are least attracted by other people's property. And it is worth reflecting that this sort of wealth makes people generous. Socrates here, from whom I obtained it, didn't supply me by quantity or weight, but handed over to me as much as I could carry away. And now I grudge nobody; I exhibit my generosity to all my friends, and I give a share of my mental wealth to anyone who wants it. What is more, you can see that I have always at hand that supreme luxury, spare time, so that I can see what is worth seeing and hear what is worth hearing and – what I value most – spend my days at leisure with Socrates. And he for his part doesn't look up to those who amass the most money, but persists in keeping company with anyone he likes.'

When Antisthenes had finished this speech, Callias said, 'By Hera, I do envy you your wealth, for two reasons especially: first, that the State doesn't treat you like a slave by imposing tasks upon you,[1] and second, that people aren't angry if you don't lend them anything.'

'No, no,' said Niceratus, 'don't envy him. You'll see me get a loan from him – of his faculty for needing nothing. Homer has taught me to amass

> Seven unfired cauldrons, talents ten of gold,
> Twenty bright cooking-pots, and horses twelve[2]

all by weight and quantity, so I never stop craving for the utmost wealth. Consequently, some people probably think I'm rather fond of money.' At this everyone roared with laughter, thinking that he had said no more than the truth.

Next somebody said, 'It's up to you now, Hermogenes, to tell us who your friends are, and to demonstrate that they have great influence and take care of you, so that your pride in them may be shown to be justified.'

1. See p. 294, n. 2.
2. *Iliad*, 9.122–3 or 264–5.

'Well, it's quite plain that both Greeks and non-Greeks believe that the gods know everything that is and will be; at any rate all States and all peoples inquire of the gods by means of divination what they ought and ought not to do. Next, it's also clear that we believe they can do us both good and harm; at least, everyone asks the gods to avert what is evil and grant what is good. Well, these omniscient and omnipotent gods are such good friends to me that, because of their concern for me, I am never beyond their notice night or day, wherever I am bound and whatever I intend to do. And because of their foreknowledge, they indicate to me the result of every action, sending me messages by utterances, dreams and omens to tell me what I ought to do and what I ought not; and when I obey these, I am never sorry for it, but when I have sometimes disobeyed in the past, I have been punished for it.'

'Well,' said Socrates, 'there is nothing incredible in this. But I would be glad to know what sort of service you render them to keep them so friendly to you.'

'Certainly,' said Hermogenes, 'a very economical kind. I praise them, which costs me nothing; I always make them a return out of what they give me; I do my best not to offend in my speech; and, when I call them to witness, I never voluntarily tell a lie.'

'Good heavens!' said Socrates. 'If that's how you keep their friendship, it seems that the gods do take pleasure in true goodness.'

The foregoing topic was treated seriously in the manner I have described.

When they came to Philippus, they asked him what he saw in making jokes that led him to pride himself upon it.

'Why, isn't it right that I should?' he said. 'Everybody knows that I make jokes and, when they have a bit of good luck, they're glad to invite me round, but, when they've had a piece of bad luck, they run away without looking behind them in case they laugh against their will.'

'Well, you certainly have a right to be proud,' said Niceratus. 'I find, with *my* friends, that it's the lucky ones who keep themselves well out of my way, but any who have had a piece of bad luck show their family tree to prove our relationship and never leave my side.'

'All right,' said Charmides. 'Now for you, my Syracusan friend: what are you proud of? I suppose it's obviously your boy?'

'Certainly not,' he said. 'I am racked by fear for him; you see, I find that some people are plotting his destruction!'

When Socrates heard this, he exclaimed, 'Good heavens! What fearful wrong do they think your boy has done them that they want to kill him?'

'No, of course they don't want to kill him,' he said, 'but to persuade him to sleep with them.'

'And apparently you think that if that happened, it would be the ruin of him.'

'Yes, indeed, absolutely.'

'Don't you sleep with him yourself, then?'

'Certainly, all night and every night.'

'I swear,' said Socrates, 'it's great luck for you to have been born with such a body that you alone have no bad effect on those who sleep with you. So you're entitled to be proud of your body, if nothing else.'

'No, really,' he protested, 'I don't take any pride in that.'

'Well, in what, then?'

'In simple-minded people, of course. They provide me with a living by gazing at my puppets.'

'Ah,' said Philippus, 'that's why I heard you the other day praying to the gods to grant, wherever you were, a glut of fruit and a dearth of wits.'

'Very good,' said Callias. 'Now then, Socrates, how do you justify your claim to pride yourself on the disreputable calling that you mentioned?'

He replied, 'Let's decide first what the duties of a pimp are. Don't hesitate to answer all the questions I ask, so that we may know how far we agree. Do you approve?'

'Certainly,' they said; and having once said 'Certainly', they all kept to this same answer for the rest of the discussion.[1]

'Do you think that it's the duty of a good pimp to represent his client to everyone he meets as a pleasing person?'

'Certainly.'

'Doesn't one means of pleasing consist in having a suitable arrangement of hair and clothing?'

'Certainly.'

'Are we aware that it's possible for the same person to give friendly and hostile looks with the same eyes?'

'Certainly.'

'Next, is it possible to speak modestly and insolently with the same voice?'

'Certainly.'

'Next, aren't there some ways of talking that are offensive and others that are conciliatory?'

'Certainly.'

'Well, wouldn't a good pimp inculcate such of these qualities as are conducive to pleasing?'

'Certainly.'

'Which would be the better – the man who can make his clients agreeable to one person or the man who can make them agreeable to many?'

Here the company was divided, some saying 'The man who can do it to most', and others saying 'Certainly'!

Socrates remarked that this too was agreed, and went on, 'Supposing that someone could represent them as pleasing to the whole city, wouldn't that in itself make him a supremely good pimp?'

'Yes, undoubtedly,' they all said.

'So if somebody could achieve this for his clients, he would be justified in feeling proud of his skill, and justified in taking large fees?' When they all agreed to this too, he said, 'I think Antisthenes here is just the type.'

1. They are teasing Socrates for his habit of questioning.

'Are you conceding your art to *me*, Socrates?' asked Antisthenes.

'Of course I am,' he replied. 'I can see that you have carried to perfection the art that follows from it.'

'What is that?'

'Procuring,' he said.

Antisthenes was very indignant. 'And what, Socrates,' he asked, 'are you aware that I have done in this line?'

'I know,' he replied, 'that you introduced Callias here to Prodicus when you saw that the one had a passion for philosophy and the other needed money. And I know that you introduced him to Hippias of Elis, from whom he learned the art of memorizing[1] – which has made him more amorous than he was before, because he never forgets anything beautiful that he's seen. And of course there was our visitor from Heraclea the other day;[2] you first excited my interest in him by praising him, and then brought us together. And indeed I'm grateful to you; I think he's a truly good person. And Aeschylus of Phlius[3] – didn't you praise us to each other so effectively that your descriptions made us fall in love and set us hunting for each other? It's because I see that you can do these things that I think you're a good procurer. It seems to me that a man who is able to recognize people who are likely to benefit each other, and who can make them desire each other, could develop friendship between States and arrange suitable marriages, and would be a very valuable ally for both States and individuals to possess. But you got angry, as if I'd insulted you by saying that you were a good procurer.'

'Well, I assure you I'm not angry now,' he said. 'If I have those qualities, my mind will soon be absolutely crammed with wealth!'

So this round of the conversation was completed.

1. On the sophist Hippias' mnemonic technique, which would have been part of one's training as an orator, see especially F. A. Yates, *The Art of Memory* (Routledge & Kegan Paul, 1966).
2. Perhaps the painter Zeuxippus, who came to Athens to teach painting (Plato, *Protagoras*, 318b).
3. An unknown character.

5

'Critobulus,' said Callias, 'are you holding back from the beauty contest with Socrates?'[1]

'Of course he is,' said Socrates. 'I expect he can see that the pimp is in favour with the judges.'

'In spite of that,' said Critobulus, 'I'm not backing out. If you've got some subtle argument, explain to me how you are more beautiful than I am. Only,' he added, 'I want the lamp brought up.'

'Well now,' said Socrates, 'I summon you first to a preliminary investigation of the case. Answer my questions.'

'Ask away.'

'Do you think that beauty is found only in man, or in other things as well?'

'I certainly believe that it's found in horses and cattle and in many inanimate objects. At any rate, I know that a shield is beautiful, and a sword, and a spear.'

'Why, how can all these things be beautiful, when they are nothing like one another?'[2]

'Surely,' said Critobulus, 'anything that is well constructed for the particular function for which we possess it, or well adapted by nature to meet our needs, is also beautiful.'

'Well, do you know what we need eyes for?'

'Obviously to see with.'

'Then in that case it would follow directly that my eyes are more beautiful than yours.'

'Why?'

'Because yours only see straight in front, but mine see sideways too, because they project.'

'Do you mean that a crab has better eyes than any other creature?'

1. See p. 243.
2. See *Memoirs*, 3.8.4–7 (pp. 158–9). The same Greek word (*kalos*) has been translated, according to context, as 'beautiful', 'fine', 'good-looking', and even 'noble'.

'In every way, surely, since it is also naturally endowed with outstandingly strong eyes.'

'All right,' said Critobulus, 'which of our noses is more beautiful – yours or mine?'

'I think that mine is,' said Socrates, 'that is, if the gods have created our noses for the purpose of smelling. Your nostrils look down at the ground, but mine are opened right up so as to admit smells from every direction.'

'Come, though: how can snubness in a nose be more beautiful than straightness?'

'Because it doesn't set up a barrier, but lets the eyes have a direct view of whatever they like. A high-bridged nose looks haughty and forms a dividing wall between them.'

'As for the mouth,' said Critobulus, 'I give you that: if it's made for biting, you can take a much bigger bite than I can. And the thickness of your lips makes your kiss softer, don't you think?'

'By your description, I seem to have an uglier mouth than a donkey's. But don't you think the following is evidence that I'm more beautiful than you are – that the Naiads, who are goddesses, are mothers of the Sileni, who resemble me more than you?'[1]

'I can't argue against you any more,' said Critobulus. 'Let them record their votes, so that I may know as quickly as possible what penalty or fine I've got to pay. Only,' he added, 'let it be a secret ballot, because I'm afraid of your and Antisthenes' wealth[2] dominating me.'

So the girl and the boy recorded their votes in secret. Meanwhile, Socrates made two arrangements: to have the lamp brought up in front of Critobulus, so that the judges might not be misled, and to fix as the token of victory given by the judges to the winner not garlands but kisses. When the votes were turned out of

1. The Naiads were water-nymphs and so belonged to the same class of nature-spirits as satyrs and Sileni, but the relationship seems unlikely. For Socrates and Silenus, see p. 242; 'Sileni' in the plural just means 'satyrs'.
2. That is, their cleverness (see p. 245), since Socrates has just publicly argued him down.

the urn and were all[1] for Critobulus, Socrates said, 'Tut, tut, Critobulus, your money doesn't seem to be like Callias'. His makes people better,[2] but yours, like most other money, is capable of corrupting both judges and juries.'

6

Here some urged Critobulus to take the kisses that he had earned by his victory, others urged him to win the consent of the dancers' master, and others uttered other pleasantries. But Hermogenes remained silent. Socrates addressed him and said, 'Hermogenes, could you tell us what drunkenness is?'

'I don't know what it is,' he said, 'which is what you're asking; but I could tell you what I think it is.'

'Well, what you think will do.'

'All right. I consider that drunkenness consists in annoying one's companions over the wine.'

'Do you realize, then,' said Socrates, 'that you're now annoying us by your silence?'

'Even while you're talking?' he asked.

'No, but when we leave a pause.'

'Has it escaped your notice that when you people are talking, there's no gap to poke even a hair in, let alone a remark?'

'Callias,' said Socrates, 'could you lend a hand to a man who's losing an argument?'

'Yes, I can,' he replied. 'Whenever the pipe is being played, we keep absolutely silent.'

Hermogenes said, 'You know how the actor Nicostratus used to recite tetrameters to the accompaniment of a pipe? Do you want me to converse with you to the sound of the pipe in the same way?'

'Yes, please, Hermogenes,' said Socrates. 'A pipe accompaniment makes a song more agreeable, and I presume that in the same

1. This is humorous exaggeration for the two votes.
2. See p. 239.

way your remarks will be improved by the tune, especially if you gesticulate to suit the words, like the pipe-player.'

'What shall the music be,' asked Callias, 'when Antisthenes here picks arguments with people at the party?'

'I think the right music for the loser of the argument would be a hiss,'[1] said Antisthenes.

As this conversation was going on, the Syracusan saw that they were paying no attention to his displays, but entertaining one another; so he felt aggrieved with Socrates and said, 'Socrates, are you the person that they call "the thinker"?'[2]

'That's nicer than if they call me "the thoughtless",' he replied.

'Yes, if you weren't regarded as a thinker about celestial things.'[3]

'Do you know anything more celestial than the gods?'

'No, no,' said the man, 'it's not in them that you're said to be interested, but in things which don't benefit us at all.'

'Even so,' said Socrates, 'I might be showing interest in the gods. It's from above that they benefit us by sending rain, and from above that they give us light. If that's a frigid answer,' he added, 'it's your fault for bothering me.'[4]

'Never mind that,' said the man. 'Tell me how many feet away from me a flea is; they say that you can solve these problems in geometry.'[5]

1. The Greek word (*surigmos*) means both a shrill tune on a pipe and a derisive hiss or cat-call.
2. See Aristophanes, *Clouds*, 266; the Syracusan evidently knows the play.
3. See also *Memoirs*, 1.1.10–11 and 4.7.6–7: it was a standard charge against philosophers that they dethroned the gods by conducting scientific inquiries into matters which were thought divine, such as the source of rain and light (see below). This is the accusation Aristophanes' play, *Clouds*, reflects, and Plato (*Apology*, 18b) uses the same phrase we find here while having Socrates deny that these are his concerns.
4. 'Frigid' was a technical term to describe various types of strained or inappropriate language (Aristotle, *Rhetoric*, 1405b35 ff.), including overdone compound words. Here Socrates chooses to take the Syracusan's 'of no benefit' (*anopheles*) as a compound of 'from above' (*an-*) and 'benefit' (*opheles*).
5. See Aristophanes, *Clouds*, 144 ff., 830 ff., and p. 9.

Antisthenes broke in, 'You're good with imitations, Philippus. Don't you think this man is imitating an intentional slanderer?'

'Yes, indeed,' he said, 'and a good many other types too.'

'But still,' said Socrates, 'you'd better not describe the type, in case you too imitate a slanderer.'

'But if I liken him to all the fine and best characters, I should be more fairly said to imitate a toady than a slanderer.'

'You're already imitating a slanderer if you say that he is better than everyone.'[1]

'Well, do you want me to liken him to worse types?'

'No, not to worse ones either.'

'Well then, to nobody?'

'Don't liken him to any of these types.'

'But I don't know how I shall earn my dinner if I say nothing.'

'Quite easily, if you keep quiet when things are better left unsaid.'

In this way the alcoholic heat of this discussion was cooled down.

7

The rest now joined in, some urging Philippus to do an imitation, and others trying to prevent it. There was an uproar, and Socrates interposed again: 'As we're all so eager to have our voices heard,' he said, 'perhaps this would be the right moment to sing together.' And with these words he started a song. When it was over, a potter's wheel was brought in for the dancing-girl, who was going to perform tricks on it. At this Socrates said, 'My Syracusan friend, it looks as if I really am a thinker, as you say; at any rate I am now considering how this boy and girl of yours can have the easiest time, and how we can get the greatest pleasure from watching them – which, I am sure, is what you want too. Well, it seems to me that to turn somersaults over sword-blades is an exhibition of danger that is quite out of place at a party. Then

1. Because this would be untrue (that is, slanderous). I read πάντων αὐτὸν βελτίω.

again, to write or read as one spins round on the wheel is no doubt a remarkable feat, but I can't make out what pleasure this could afford either. Nor, again, is it more pleasant to watch attractive young people twisting their bodies round into hoops than to see them in repose. In fact, it isn't at all uncommon to find things to wonder at, if that's what one wants: there are puzzling things right before our eyes. We can wonder why on earth it is that the lamp gives light because it has a bright flame, whereas the bronze mirror, although it's bright, doesn't make light, but shows the reflections of other things in itself; and how it is that oil, which is liquid, feeds the flame, but water, because it's liquid, puts the fire out. However, even these topics don't coincide with the aims of drinking. But, if they danced, with a pipe accompaniment, figures representing Graces and Seasons and Nymphs,[1] I believe that they would have an easier time and the party would be more graceful!'

The Syracusan said, 'Yes, indeed, you're right, Socrates, and I will put on displays which you will enjoy.'

8

He went out amid applause. Socrates once more introduced a new subject.

'Gentlemen,' he said, 'we are in the presence of a great deity, as old in time as the eternal gods, and yet most youthful in appearance, who pervades all things in his greatness and is enshrined in the heart of man: I mean Love.[2] Isn't it natural that we should make some mention of him, especially since we are all his worshippers? I can't name a time when I haven't been

1. The Graces were goddesses of grace and beauty, often associated with Aphrodite; the Seasons were nature-spirits who presided over the several stages of the year and the gifts of the earth; the Nymphs haunted natural objects such as woods, springs and mountains; all were represented in art as beautiful young women.
2. In Plato's version of a party attended by Socrates (*Symposium*), love is the main topic.

continuously in love with someone;[1] I know that Charmides has acquired a number of admirers, and has lost his own heart to more than one; and Critobulus, who still has his admirers, is already setting his heart on others. Then Niceratus too, as I hear, is in love with his wife and is loved by her in return. And Hermogenes – don't we all know that, whatever true goodness is, he is wasting away with love of it? Don't you see how serious his brow is, how calm his countenance, how measured his speech, how gentle his voice, how cheerful his disposition? And how, although he enjoys the friendship of the most holy gods,[2] he shows no disdain for us mortals? Have you alone, Antisthenes, no love at all?'

'Yes, by heaven, I have!' he replied. 'A violent love for you!'

Socrates replied banteringly, with mock coyness, 'Don't bother me just now; you can see that I'm otherwise engaged.'

Antisthenes responded: 'How blatantly you always behave like this, pimping for your own favours! At one time you offer the divine as a pretext for not talking to me,[3] and at another your reason is that you're attracted by someone else.'

'For heaven's sake, Antisthenes,' said Socrates, 'all I ask is that you leave me a little bit intact. The rest of your unkindness I bear, and will continue to bear, in a friendly spirit. But let's draw a veil over your love for me, because it's inspired not by my mind, but by my beautiful body! That you, Callias, are in love with Autolycus is known to the whole of our city and, I expect, to a good many foreigners too, the reason being that you are both sons of famous fathers,[4] and distinguished men yourselves. I have always admired your nature, but now I admire it much more, because I see that the person you love is not pampered by luxury or enervated by effeminacy, but displays to the eyes of all his strength, endurance, courage and self-discipline. To be attracted by these qualities is evidence of the lover's own character.

1. See *Memoirs*, 4.1.2 (p. 177), and p. 222.
2. See p. 248.
3. See pp. 34–5.
4. Callias' father Hipponicus belonged to a famous and wealthy family, but Autolycus' Lycon seems to have had little claim to distinction.

'Whether there is one Aphrodite or two, Celestial and Common,[1] I don't know: Zeus has many titles, although he is regarded as the same deity. But I do know that there are different altars and shrines for each of them; and that the rites are more casual for the Common, and of a devouter kind for the Celestial goddess. One might guess that the former inspires physical love, while the latter inspires love of the mind, of friendship, and of noble deeds. That, I believe, is the sort of love that possesses you, Callias. I base my belief on the true goodness of the one you love, and on the fact that I see you invite his father to be present when you are together, because there is nothing in these associations that need be concealed from the father by a truly good lover.'

'I swear, Socrates,' said Hermogenes, 'the thing I admire most in you – and there are many others – is that, at the same time as paying Callias a compliment, you instruct him in how he ought to behave.'

'Quite so,' he replied, 'and to increase his pleasure even more, I want to show him evidence that love for the mind is much better than physical love. We all know that without affection there can be no companionship worthy of the name. Now, the affection of those who admire the character is recognized as a pleasant and acceptable compulsion; but many of those whose desires are sensual criticize and dislike the characters of those whom they love. And even if they are fond of them in both ways, the bloom of youth, as we know, quickly passes its prime, and when this fails, the affection must fade along with it; but so long as the mind is progressing towards greater wisdom, the more lovable it becomes. Then again, involvement with physical beauty entails a sort of satiety, so that one is bound to lose interest in a favourite in just the same way as repletion makes one lose interest in food; but affection for the mind, being pure, is less liable to satiety. Yet this does not imply, as might be supposed, that Aphrodite is any the less concerned with it: on the contrary, the prayer in which we ask the goddess to imbue our speech and action with her charm is

1. Aphrodite was worshipped under both these titles: this is not entirely a philosophical fancy.

manifestly fulfilled. That a mind blooming with non-servile attractiveness and with a modest and noble character – which even among its contemporaries combines authority with friendliness – that such a nature admires and loves its beloved needs no explanation; but I shall prove to you that it is natural also for such a lover to have his love reciprocated by his beloved.

'In the first place, who could hate a person by whom, he knows, he is considered truly good, and secondly who, he can see, is more concerned about what is good for his favourite than what is pleasant for himself, and moreover whose affection, he trusts, could not be diminished even by the calamity of a disfiguring disease? Must not those whose affection is mutual look at each other with pleasure and converse in amity; must they not trust and be trusted, be considerate to each other, share pleasure in their successes and sorrow if anything goes wrong; must they not continue in happiness so long as they are together and in good health, and, if either falls ill, must not the other keep him company much more constantly; and must they not care for each other even more in their absence than in their presence? Aren't all these characteristics filled with Aphrodite's charm? It's this sort of conduct that maintains people's mutual devotion to their friendship and their enjoyment of it even into old age.

'As for the lover whose attachment is physical, why should the boy return his affection? Because he assigns to himself the gratification of his desires, leaving the boy to the extremity of shame? Or because the favour that he is eager to exact cuts the favourite off completely from his family and friends? Then again, the very fact that he uses not force but persuasion makes him more detestable, because a lover who uses force proves himself a villain, but one who uses persuasion ruins the character of the one who consents.[1] Again, is one who sells his youthful beauty for money any more likely to love the purchaser than one who trades in the market? Certainly, the fact that he is young and his partner is not,

1. This notion was enshrined in Athenian law, under which the penalties for rape were less severe than those for adultery: see Lysias, 1.32–3.

or that he is beautiful and his partner is so no longer, or that he is not in love and his partner is – this will not stir his affection. A boy does not even share the man's enjoyment of sexual intercourse as a woman does: he is a sober person watching one drunk with sexual excitement. In view of all this, it is no wonder if he even develops contempt for his lover. Investigation would also show that no negative result has ever been caused by those who are loved for the sake of their characters, whereas the shameless form of intercourse has led before now to many atrocious deeds.

'I shall now show that the association is more servile for the lover of the body than for the lover of the mind. The person who teaches you to say and do what you ought may fairly be held in honour, as Chiron and Phoenix were by Achilles,[1] but the one who has a physical craving may reasonably be treated like a mendicant, because he always follows his favourite round, begging and soliciting either a kiss or some form of physical contact.

'Don't be surprised if I am rather outspoken. It's partly because the wine helps to carry me away, and partly because the love which is my constant companion spurs me on to speak out against its adversary. It seems to me that a person who concentrates on outward appearance is like one who has rented a plot of land: his object is not to increase the value of the land, but to secure for himself as many crops as he can. But the man who desires friendship is more like the owner of his own holding; at any rate, he gathers together from every quarter whatever he can get to increase the worth of the one he loves. Besides, a favourite who knows that enough outward beauty will enable him to dominate his lover is likely to take little trouble over any other quality; but if he knows that, unless he is truly good, he will not retain the friendship, then it is natural that he should care more about virtue.

'But the supreme advantage enjoyed by one who is eager to convert his favourite into a good friend is that he is compelled to cultivate goodness himself, because, if he behaves wickedly, it is

1. Chiron the Centaur and Phoenix were both tutors of Achilles.

impossible for him to make his companion good; and if he shows himself shameless and dissolute, it is impossible for him to make the one he loves self-controlled and disciplined.

'I feel moved also to invoke myth to show you, Callias, that not only men but gods and demi-gods set love of the mind above physical gratification. All the mortal women whom Zeus loved for their physical beauty he left mortal after he had had sex with them, but all those men who won his regard by their nobility of mind he made immortal. Examples of these are Heracles and the Dioscuri;[1] and we are told of others as well. I myself maintain that Ganymede[2] too was carried off by Zeus to Olympus on account not of his body but of his mind. His very name supplies the evidence. Homer, as you know, has the phrase "and he is glad to hear it", which means "and he is pleased to hear it". And somewhere else there is the phrase "in his heart knowing shrewd counsels". This in turn means "in his heart knowing wise advice".[3] Putting these two together, we find that Ganymede is held in honour among the gods by a name which means not "pleasing in body" but "pleasing in mind". Besides, Niceratus,[4] Homer has made Achilles exact his famous vengeance for Patroclus not because Patroclus was his lover, but because he was a friend and was killed.[5] Also, Orestes and Pylades, and Theseus and Pirithous,[6] and many others among the greatest heroes are celebrated in song for having jointly performed the greatest and noblest exploits, not because they slept together, but out of mutual admiration.

1. Castor and Polydeuces (Pollux), sons of Zeus by Leda. They were immortal on alternate days.
2. Son of Tros or some other Trojan prince; he became cup-bearer to the gods and Zeus' catamite.
3. The fragments do not occur in extant Homeric poems. Socrates derives Ganymede's name from *ganusthai* (to be glad) and *medea* (counsels).
4. Socrates turns to address Niceratus now because of his professed expertise in Homer (pp. 236–7, 239–41).
5. See Homer, *Iliad*, 16–24.
6. Orestes, son of Agamemnon, was proverbially close to his friend Pylades, who helped him in his revenge against Clytemnestra; Pirithous fought with Theseus against the centaurs and together they braved Hades.

'Take the case of noble deeds in our own day: wouldn't you find that they are all done to win praise by men who are willing to endure hardship and danger rather than by those who are accustomed to choose pleasure before glory? And yet Pausanias, the lover of Agathon the poet,[1] in his defence of those who wallow in debauchery[2] has said that an army composed of boys and their lovers would be braver than any other, because he said he thought that they would be most ashamed to desert one another – a remarkable statement, that those who make a habit of disregarding censure and acting shamelessly towards each other should be most ashamed of doing something shameful! And he adduced as evidence the fact that this was the policy of both Thebes and Elis[3] – at any rate, he said that, although they slept with their favourites, they nevertheless had them posted by their sides for battle. This was his evidence, but the cases are not equivalent, because pederasty is an accepted custom with those peoples, but with us it is a matter for reproach. Also, it seems to me that those who arrange the ranks like that are probably not sure that their favourites will acquit themselves like brave men if they are separated. The Spartans, who believe that, if a man so much as entertains a carnal desire, he can no longer attain any truly good object,[4] train their favourites to such a perfect pitch of bravery that even among strangers, even if they are not stationed in the same rank as their lovers, they are just as much ashamed to desert the comrades at their side. This is because the goddess that they believe in is not Immodesty but Modesty.

'It seems to me that we should all come to an agreement on the subject that I am discussing if we looked at it from this point of

1. For Pausanias and Agathon, see Plato, *Protagoras*, 315d–e and *Symposium*, 193b.
2. Xenophon refers to Pausanias' speech in Plato's *Symposium* (180c–185c); see further p. 220.
3. Xenophon here conflates bits of two speeches from Plato's *Symposium*. Pausanias refers to 'Elis and Boeotia' (182b), but only as countries where pederasty is taken for granted. The notion of an army composed of 'lovers and their favourites' is introduced by Phaedrus (178e).
4. An outstanding case of Xenophon's admiration for Sparta.

view: of two boys, each loved in one of the two ways, which would more confidently be entrusted with money or one's children or favours? I imagine that even the person who is involved with the external beauty of his beloved would be more ready to commit all these things to the one who is loved for his mind.

'As for you, Callias, I think you should be grateful to the gods for implanting in you a love of Autolycus. It's easy to see that he is eager for honour, because he endures a great many hardships and discomforts for the sake of being proclaimed victor in the pancration.[1] Now, if he thought that he would not only distinguish himself and his father, but be enabled by his manly prowess both to help his friends and to raise the prestige of his country by winning victories over its enemies, and that he would consequently be admired and famous among both Greeks and foreigners, don't you think he would treat with the deepest respect the person who he thought would be his most effective helper to this end? So if you want to find favour in his eyes, you should consider what sort of knowledge enabled Themistocles to liberate Greece, and what sort of wisdom it can have been that earned Pericles the reputation of being his country's best adviser; you must consider what sort of profound reflection preceded Solon's provision for our city of a matchless legal code;[2] and you must also inquire what sort of qualities the Spartans cultivate that make them regarded as the best leaders. You are their representative[3] at Athens, and the most important of them are always given hospitality at your house. You may be sure that your country would readily put itself in your charge, if that is your wish, because you have the essential qualifications. You are of noble birth, a priest of the gods who were instituted by

1. See p. 227, n. 4.
2. Themistocles, Pericles and Solon were the outstanding Athenian statesmen of the past. Solon instituted its democracy; Themistocles was instrumental in defeating the Persian invasion; Pericles guided the city at the time of its greatest glory.
3. Diplomatic representative (*proxenos*); although an Athenian citizen, he looked after Spartan interests in Athens.

Erechtheus and who marched with Iacchus against the barbarians;[1] and now at the festival you are thought to be a more distinguished holder of that sacred office than any of your predecessors,[2] and you have a body which is the most attractive in the city and capable of enduring hardships. If you think that I have spoken more seriously than is appropriate over our wine, don't be surprised at that. I have always shared my country's love for those who are naturally good and make virtue their keen ambition.'

The others began discussing what had been said, but Autolycus kept his eyes fastened on Callias. Callias, with a glance at him, said, 'So are you going to play the pimp, Socrates, between me and the State, so that I may engage in politics and always be in favour with the State?'

'Yes, indeed,' he replied, 'if they see that your interest in goodness is not superficial but genuine. A false reputation is soon exposed when put to the test, but, unless a god interferes, true manliness by its actions always helps to make renown more glorious.'

9

That was the end of this discussion. Autolycus got up to walk home, because it was time for him to go. As his father Lycon was going out with him, he turned back and said, 'I swear, Socrates, it does seem to me that you are a truly good man.'

At this point a sort of throne was set up in the room, and then

1. Erechtheus was a semi-divine legendary king of Athens who, *inter alia*, instituted the worship of Athena and Poseidon at Athens. Iacchus was a deity associated with the mystery cult of Demeter at Eleusis. Just before the crucial battle of Salamis (480) against the Persians, the shout of 'Iacchus' swept in the form of a cloud from Eleusis over the Persian fleet, signalling its impending defeat (Herodotus, 8.65). Athena and Poseidon could be said to be present, because Athena was guardian of the city, and Poseidon's domain was the sea (Salamis being a sea-battle).
2. The festival referred to must be the Panathenaea, the occasion of this dinner-party (p. 227). Callias was also a hereditary torch-bearer at the Eleusinian festival.

the Syracusan came in and said, 'Gentlemen, Ariadne will enter her and Dionysus' bedroom;[1] and after that Dionysus will arrive after having had a few drinks with the gods, and will go in to her; and then they will frolic with each other.'

Hereupon first Ariadne came in dressed up as a bride and sat down on the throne and, although there was still no sign of Dionysus, the Bacchic music was being played on the pipe. At this point the choreographer won admiration, because, as soon as Ariadne heard it, she acted in a way that showed unmistakably that she was delighted at it; she did not go to meet her bridegroom or even stand up, but she obviously could hardly keep still. When Dionysus caught sight of her, he came dancing across and sat down on her lap in the most affectionate way imaginable, flung his arms around her and kissed her. She conveyed the impression of shyness, but nevertheless returned his embraces lovingly.

When the guests saw this, they clapped and shouted, 'Encore!' Dionysus got up and helped Ariadne to stand up too; and then there was an opportunity to watch the figures they danced as they kissed and embraced each other. When the guests saw that Dionysus really was handsome, and Ariadne young and pretty, and that they were not pretending but actually kissing with their lips, they were all carried away with excitement as they watched. They heard Dionysus asking her if she loved him, and the girl vowing that she did, in such a way that not only Dionysus but the whole company would have sworn with one voice that the two young people really did love each other. They did not seem to have rehearsed their movements; it seemed as if they were free at last to do what they had long desired.

When the guests eventually saw them in each other's arms and going off as if to bed, the bachelors swore that they would get married, and the married men mounted their horses and rode away to their own wives with the same end in view. Socrates and

1. The Syracusan is fulfilling his promise of 7.5 (p. 257). Ariadne helped Theseus to escape from the labyrinth and fled with him from Crete; but he left her on the island of Naxos, where Dionysus found her and married her.

those who were still left set out to walk with Callias to the home of Lycon and his son. That is the way in which this party came to an end.

THE ESTATE-MANAGER

TRANSLATED AND INTRODUCED BY ROBIN WATERFIELD

INTRODUCTION

The Latinized Greek title of *The Estate-manager* is *Oeconomicus*. The Greek *oikonomikos* means 'one skilled at managing an *oikos*', where *oikos* means first a 'house', and then by extension all the people and things which occupy a house – a 'household' – and then by a little further extension all one's property – an 'estate'.

One reason why I prefer to translate the title, rather than transliterate it, is that *oikonomikos* is the root of the English word 'economics', and one occasionally comes across careless statements to the effect that the work is an early treatise on economics. This is not the case. For a work to be concerned with economics, properly speaking, it must at the very least include some analysis of economic factors; Xenophon draws our attention to various aspects of human life which in the hands of an analyst could be regarded as economic factors, but he goes no further than drawing our attention to them: they are not analysed and they do not play a part within the broad scale of a concept such as 'the economy'.

I believe that ancient writers never came anywhere near what we would call scientific economics. Aristotle occasionally seems to be heading in that direction, but his framework is quite different from an economic framework.[1] But consider the following passage from Plato (*Republic*, 369b–c):

1. See M. I. Finley, 'Aristotle and Economic Analysis', in J. Barnes *et al.* (eds.), *Articles on Aristotle*, vol. 2: *Ethics and Politics* (Duckworth, 1977), pp. 140–58.

A State comes into being, in my opinion, when each of us finds that he is not self-sufficient, but lacks many things . . . So A calls in B with regard to his need of X, and calls in C with regard to his need of Y; and we lack many things, so we gather many people together into one place of habitation, as our partners and allies . . . and people give and take in exchange.

Here we have what may be called an economic interpretation of history, based on the idea of division of labour. But the ideas remain half-formed in economic terms, and are not developed into a science of economics with analysis of factors such as labour, wealth, productivity, prices, supply, demand, trade, national income and so on. The problem is succinctly stated by Joseph Schumpeter:[1]

Common-sense knowledge goes in this field much farther relatively to such scientific knowledge as we have been able to achieve, than does common-sense knowledge in almost any other field. The layman's knowledge that rich harvests are associated with low prices of foodstuffs or that division of labour increases the efficiency of the productive process are obviously prescientific and it is absurd to point to such statements in old writings as if they embodied discoveries.

In short, the context of Plato's remarks is not scientific economics, but Greek theories on the origins of things, which were developed in the fifth century. We find the sophists in particular expressing opinions on the origin of language, religion and society. Views on the origin of society are the immediate context of Plato's remarks; the most famous such theory is that of Protagoras, retold in Plato's *Protagoras*, 320c–322d, where it is suggested that it was man's defencelessness against the elements and other animals that first caused him to band together.

In *The Estate-manager* too we find reflections on origins. In 7.18–28 Ischomachus expatiates on the origins of the physical and psychological differences between men and women; and a theme throughout the book is that agriculture is the foundation of

1. *History of Economic Analysis*, p. 9, quoted by Finley, op. cit., p. 141.

civilization (e.g. 5.1–17). But none of these remarks, in Xenophon or elsewhere, should be seen as economics or even proto-economics.

While we are on the subject of what *The Estate-manager* is not, we should also note that it is not an agricultural handbook. Technical treatises on the subject did exist before Xenophon's time: Aristotle (*Politics*, 1258b–1259a) mentions two authors, Charetides of Paros and Apollodorus of Lemnos, and we know that the fifth-century philosopher Democritus of Abdera also wrote on the subject.[1] Xenophon, however, is not intending to write a technical handbook, and even sneers at those who have done, calling them 'people who give the most detailed verbal account of farming, but never actually work on a farm' (16.1). It is true that agriculture plays a major part, but only as an object of eulogy. Even the four chapters (16–19) which do give some detail about agricultural methods are included only to support the general eulogistic thesis that agriculture is 'generous'; the technical details are almost entirely a matter of observation and common sense (only sowing is treated as involving any skill).

The thesis that farming is not a matter of specialist skill, but only common sense, is easily disproved by reflection on chapter 2, on 'Agriculture', of H. Michell's book *The Economics of Ancient Greece* (Cambridge University Press, 1940), which, despite a rather quixotic introductory chapter, is important reading. Greek farmers were working under difficult conditions and over the centuries had gained a great deal of skill and specialized knowledge in all areas of farming. *The Estate-manager* is informative, but only scratches the surface of Greek farming lore. Xenophon's attitude, through the mouth of Ischomachus, is that of the amateur farmer, the country gentleman who rides about his estate on horseback, supervising his labourers who (and especially the

1. Moreover, the medical treatises attributed to Hippocrates, at least some of which were written before or during Xenophon's lifetime, not infrequently used the growth or propagation of plants to illustrate theories about human beings.

foreman), one may reasonably suppose, knew a great deal more about farming techniques than he did. Xenophon could write technical handbooks, as his *Cynegeticus* and *Hipparchicus*, on hunting and cavalry command respectively, demonstrate; but *The Estate-manager* is not one of them.

Agriculture, at a broad, non-technical level, does play a major part in the book, however, and the purpose is, as mentioned, to praise it. We need to set this eulogy in context, since the modern reader is likely to have or gain some false preconceptions.

Given the quantity of praise Xenophon lavishes on the joys of owning a farm, we are likely, when we read of Ischomachus visiting his farm (11.14–18), to form a mental picture of a vast estate of thousands of acres. It is surprising, then, to read that Ischomachus can leave Athens early in the morning, walk out to one of his farms, supervise the labourers, go for a ride, walk and jog back to Athens, and still be back in time for a late-afternoon meal! In fact, his main farm is likely to have been between 100 and 200 acres at the most. We do hear of the possibility of someone owning 1,000 acres (Plato, *Theaetetus*, 174e), but this means that he would have owned a number of farms, not a single one of 1,000 acres. Even Alcibiades, for all his great wealth, had only 200 acres (Plato, *Alcibiades I*, 123c).

Likewise, when we hear about the slave labourers on Ischomachus' farm, our minds should not leap to the Hollywood image of scores of slaves picking cotton on a Louisiana estate at the beginning of the last century. Not very many people are needed to work 100 acres or so: Ischomachus' workforce would have been between five and ten men. It is in this context that his remarks about the importance of one man working flat out (20.16–17) make sense.

The workforce would have been all, or mainly, slaves. The Athenian economy depended on slave-labour. The aristocratic Athenian citizen's rather supercilious attitude to manual labour (see, for example, 4.1–3) fed and was fed by his reliance on slaves; the political system, in which every male citizen could play a part by taking time off work to vote in the Assembly or do jury service, could not have existed without slaves to do the everyday work.

Once we appreciate the small scale of Ischomachus' farm, it should become clear that the eulogy of farming is not based on its financial profitability. Moral profit rightly receives more emphasis throughout the book; it has been estimated that even a very large estate yielded only about an 8 per cent return per annum (Michell, op. cit., p. 86). The only time in *The Estate-manager* that we hear about making substantial profit out of agriculture (20.22–24) is where it comes from buying up farms which have become derelict (as a result of war or debt) and then improving and reselling them.

It must be remembered (as any visitor to modern Greece knows) that no great proportion of the land is suitable for cultivation. In particular, Attica, the district around Athens which is the setting for *The Estate-manager*, is often mountainous and even more often unsuited to grain-production. Ischomachus talks of growing grain as well as fruit trees, but Athens was never self-sufficient in grain and had the constant problem throughout its history of how to feed its population (see pp. 155, 356). Olives, figs and vines were Attica's paying crops.

In short, in spite of Xenophon's rosy portrait, life was not easy on Ischomachus' farm. It was too small to yield a large profit, and the soil and climate were unfavourable.[1] If Xenophon contrives to give us a picture of prosperity, it is almost certainly an idealized picture. It is true that some landowners (and some craftsmen) were well off; but they were few, and are only prominent in Greek literature because it was their peers who were writing that literature. Herodotus' memorable dictum (7.102) that 'Poverty is the ever-present sibling of Greece' is closer to the reality; and where Attica is concerned, Xenophon remarks (referring to the silver mines at Laurium) in a late treatise (*Poroi*, 1.5, on Athens'

1. The toughness of farming in Greece makes Ischomachus' remarks on the necessity of women doing the indoor work (7.18–28) seem slightly less bigoted and more realistic.

revenues) that in his opinion mining Attica is more profitable than cultivating it.

If *The Estate-manager* is neither an economics book nor an agricultural treatise, what is it? A minimalist view would be that it is, as the title implies, a treatise on the activities of an estate-owner: what he must do, when and how, as well as how he should treat his wife and slaves. Aristotle also covered these topics in the first book of his *Politics*, and these two sources – Xenophon and Aristotle – started a minor tradition of treatises on the subject: we know of a number of authors who wrote *Oeconomica*, and we have two surviving representatives – in the first book of the pseudo-Aristotelian treatise with that title (written probably about 300 BC)[1] and in the substantial fragments of a similar work by the Epicurean philosopher Philodemus of Gadara (written *c.* 50 BC). It is not going too far to say that all but a few sentences in pseudo-Aristotle's *Oeconomica* contain sentiments drawn from either Aristotle or Xenophon; Philodemus too drew heavily on Xenophon.

So Xenophon contributed towards the founding of a literary topic. But did he invent the topic? We have only a fraction of the fifth-century literature we would like to have, but, even with that qualification, there seems to be no reason not to credit Xenophon with an initiatory role (Aristotle's *Politics* was written well after Xenophon's death). This is not to say that the work represents a great pioneering feat. Xenophon drew largely on his own experience and on oral lore, but there were also relevant writings which could have been available to him. The most significant of these is Hesiod's epic poem *Works and Days* (written *c.* 700), which is a mine of practical information on the very topics Xenophon covers. Hesiod also wrote other relevant poems, which are now lost to us: *Great Works* covered agriculture at greater length than

1. This is worth reading for comparison with our piece. It is available in translation, as a section of vol. 10 of *The Works of Aristotle*, translated into English under the editorship of W. D. Ross; *Oeconomica* is translated by E. S. Forster.

Works and Days, and *Precepts of Chiron* seems to have contained practical as well as purely moral advice.

Hesiod's surviving poem consists of a series of homilies and, due to his method of composition (which was derived from the oral, bardic tradition), is often loose and unconnected. What makes Xenophon's work original is his methodical approach: at the beginning he declares that estate-management is to be considered as a science, and he proceeds to give a reasonably orderly account of the topics which fall under this generic science. The science of estate-management is defined in chapter 1 as 'knowing how to make use of assets so that they are profitable', and the rest of the book is meant to show, particularly in the person of Ischomachus, how a good estate-manager makes use of his assets. The discussion of each asset (wife, slaves, house, farm, etc.) is announced, and transitions from topic to topic are clear; even the elements which contribute towards each topic are neatly enunciated, as in Ischomachus' five-point programme for training his foremen (chapters 12–14). No doubt even without Xenophon, Aristotle would still have formulated his idea that estate-management is a science (and falls under the even more generic science of politics); but Xenophon deserves credit for being the first rationally to delineate the areas with which estate-management is concerned.

I have mentioned the 'minimalist' view that *The Estate-manager* is exactly what it appears to be – a treatise on estate-management. But there is an extra dimension: the work is couched as a Socratic dialogue, and therefore Socratic themes (or rather Xenophon's Socratic themes) play a part. Xenophon doubtless used the literary form of a Socratic dialogue in this instance partly to make the subject-matter more digestible, but that is not the whole story.

For Xenophon's Socrates, to be a good estate-manager is part of what it is to be a 'truly good' person (see p. 60). Thus the topic of estate-management occasionally crops up in *Memoirs*: the most important passages are 1.2.64, 1.5.3, 2.1.19, 3.4.7–12, 4.1.2 and

4.5.10. These passages all show that estate-management is a good thing, and that good people are good at it; but 2.1.19 and 4.5.10 also show *why* good people are good at it: they can manage themselves – they have self-discipline. And the pairing of estate-management with State-management (for example, 2.1.19, 4.4.16, 4.5.10) or army-management (3.4.7–12) implies that self-discipline is the foundation of all kinds of external management.[1]

This relationship between self-discipline and estate-management also emerges clearly from *The Estate-manager*. This is achieved partly by implication: Ischomachus demonstrates the discipline of his personal regimen (11.7–20) and we are meant to see what a good manager he is. Mainly, however, the thesis is backed up by argument: Socrates argues that failure at estate-management is due to lack of self-discipline (1.16–23); Ischomachus insists that a prerequisite for positions of managerial responsibility on his estate is self-discipline (9.11, 12.11–14), and that unprofitable farming is due to carelessness (20.2–20).

It is only in the context of *The Estate-manager* as a quasi-philosophical, moral treatise that the eulogy of farming makes full sense. No doubt there are some more prosaic motives behind the praise. Xenophon may have recently taken up farming himself, and have been enthusiastic about it; he may be reflecting the Athenian citizen's proprietorial love of the land; it has even been suggested that he was trying to encourage people to move back to abandoned farms. But it is the moral benefit of farming that is stressed throughout: farming inculcates self-discipline and all the manly virtues (5.4, 5.12–13); it trains people to want to protect their country and to be good at doing so (5.5, 5.7); it teaches men to rule others (5.15–17). These references are all from Socrates'

1. This notion is not alien to Plato: in *Republic* his philosophers are to be induced to govern the city because they have proved themselves capable of self-government (485e), and controlling one's emotions and appetites by reason is precisely analogous to the philosopher members of the State controlling the other classes (427d–444e). Is this analogy between individual control and political control another Socratic principle (see pp. 22–6)?

remarks on farming; Ischomachus' role is to stand as a living model of all that Socrates says.

It should be clear by now that there is a substantial element of Socratic philosophy at work in *The Estate-manager*. The analogy between internal and external management or discipline is extended. At 13.5 Socrates becomes very excited by Ischomachus' claim that he can teach his foremen to wield authority on a farm, since this implies that Ischomachus can teach kingship, regarded by both Xenophon and Plato as the highest form of political constitution (see also *Memoirs*, 4.6.12); and in the final two chapters (20–21) the analogy between wielding authority on an estate and doing the same in an army is developed at some length.[1] The concluding chapter is supposed to be a resounding climax. Xenophon's artistry often falls short of his intentions, but it is clear that conjoined with the theme of estate-management are the philosophical themes of self-discipline and of kingship, which is a constant topic in Greek political theorizing.[2]

What is it, in Xenophon's view, to be a kingly ruler? It is, first and foremost, to have thorough knowledge of the field in which you hope to rule (for example, *Memoirs*, 3.3.9, 3.9.10). Where kingship itself is concerned, the knowledge required is knowledge of how to deal with people: this is a constantly reiterated theme in the descriptions of the Xenophontic 'truly good' man. By displaying this knowledge, the ruler commands obedience from his subordinates (for example, *Socrates' Defence*, 20; *Memoirs*, 4.6.12).[3]

It is a familiar Socratic notion that a person with knowledge

1. See also *Memoirs*, 3.4. It is pointed out on p. 144, n. 1 that, because Xenophon's thoughts on this issue – that all management is in principle the same – are entirely general, he can go astray. However, on the importance and originality of Xenophon's analogy with an army, see N. Wood, 'Xenophon's Theory of Leadership', *Classica et Mediaevalia*, 25 (1964), pp. 33–66.
2. See, for example, T. A. Sinclair, *A History of Greek Political Thought* (Routledge & Kegan Paul, 1951). Xenophon also covers the topic of kingship in *Hieron* and *Cyropaedia*.
3. Drawing on all of Xenophon's works, Wood (op. cit.) elaborately details the characteristics of Xenophon's ideal leader.

ought to be the leader; and Plato's Socrates, like Xenophon's, points out that in most areas of life, at any rate, experts are given authority by others because of their knowledge (for example, *Protagoras*, 319b–c; see also, in later dialogues, *Republic*, 489b–c, *Theaetetus*, 170a–b). We are on fairly safe ground, then, in attributing this idea to the historical Socrates, and we find again that Xenophon is truly reflecting Socratic philosophy.

Xenophon also goes a little further in *The Estate-manager*. There was a current debate, which started in the fifth century, about whether virtue, or any part of it, came from education or natural talent (the debate is reflected elsewhere in Xenophon's work: see pp. 160, 231, 332 and 359). Plato's Socrates is ambivalent about the issue. *Meno*, for instance, is devoted to the question: it concludes that if virtue is knowledge, it is presumably teachable; but there seem to be no teachers of it, so perhaps it is due to divine dispensation after all (compare *Euthydemus*, 282c). There is irony in the comment on the lack of teachers of virtue because there were many who claimed to teach it, but even the main conclusion is hypothetical: *if* virtue is knowledge, then it is teachable.

Xenophon's Socrates is similarly ambivalent. The impression we could have had from the rest of Xenophon's Socratic writings (despite, for example, *Memoirs*, 3.1.6., 3.9.1–3) is that since virtue is knowledge, it is a matter of education. But *The Estate-manager* ends on a less certain note: training *and* natural talent *and* divine dispensation are all required. No one, then, can write a manual on kingship since natural talent is not a skill which can be taught. But since of the three necessary ingredients, only education is within human control, Xenophon rightly stresses that any aspiring leader must ensure that he has knowledge.

I hope to have demonstrated that there is a substantial element of philosophy underlying *The Estate-manager*, as we have also found as regards *Memoirs* and *The Dinner-party*. In short, it contains Xenophon's answer to the question of what type of knowledge is meant in the Socratic equation of virtue and knowledge: it is managerial knowledge, applied to oneself and one's environment. It is interesting to note that Plato too, in

Euthydemus, 291b ff., has Socrates seriously consider the idea that the supreme knowledge, to which everyone ought to aspire, is kingship.

Moving away from the broad level, it is also worth pointing out that *The Estate-manager* contains the most typically subtle Socratic argument (in the Platonic sense of 'Socratic') in the entire volume (1.7 ff.). The argument depends on three cognate words: *chresthai*, *chresimos* and *chremata*. I have translated these respectively as 'make use of', 'useful' and 'assets'. I have chosen to translate *chremata* as 'assets' because the English word can be ambiguous in the same way as the Greek word. On the one hand, my assets are, neutrally, my property; on the other hand, something is an asset to me only if it is useful.

Once this subtlety is appreciated, the argument becomes quite delightful. I shall call 'assets' in the first sense 'property-assets', and in the second sense 'useful assets'. Under Socrates' prodding, Critobulus argues that only beneficial things are assets – that is, useful assets – and that a possession which one does not know how to make use of is therefore not an asset. In fact, says Critobulus, a useless possession only becomes an asset if one sells it.

This is all fair enough – but only if 'assets' means 'useful assets'. The argument is equally capable of being read, however, as concerning property-assets, since these are the original and concluding terms of the argument. From this point of view, we see that Socrates has forced Critobulus into an exquisite paradox: a useless possession only becomes a piece of one's property if one sells it!

The paradox does more than just add a humorous twist. The immediate point of the argument has to do with useful assets: even selling a possession does not convert it into a useful asset unless one knows how to make proper use of money.[1] When later

1. This is a typically Socratic point. In Plato's *Euthydemus* (280b–e), for instance, exactly the same point is made, and it is added that since it is knowledge that enables one to make proper use of things, then knowledge is the only good thing there is.

(2.2 ff.; compare, for example, *Socrates' Defence*, 18) Socrates claims to be rich, even though poor, he is continuing the paradox. The implication is that he is rich because, even though his property-assets are few, they are all useful assets. The same point is made when, later still (3.2–3), tidiness is praised because it converts property-assets into useful assets (Ischomachus also fulsomely praises tidiness in chapter 8). Since the aim of estate-management is to make a profit by correctly managing one's estate, the paradox of useful assets and property-assets is of central importance.

The Estate-manager is not entirely without artistic merit. By the time you have read the conversation with Critobulus, you will have a reasonable picture of Critobulus in your mind; and likewise of Ischomachus and his wife by the time you have reached the end of the book. Nor is Ischomachus as unsympathetic a character as some have said (for example, Rose, quoted on p. 55, n. 1): by our lights, his attitude towards his wife and his slaves is chauvinistic and overbearing; but given that in both regards ancient Greek society allowed the man great licence, it is to Ischomachus' credit that he does not exploit it too much. He is gentle and considerate towards his wife (as well he might be, considering that he is probably twenty years older than her), within the confines of a system in which she could not be his equal; and he rewards his slaves if they deserve it.

So he shows some skill in economical portraiture; and the plainness of his writing admirably reflects the often practical nature of his subject-matter. In fact, considering the dreariness of the topic, it is astonishing how readable and enjoyable the work is. On the debit side, however, is Xenophon's occasional lack of skill with words, which we have noted before.[1] My least

1. Contrast the extravagant praise of H. G. Dakyns ('Xenophon', in E. Abbott (ed.), *Hellenica* (Rivingtons, 1880), pp. 379–80; see also H. G. Dakyns (trans.), *The Works of Xenophon*, vol. 3, part 1 (Macmillan, 1897), p. xlix)): 'It is full of the Xenophontean limpidity, the little bells of alliteration, the graceful antithetic balance; the sweet sounds helping out the healthy sense, as of a fragrant air breathed upon us from fresh and well-worked fields . . .'

favourite sentence in Xenophon's Socratic writings (apart from the rhetorical passages mentioned on p. 8) occurs at 7.9: having asked Ischomachus for an account of how he educated his teenage bride, Socrates says, 'I'd rather hear you describe this than the most spectacular athletic competition or horse-race.' Could there be a more awkward or inappropriate comparison than this?

It is tempting to try to find an artistic awareness in the relationship between the two parts of the book – the dialogue with Critobulus and the dialogue with Ischomachus. It would be artistically pleasing to find that in the first part Socrates enunciates general notions or makes suggestions about estate-management, and that in the second part Ischomachus embodies and confirms these notions, and proves that they do belong to the 'truly good' man. There are certainly some overlapping themes, and, in fact, each part of Socrates' discussion of the elements of estate-management is later echoed by Ischomachus. Socrates says that houses should be practical, not ornamental (3.1); so does Ischomachus (9.2–5). Socrates commends tidiness (3.2–3), and Ischomachus expands on the theme at great length (8.1–9.10). Socrates' elusive comments on the correct management of slaves (3.4) are elaborated by Ischomachus (9.11–13, 12.1–14.10). Socrates' observation that farming can be either profitable or unprofitable (3.5–6) and his reasons for this (1.17–23) are corroborated by Ischomachus (20.2–26). Socrates' remarks on the importance of training a young wife (3.10–15) are borne out by Ischomachus (7.5–10.13).

I think, however, that these echoes can be attributed simply to repetition rather than artistry in the sense of a thematic substructure to a unified work. It is my strong impression that the two parts of *The Estate-manager* were composed at different times (see also p. 7) and then later cobbled together by Xenophon – although it is difficult to prove this conclusively.

The most important factor is that the conversation with Critobulus is obviously part and parcel of *Memoirs*, whereas the conversation with Ischomachus is not, since Socrates is there being taught, rather than doing the teaching. Moreover, there are others present at the conversation with Critobulus (see 3.1, 3.12), which is Socrates' usual environment, as distinct from his solo conversation with Ischomachus. The very beginning of *The Estate-manager* is significant in this regard: Xenophon says, 'I *also* once heard *him* discussing estate-management . . .' The conversation with Critobulus was surely conceived as one of the *Memoirs*; it is not a separate work, as the 'also' and lack of mention of Socrates by name prove. Many chapters of *Memoirs* start in a similarly oblique manner.

We should also consider that if *The Estate-manager* had been conceived and composed as a single piece, Xenophon would have concluded the book by having Socrates say, at the very least, something like, 'And that, Critobulus, was my conversation with Ischomachus.' The whole conversation with Ischomachus is supposed to be related by Socrates to Critobulus, yet the book ends abruptly with Ischomachus still the protagonist.

So my impression is that Xenophon had written the conversation with Critobulus – or perhaps some part of it, since the first chapter, say, could stand on its own – as one of the conversations in *Memoirs* (possibly part of either Book 3 or Book 4, since there is no sign of defence of Socrates in our dialogue – see p. 54), but later wanted to devote a whole work to estate-management and wrote 6.11–12 as a link to stitch in the conversation with Ischomachus.

The dramatic date of the conversation with Critobulus, and therefore of the whole piece in the sense that the conversation with Ischomachus is supposed to be part of Socrates' conversation with Critobulus, is easy to pinpoint. Cyrus the Younger died in 401 (see 4.18), and Socrates died in 399. The Peloponnesian War ended in 404, and there is peace at the time of the conversation (2.6), which must therefore have occurred at some time between 401 and 399.[1] There is one anachronism: Aspasia, mentioned as if alive at 3.14, was probably dead before 401.

1. Note again (see pp. 21, 58) that Xenophon cannot have been present at the conversation, as he claims, since he did not return to Athens after Cyrus' death (see p. 7).

All we can safely say about the dramatic date of the conversation with Ischomachus is that it precedes the conversation with Critobulus, since Socrates recounts it to Critobulus, and that it is again peacetime, since Ischomachus can come and go from Athens as he pleases (11.14–18) – during the war the countryside was invariably ravaged and even occupied by the enemy. There are two possibilities, therefore: the conversation could have taken place either before 431, when the Peloponnesian War began, or between 404, when it ended, and 401, the upper terminus of the conversation with Critobulus.

I would leave the matter there were it not that further discussion will also serve to tell the reader some of what we know about Ischomachus from other sources (see also p. 310, n. 2), as well as introduce a scenario which, especially if relevant, would supply a delightful contrast to Xenophon's portrait of Ischomachus' wife as a model of Greek meek-and-mild feminine virtue.

We find the name 'Ischomachus' in several other authors.[1] The following three mentions are relevant in the present context. Araros, the son of Aristophanes and himself a comic poet, mentions a living Ischomachus in Fragment 16. Araros did not put on any of his own plays until after 375 BC. The second mention is by the orator Lysias (19.46); this speech is most plausibly dated to *c.* 388 and mentions Ischomachus as dead – probably recently.

The third mention gives, or implies, more detail. Andocides, in a court speech (*On the Mysteries*, 124–7, written in 399), tells a wonderfully scurrilous story about Callias. He reports that Callias' second marriage was to a daughter of Ischomachus and his wife Chrysilla. Within a year, however, Andocides claims, Callias had also installed Chrysilla in his home as his mistress. The daughter, after attempting suicide, leaves Callias. Eventually, Callias gets rid of Chrysilla too, but she is already pregnant by him and, after another unspecified length of time, Callias takes

1. For a thorough account, see J. K. Davies, op. cit. (p. 6, n. 2), pp. 264–8.

her back (she is by now described as an old woman) and acknowledges the child, a boy, as his own, although he had previously disowned him.

Now, it was standard practice in Athenian courts to slander one's opponent; but notwithstanding, there are still facts involved which Andocides' audience would have known and he therefore could not have falsified. So, assuming that Chrysilla could not have moved in with Callias unless Ischomachus were dead, what dates can we attach to these facts?

It is the son of Callias and Chrysilla who allows us roughly to date these events. Andocides was the legal guardian of a girl of whom Callias wanted to become guardian. After some manoeuvring, in 400 BC, Callias had entered a claim for guardianship of the girl in the son's name. The son must therefore have been over eighteen years old – a citizen and entitled to guardianship. If we suppose, then, that he was born *c.* 420, then Chrysilla must have moved in with Callias *c.* 422, and Ischomachus must have died some time before that.

Now clearly, if Andocides' story refers to our Ischomachus, and if Chrysilla could not have moved in with Callias unless Ischomachus were dead (rather than their being divorced), then the dramatic date of Socrates' conversation with Ischomachus must be in the peacetime before 431. In fact, even if divorce rather than death were involved, the same dramatic date would still obtain. Chrysilla could be described as old by 410 at the latest, and has a daughter who is of marriageable age by *c.* 423. We can deduce, therefore, that the daughter would have been born *c.* 438 at the latest, and her mother, Chrysilla, *c.* 455 at the latest. If Chrysilla is the wife of our Ischomachus, then they were married *c.* 440, and Ischomachus, who is much older than his wife, was born *c.* 470. At the time of the conversation with Socrates, our Ischomachus is at the prime of life – old enough to have prestige in Athens, but young enough to take vigorous exercise. If the peacetime referred to *follows* the Peloponnesian War, Ischomachus would be getting on for seventy years old and hardly capable of jogging back from his farm to Athens after a hard day

(11.14–18). Besides, he and his wife do not yet have children (7.12).

If Andocides means our Ischomachus, and he divorced Chrysilla rather than dying, then Lysias could be referring to the same person, while Araros must be referring to a different Ischomachus.[1] However, if we prefer the later dramatic date for Socrates' conversation with Ischomachus, after the Peloponnesian War, then Araros is more likely to be referring to our Ischomachus, and Andocides and Lysias are talking about someone else.

It would be a pity if we could not tip the scales in this issue one way or the other. At 6.13–14 Socrates implies that it was not long after he began his quest for true goodness that he introduced himself to Ischomachus. If this quest is synonymous with Socrates' philosophical work (which is not implausible either in itself or by comparison with, for example, Plato, *Apology*, 21b ff.), then Xenophon could not be dating Socrates' meeting with Ischomachus as late as *c.* 403, since Socrates was flourishing philosophically long before that. If this factor tips the scales, then it has the delightful consequence that the scandalous Chrysilla is Ischomachus' wife, and Ischomachus possibly divorced her! This would show just how unreal and idealized Xenophon's portraits of people could be.

When all is said and done, however, probably the only safe conclusion is that Xenophon is writing fiction and is not concerned with accurate historical settings for his work. And we should not let the reality of Chrysilla detract from the charming (and, for us, unique) view Xenophon affords us behind the doors of a Greek household.

The date of composition of *The Estate-manager* is impossible to assess. The best that can be said is that the conversation with Critobulus seems to be of a piece with *Memoirs*, 3 and 4 (see pp. 283–4); but since it is likely that individual chapters of *Memoirs*

1. For further evidence of this other Ischomachus, who died in the 340s, see Davies, loc. cit. (p. 285, n. 1).

were written at differing times (see p. 54), this consideration does not help at all. The subject-matter as a whole – especially the eulogy of farming – is likely to have been inspired by Xenophon's own experiences when he was settled on an estate by the Spartans in 394 (see p. 7): this would have been his first experience of farming; his family's estates in Attica would have been largely inaccessible while he was in Athens, owing to the Peloponnesian War which ended only three years before his departure in 401. But, especially since the characters and scenery of the book are all Athenian, it could even have been written after Xenophon's return to Athens in 365. In short, no precise or even approximate date is feasible.

THE ESTATE-MANAGER

I once heard him discussing estate-management as follows. 'Tell me, Critobulus,' he asked, 'is estate-management the name of a branch of knowledge, like medicine, metalwork and carpentry?'

'I think so,' said Critobulus.

'You know how we can attribute a function to each of those skills? Can we do the same for estate-management?'

'Well, I think that a good estate-manager is one who manages his own estate well,' said Critobulus.

'What about if he were entrusted with someone else's estate?' asked Socrates. 'Wouldn't he be able to manage it as well as he does his own, if he chose to? I mean, an expert carpenter could do for someone else just as good a job as he does for himself; and the same goes for an estate-manager, I imagine.'

'I think you're right, Socrates.'

'So,' said Socrates, 'is it possible for an expert at this skill, even if he happens to have no property himself, to earn a salary by managing someone else's estate, just as he could by building him a house?'

'Yes, indeed,' said Critobulus. 'He could earn a great deal of money, if he were able to take over an estate, pay all necessary expenses and increase the estate by providing a surplus.'

'So what do we think an estate is? The same as a house? Or is it the case that all possessions outside the house are also part of an estate?'

'Well,' said Critobulus, 'I think that *all* someone's possessions, even if he has them in different cities, are part of his estate.'

'Now, some people have acquired enemies, haven't they?'

'Certainly, lots of them in some cases.'

'Shall we include enemies among their possessions?'

'But it would be absurd,' said Critobulus, 'to pay someone wages for increasing the number of one's enemies!'

'Wait, though – we decided that a person's estate was the same as his property.'

'Yes, indeed,' said Critobulus, 'it is any *good* thing he possesses. But I most certainly do not include bad possessions among his property.'

'You're apparently describing as his "property" whatever is useful to an individual.'

'Quite so. I count harmful things as liabilities rather than as assets.'

'So suppose someone buys a horse, but doesn't know how to make use of it, and falls off and is injured – then the horse isn't an asset?'

'No, it isn't, if assets are good.'

'So a person's land isn't an asset either, if his working it results in a loss.'

'No, not even his land is really an asset, if it promotes hunger instead of nourishment.'

'And the same goes for his flocks too: if someone incurs a loss through ignorance of how to make use of flocks, then his flocks wouldn't be assets either, would they?'

'Not in my opinion, anyway.'

'In short, you reckon (or so it seems) that whatever is beneficial is an asset, and whatever is harmful is not.'

'Just so.'

'It follows that the same things are assets if one knows how to make use of them, and are not assets if one doesn't. For instance, pipes are assets in the hands of someone who knows how to play them adequately, but someone who doesn't might as well have useless stones.'

'Unless he sells them.'[1]

1. I follow Thalheim in attributing this to Critobulus, rather than treating it as a subordinate clause in Socrates' previous speech.

'So our impression is that, for those who don't know how to make use of them, pipes are assets if they sell them, but are not assets if they don't sell them but hang on to them.'

'Yes, Socrates, and the stages of our argument are perfectly consistent, based on the premiss that beneficial things are assets. Unsold pipes are not assets, because they are useless; sold pipes are assets.'

Socrates' response was as follows: 'Yes, *if* the seller knows how to sell. But if he sells the pipes for something else which he doesn't know how to make use of, then it follows from your argument that pipes are not assets even if they're sold.'

'You seem to be implying, Socrates, that not even money is an asset, unless one knows how to make use of it.'

'Yes, but you too agree that assets are things which can benefit a person. At any rate, if the use that someone makes of his money is, for example, to buy a concubine and consequently to damage his body, mind and estate, then how can his money benefit him?'

'It cannot – unless we are going to claim that even the plant called henbane, which makes you mad if you eat it, is an asset.'

'So if one doesn't know how to make use of it, Critobulus, then money must be kept at such a distance that it isn't even included among one's assets. Now, what about friends: if one knows how to make use of them, so as to derive benefit from them, then how should they be described?'

'Most emphatically as assets,' said Critobulus. 'They deserve the description far more than cattle, provided they are more beneficial than cattle.'

'So it follows from your argument that enemies too are assets for someone who is capable of deriving benefit from them.'

'I agree.'

'Therefore, it is the job of a good estate-manager to know how to make use of enemies too in such a way that benefit is derived from them.'

'Indubitably.'

'All right. Now, you can see, Critobulus, how many estates

belonging to private individuals, and those of despots too, have been increased as a result of war.'

'I'm happy with some of what you're saying, Socrates,' said Critobulus, 'but what about the fact that we come across people who have the relevant branches of knowledge, the resources to work their estates and the ability to increase them, but who, as we can recognize, are not prepared to do it and hence derive no benefit from their knowledge? What do we make of them? Aren't we bound to say that in their case neither their expertise nor their property is an asset?'

'Are you trying to raise the topic of slaves with me, Critobulus?' asked Socrates.

'No, not at all,' he replied. 'I'm talking about people, some of whom, at least, are regarded as definitely well born, and who I can see are experts in war and peace, but are not willing to do anything with their expertise; and the reason, in my opinion, is precisely that they have *no* masters set over them.'

'Of course they have masters,' said Socrates. 'After all, they pray for happiness and want to do things from which they might derive good, but are prevented from doing these things by their rulers.'

'And who are these invisible rulers?' asked Critobulus.

'They're not invisible at all,' said Socrates. 'They are exceedingly conspicuous. And even you must see that they are the worst kind of rulers, if you regard laziness and mental flabbiness and irresponsibility as bad. There are others too – mistresses and deceitful with it – who pretend that they are pleasures, such as gambling and pointless parties; as time goes on, it becomes clear even to the victims of their seduction that they are afflictions disguised as pleasures, and that their rulership prohibits beneficial activity.'

'But there are other people, Socrates, who do not have these masters to prevent them from working, but who in fact are very enthusiastic about work and about arranging incomes for themselves; nevertheless, they squander their estates and are surrounded by difficulties.'

'These people are slaves too,' said Socrates, 'with very harsh masters set over them; some are ruled by gluttony, some by sex, some by drink, some by stupid and costly ambitions. These are such harsh rulers of the people they govern that, as long as they see them flourishing and capable of work, they force them to take the fruits of their labours and spend them on their own desires; and when they see that old age has made them incapable of work, they abandon them to wretched senility, and try to enslave others instead. No, it is just as crucial to fight for one's freedom against these opponents, Critobulus, as it is to fight against those who try to enslave you by force of arms. In fact, when people are enslaved by enemies who are truly good, they are often forced by their masters' reprimands to become better and to live the rest of their lives with fewer constraints. But mistresses like the ones I mentioned never stop preying on people's bodies and minds and estates as long as they rule them.'

2

Next, Critobulus spoke somewhat as follows: 'I don't think you need tell me any more about them: when I examine myself, I think I find that my control over them is adequate. So if you were to advise me how to increase my estate, I don't think it would be these mistresses, as you call them, who would prevent me from doing it. So don't hesitate to give me all the good advice you have. Or have you decided, Socrates, that we are rich enough and don't need further assets?'

'If you're including me,' said Socrates, 'no, I don't think I need any further assets: I'm rich enough. But I think that you are very hard up, Critobulus, and indeed there are times when I feel very sorry for you.'[1]

Critobulus said with a smile, 'In all honesty, Socrates, how much do you think the sale of your property would fetch compared with mine?'

1. See *The Dinner-party*, 4.29–33 (p. 245).

'I think,' said Socrates, 'that if I were lucky in the buyer I found, all my property, including my house, would quite easily fetch five minae;[1] yours, however, I'm absolutely certain, would fetch more than a hundred times that.'

'And although you realize this, do you still think *you* need no further assets, and feel sorry for *my* poverty?'

'Well, you see, my property is enough to supply me with all my needs; but you cut such a dash and have such a reputation that I don't think you'd have enough even if you had three times more than what you possess now.'

'What do you mean?' asked Critobulus.

Socrates explained: 'In the first place, I see that you are obliged to offer many large sacrifices to the gods; otherwise, I think, both gods and men would object. Next, it is incumbent on you often to entertain visitors from abroad, and to do so generously. What is more, you have to invite your fellow citizens to dinners and do them favours; otherwise, you'd lose your supporters. Furthermore, I notice that the State is already requiring great expenditure from you on things like horse-rearing, financing choruses and athletic competitions, and on administration; and if there should be a war, I'm sure that they will require you to finance triremes and will make you pay an almost unbearable amount of tax.[2] And if you give the impression of not doing enough in any of these areas, I have no doubt that the Athenians will retaliate as severely as if they had caught you stealing from them. In addition, I see that you think you are rich, and you don't bother about arranging an income; instead, you give your attention to childish pursuits, as if they were all you had to do. These are the reasons why I feel sorry for you and am worried in case you are ruined. Now, if *I* needed something, you know as well as I do that there are people who would help me out and whose contributions would not have to be at all large to overwhelm me with more than I need to live.

1. Not much: about the equivalent of a low annual income.
2. There was no regular system of taxation in Athens, except in wartime; but the rich were expected to undertake the sorts of things Socrates mentions. See also p. 143, n. 2.

Your friends, however, although they have enough for their own situations and are therefore far better off than you, since you do not have enough, still look to you for your help.'

'I can't say you're wrong in all this, Socrates,' said Critobulus. 'But now is the time for you to take charge of me and make sure that I don't become really pitiable.'

In response, Socrates asked, 'Don't you think you're behaving strangely? Not long ago, when I claimed to be rich, you laughed at me for my ignorance of what wealth is, and you wouldn't let go until you'd argued me down and forced me to admit that my property is not even a hundredth of yours; but now you are telling me to take charge of you and to make sure that you don't really become utterly impoverished.'

'That, Socrates,' he said, 'is because I see that you know how to create a surplus, which is one of the activities that bring in money. So I look forward to someone who can create a surplus from meagre resources having little difficulty in creating a substantial surplus from substantial resources.'

'Don't you remember that point earlier in the discussion – it was when you weren't letting me get a word in edgeways, and you said that horses are not assets for someone who doesn't know how to make use of horses, and likewise for land, flocks, money and anything else whatsoever which someone doesn't know how to make use of? Now, it is things like these from which income is derived, so how do you imagine that I know how to make use of any of them, when I've never had any of them in the first place?'

'But our opinion was that there is a science of estate-management, which is not dependent on whether or not someone happens to have assets; so there's nothing to stop you having this branch of knowledge, is there?'

'Yes, there certainly is – the same thing which would stop a person knowing how to play the pipes, if he himself had never owned pipes or been lent someone else's with which to learn. That's exactly my situation as regards estate-management. I have not had the chance to learn from having owned the instrument myself – the instrument in this case being assets – nor has anyone else ever lent me his own assets to practise on, until your offer just now. But as you know, complete beginners at playing the lyre tend to ruin their lyres; so if I tried to learn estate-management on your estate, the chances are that I would ruin it.'[1]

'Socrates,' Critobulus replied, 'you're trying hard to avoid lending me a helping hand; there are burdens I must bear, and you are not prepared to make them any easier for me.'

'You completely misunderstand me,' protested Socrates. 'I'll do my very best to explain to you anything I can. But I think that if you had come for fire and I didn't have any to hand, and I directed you somewhere else, where you could get it, you wouldn't have criticized me; and if you were asking me for water, and I didn't have any, but I took you elsewhere for it, I'm sure that you wouldn't have criticized me for that; and if you wanted to learn music from me and I pointed you to people who were far better than me at music and who would thank you for coming to learn from them, then would you still find fault with my conduct?'

'That wouldn't be fair at all, Socrates.'

'Well, Critobulus, I'll point you in the direction of other people who are far better than me at the matters which you are currently so keen to learn from me. I admit that I have looked into the question of who in Athens are the greatest experts at things. You see, I once noticed that some people get very poor, others very rich, as a result of the same activities; I was surprised, and I thought it worth investigating why this should be so. My investigations led me to the conclusion that this occurs quite naturally: I saw that those who act casually incur losses, while those who work hard and apply themselves act more quickly, more easily and more profitably. Now, suppose you learn from the latter people, if you want; then, in my opinion, provided God does not oppose you, you would become a very good businessman.'

1. The point that actual experience is needed to make one expert in anything like this is valid, of course, but it is effectively ignored in the rest of the dialogue: Socrates tells Critobulus that he can learn by being taught by experts, and then recounts the instruction he himself received from one such expert.

3

In response, Critobulus said, 'Now look, I'm not going to let you go, Socrates, until you have demonstrated what you promised to demonstrate in front of our friends here.'[1]

'Well then, Critobulus,' said Socrates, 'what if I demonstrate that, in the first place, some people spend a lot of money on building useless houses, whereas others spend far less and build perfectly adequate houses? If I do this, will I, in your opinion, be demonstrating that this is one of the things that fall within the domain of estate-management?'

'Certainly,' said Critobulus.

'What if I next demonstrate to you the corollary of this? That some people own a great many possessions of all sorts, are unable to make use of them when they need to, don't even know whether they are safe and sound, and hence cause themselves, and their servants, a great deal of irritation. On the other hand, those who have not more but fewer possessions have them immediately available and are able to make use of the ones they need.'

'Isn't the reason for this, Socrates, that the first lot of people drop their things here, there and everywhere, whereas the others keep everything arranged and in place?'

'Yes, of course,' said Socrates, 'and everything is arranged in the proper placc, not at random.'

'I suppose you're implying,' said Critobulus, 'that this too falls within the domain of estate-management.'

'What if I further demonstrate to you that in some cases all the slaves are kept in chains, as it were – and these are the ones who constantly run away – whereas in others they are free and happy both to work and to stay? Will you think that I am demonstrating something remarkable, which also falls within the domain of estate-management?'

'Yes, I most certainly will,' said Critobulus, 'very much so.'

'And what about people who work almost identical farms, some of whom complain that they are being ruined by farming,

1. There are assumed to be others present at this discussion.

and cannot make a living, while others gain from their farms everything they need, both in quantity and quality?'

'Yes indeed,' said Critobulus. 'I mean, presumably there are people who spend money not only on necessities, but also on things which are bad for themselves and for their estates.'

'There probably are people like that,' said Socrates, 'but I'm not talking about them. I'm referring to people who don't have money to spend even on necessities, despite claiming to be farmers.'

'Why would this happen, Socrates?'

'I'll take you to meet them too,' said Socrates, 'and when you observe them, you'll understand the reasons, I'm sure.'

'I certainly will, if I can,' he said.

'Well, you must observe them, and then you'll discover by experience whether you find it comprehensible. I'm well aware of your current practice: when there's a comedy to be seen, you get up very early in the morning and walk a very long way, and try hard to persuade me to come and watch it with you; but you've never invited me to any production like the one I've mentioned.'

'So you think me ridiculous, Socrates.'

'Far less than you do yourself, surely,' he said. 'And what if I demonstrate to you that stud-farming has led some people to indigence, but others to considerable prosperity and the ability to revel in their gains?'[1]

'Well, I've seen both types – I know them well – but I am still just as far from joining the profit-makers.'

'That's because you watch them as you watch tragic and comic actors, which you do not do with a view to becoming a playwright, I imagine, but to enjoy what you see or hear. That's how it should be, I suppose, since you don't want to become a playwright; but since you are forced to be involved with stud-farming, don't you think it would be stupid not to ensure that you tackle the business professionally, bearing in mind especially

1. Horse-farming was very rare in Attica: sheep and goats were more usual livestock.

that where horses are concerned, those whose use brings advantage are also those whose sale brings profit?'[1]

'Are you suggesting that I break in horses when they're young, Socrates?'

'No, of course not – no more than I would suggest that you buy farm-hands and train them from childhood; but I think that there are times in the lives of both horses and people when immediate use can be made of them *and* they can go on improving.[2] Next, I can demonstrate that some people treat their wives in such a way that they gain their cooperation in the job of increasing their estates, but others treat their wives in a way guaranteed to maximize the destitution of their estates.'

'And should one attribute this to the husband or the wife, Socrates?'

'If a sheep is in a bad way,' replied Socrates, 'we usually blame the shepherd; if a horse's behaviour is unruly, we blame the trainer. As for a wife, if she has faults even though her husband has tried to teach her virtue, then it would probably be fair to blame the wife; but if he doesn't teach her what is truly good and then finds her ignorant of it, wouldn't it be fair to blame the husband? Now, we're all friends here, Critobulus, so you must be absolutely honest with us. Don't you entrust more of your affairs to your wife than to anyone else?'

'Yes,' he replied.

'And is there anyone to whom you speak less than you do to your wife?'

'There aren't many, if any.'

'Didn't you marry her when she was very young indeed and had had the least possible experience of the world?'[3]

1. Compare pp. 290–91 on making use of things and profit. The 'usefulness' of a horse lies in its manageability: this is clearer in the Greek than the English, and introduces Critobulus' next question.
2. In other words, Critobulus is to do with horses exactly what Ischomachus later recommends for farms (pp. 355–6): buy them (not necessarily when young), improve them and resell them.
3. Brides were often in their mid-teens, even if the man was considerably older.

'Yes, she was very young.'

'So it would be far more remarkable for her to know how to speak or behave properly than for her to make mistakes.'

'But what about the people you mention who have good wives, Socrates? Did they educate them by themselves?'

'There's nothing like inquiry. I'll get you to meet Aspasia,[1] and she'll give you a far more knowledgeable account of all this than I can. My opinion is that when a wife is a good partner in the house, her contribution is just as beneficial as the husband's. For the entry of wealth into the house is generally due to the husband's activities, but expenditure is generally due to the wife's housekeeping: if both of these jobs are done well, households flourish; but if they are done badly, households suffer. And if you feel a need to know about any other branch of knowledge, I think that I can direct you to someone who does an admirable job in it.'

4

'But do you need to do this for every branch of knowledge, Socrates?' asked Critobulus. 'I mean, it isn't easy to get hold of proper craftsmen of every craft, nor is it possible to become expert at them oneself.[2] So why don't you concentrate on the branches of knowledge which you think finest and to which I particularly ought to apply myself? Show me which they are and who works at them, and help me yourself by explaining whatever you can about these matters.'

'You're right, Critobulus. I mean, the manual crafts, as they are called, have a bad name[3] and are not rated at all highly in our countries. There are good reasons for this. You see, those who work at them and apply themselves to them are forced to be sedentary and spend their time out of the sunlight, and sometimes even to spend their days by the heat of a fire.[4] As a result their

1. See p. 126, n. 1.
2. Reading αὐτῶν αὐτόν.
3. Contempt for manual labour was common among upper-class Greeks.
4. In fact, it is not impossible that the Greek word translated here as 'manual' is derived from a word for 'forge', though Xenophon is not playing with any such etymology here.

bodies are ruined, and this physical debilitation is accompanied by considerable weakening of their minds too. These so-called manual crafts give people no time to bother with friends or country, and consequently their practitioners are thought to be bad at dealing with friends and at defending their countries. In fact, it is a rule in some countries, and especially those with a reputation for military prowess, that only non-citizens can work at manual crafts.'[1]

'So which crafts do you think we ought to be involved with, Socrates?'

'Could we possibly be ashamed if the king of Persia was our model? I mean they say that he regards agriculture and the art of war to be among the finest and most essential pursuits, and applies himself thoroughly to them both.'

In response to this, Critobulus said, 'Do you trust this report, Socrates? Do you believe that the king of Persia makes any place at all among his occupations for agriculture?'

'Perhaps we'll find out if he does, Critobulus,' said Socrates, 'if we look at it this way. We agree that he pays close attention to military matters, because he has ordered the leaders of every nation which pays him tribute to maintain a quota of cavalry, archers, slingers and wicker-shield bearers[2] for the purpose of controlling his subjects and defending the country in the event of a hostile invasion; and apart from these troops, he maintains garrisons in the city keeps. There is an official who has been given the job of maintaining the garrisons, and every year the king organizes a review of the troops, both those who receive pay and those who are otherwise instructed to bear arms; all the troops, except for those in the city keeps, are assembled at appointed places of muster. He personally inspects those who are stationed near his residence, and he sends trusted officers to inspect those who are stationed far away. Those commanders of garrisons or districts or provinces[3] who turn out with the full quota and have

1. Sparta is the country Xenophon has in mind.
2. Light-armed Persian infantry used a distinctive wicker shield.
3. A province commander is perhaps better known as a 'satrap'.

their men equipped with good-quality horses and weapons are promoted by him and enriched with generous gifts; but those commanders who are found to be neglecting their commands or making a profit out of them are severely punished by him and others are appointed to their posts. So, we reckon that these actions of his show beyond the shadow of a doubt that he applies himself to military matters.

'Moreover, he personally assesses as much of his land as he sees when he passes through it; and however much he doesn't see himself, he sends trusted men to inspect. And those rulers who are able to show him a populous domain and land which is being worked and has plenty of the local trees and crops – to these he assigns extra land, and he enriches them with gifts and rewards them with official posts; but those whose land he finds unworked and sparsely populated because of their strictness or oppression or neglect are punished by him and deprived of their command, and others are appointed to their posts. Do we reckon that these actions of his show that he pays less attention to ensuring that his land is worked by its inhabitants than to ensuring that it is well protected by its garrisons?

'He has also arranged for there to be distinct officers for each of the two spheres: some govern the inhabitants and labourers, and collect tribute from them; others command the soldiers and garrisons. If the commander of a garrison fails to protect the land well enough, then the person who governs the inhabitants and oversees their labour informs against the commander, on the grounds that the inhabitants are unable to work the land because it is undefended; on the other hand, if the garrison commander is making sure that no warfare interrupts the labour, but the governor is still causing the land to be sparsely populated and unworked, then the garrison commander informs against *him*. This makes sense because, by and large, badly worked land cannot maintain garrisons or pay tribute. Wherever a province commander is appointed, however, both these jobs are in his hands.'

At this point Critobulus said, 'Well, if the king of Persia does all this, Socrates, then I don't think that he pays less attention to agricultural matters than to military matters.'

'But that's not all,' said Socrates. 'He ensures that not only all the places where he has residences, but also all the places he travels to, have parks, which are called *paradeisoi*,[1] filled with all the truly good produce of the earth; he himself spends as much time as possible in these parks, except when the weather prevents him.'

'Well, Socrates,' said Critobulus, 'of course he ensures that these *paradeisoi*, where he himself spends time, are made as beautiful as possible with trees and all the other beautiful things the earth produces.'

'And, Critobulus,' said Socrates, 'some say that when the king is handing out rewards, the first to be summoned are those who have excelled in war, on the grounds that plenty of land ready for crops is no use at all unless there are people to defend it; then the next to be summoned are those who have done particularly well at cultivating their lands and making them productive, the given reason being that even the defenders would be unable to live without people to work the land. In fact, Cyrus, who was the most renowned member of the Persian royal family,[2] is said to have once told the people he'd summoned for rewards that it would be fair if he himself received the rewards for both activities, since he was pre-eminent both at cultivating the land and at defending it when it had been cultivated.'

'Well,' said Critobulus, 'if Cyrus said that, then he prided himself just as much on making the land productive and cultivating it as on his skill at warfare.'

'Yes, he certainly did,' said Socrates. 'And if Cyrus had lived, he would probably have been an excellent ruler. There's plenty of evidence to suggest it, but especially significant is the fact that,

1. A Hellenization of the Avestan word *pairi-daeza* ('walled garden') and the origin of the English word 'paradise'.
2. Not Cyrus the Great (who ruled from 559 to 529), the subject of Xenophon's eulogistic *Cyropaedia*, but Cyrus the Younger, whose ill-fated campaign against his brother, King Artaxerxes, in 401, is described in Xenophon's *Anabasis*; Xenophon himself was a mercenary on this campaign.

during the course of his expedition against his brother, to fight him for the throne, not a single man is said to have deserted from Cyrus to the king, whereas thousands upon thousands deserted from the king to Cyrus. I count it as highly indicative of good leadership when people obey someone without coercion[1] and are prepared to remain by him during times of danger. While Cyrus was alive, his friends fought next to him; and when he was killed, they all died with him, fighting around his corpse – all except Ariaeus, that is, who, as it happened, was positioned on the left wing.[2]

'While we're on the subject of Cyrus, there's a story (which Lysander himself once told someone he visited in Megara) that, when Lysander[3] came to him, bringing gifts from his allies, Cyrus acted kindly towards him in many ways, but especially by showing him the *paradeisos* in Sardis. When Lysander marvelled at how beautiful the trees were, how regularly they had been planted, how straight the rows were, how all their angles made for beauty, and how, as they walked around, they frequently came across pleasant scents, he expressed his admiration by saying, "I find the beauty of all this quite astonishing, Cyrus, but I am far more in awe of whoever measured and arranged everything for you."

'Cyrus was delighted at this and said, "Well, Lysander, it was I who did all the measuring and arranging, and I even planted some of the trees myself."

'Lysander looked at him, saw the fineness of the clothing he was wearing, smelled his perfumes, noticed the fineness of the necklaces and bangles and the rest of the jewellery he had on, and said, "What do you mean, Cyrus? Did you really do some of this planting with your own hands?"

'"Does that surprise you, Lysander?" Cyrus replied. "I swear

1. See *Memoirs*, 3.3.9 (p. 141).
2. According to *Anabasis*, 1.9.31 (which is verbally echoed in our passage), Ariaeus fled when he saw Cyrus fall.
3. The Spartan military leader at the end of the Peloponnesian War; he enlisted Persian aid to help Sparta finally defeat Athens. The episode which follows probably took place in 407 BC (*Hellenica*, 1.5.1 ff.).

to you by Mithras that, my health permitting, I never ate without having first worked up a sweat by undertaking some activity relevant either to the art of war or to agriculture, or by stretching myself in some way or other."

'Lysander's own report is that when he heard this, he applauded Cyrus and said, "You deserve your good fortune, Cyrus: you have it because you are a good man."

5

'I am telling you this, Critobulus,' said Socrates, 'because even those who are very well off cannot distance themselves from agriculture. You see, it is plausible to claim that the practice of agriculture is simultaneously a source of pleasant living, of increasing one's estate, and of training the body for being able to do everything a free man ought to be able to do. In the first place, thanks to those who work it, the land bears not only the means for people to live, but also bears the means for them to live pleasantly; in the second place, it provides all the things people use to decorate their altars and their votive offerings, and all the things with which they decorate themselves – and the land does not merely provide these things, but also causes them to have the most pleasant scents and appearances; in the third place, it grows many savouries,[1] and feeds others (since livestock-breeding goes hand in hand with land-cultivation), and results in people both being able to please the gods by offering sacrifices and having stock for their own disposal.

'The land provides the greatest abundance of good things, but doesn't allow them to be taken without effort. It trains people to endure the cold of winter and the heat of summer. It exercises and strengthens smallholders who work it with their hands. It makes men of those who cultivate it diligently, by having them wake early and making them exert themselves as they go about their business. For on estates as well as in cities, the most vital jobs are always urgent.

1. See p. 175, n. 1.

'Moreover, if one wants to help one's country by serving in the cavalry, agriculture, more than anything else, is capable of contributing towards maintaining one's own horse; if one is in the infantry, agriculture makes one's body vigorous. And the land goes some way towards stimulating an interest in the effort that hunting requires,[1] since it makes it easy to maintain a pack of hounds and at the same time nourishes wild animals. And while both horses and hounds are benefited by agriculture, they in turn benefit the estate – the horse by carrying the manager early in the morning to his job and by giving him the opportunity to leave it late, the hounds by keeping wild animals from damaging crops and flocks, and by reducing the risks of living in isolation.

'The land also plays a part in encouraging farmers to take up arms to assist their country, because its crops grow out in the open for the victor to take. What area of expertise produces better runners, throwers and jumpers than agriculture? What area of expertise offers more rewards to its practitioners? What area of expertise admits an acolyte more gratifyingly, freely allowing anyone who approaches to take what he needs? What admits strangers more generously? Where else than on an estate is it more feasible to pass the winter with no shortage of fire and with warm baths? Where else than in the country with its water, breezes and shade, is it more pleasant to spend the summer? What other area of expertise supplies the gods with more appropriate first-fruits or gives rise to more popular festivals? What is more congenial to one's servants, or gratifying to one's wife, or welcome to one's children, or agreeable to one's friends? I think it highly unlikely that any free man has ever acquired any possession more gratifying than this, or discovered a more pleasant pursuit, or one which enhances his livelihood more.

'Furthermore, the land also freely teaches justice to those who are capable of learning; for it does people favours in proportion to how well they serve it. So if people involved in agriculture – with

1. This may seem out of place, but for Xenophon on the moral and military benefits of hunting, see his *Cynegeticus*.

its vigorous and manly training – are ever forced away from their work by a massed army, they are well equipped in body and mind, if God should not oppose them, for being able to invade their opponents' territory and take provisions. It is not uncommon in war for it to be safer to take weapons rather than farming implements on a foraging expedition.

'Agriculture also contributes towards training people in co-operation. Going against hostile forces requires more than one person; so does working the land. Someone who wants to become a good farmer, then, must ensure that his labourers are both keen and obedient; someone who is going to lead an expedition against hostile forces must arrange for the same results, by rewarding those who act in a manner appropriate to good soldiers and by punishing those who lack discipline.[1] It is often just as important for a farmer to encourage his labourers as it is for a general to encourage his troops. And slaves need good prospects for the future just as much as free men – or even more – to make them prepared to stay put.

'Whoever it was who said that agriculture is the mother and nurse of all other arts was right, because when agriculture is faring well, all the other arts are strengthened too; but wherever the land is forced into barrenness, all the other arts, whether based on land or sea, are more or less smothered.'

In response to this speech, Critobulus said, 'You're quite right in this, Socrates, I think. But it is beyond human ability to foresee the majority of factors relevant to agriculture. I mean, hailstorms and occasional frosts, droughts, sudden rainstorms, crop-diseases – all these and other factors often undo well-planned and well-executed work. And even the most well-bred flocks are sometimes utterly ruined by the occurrence of disease.'

'Critobulus,' Socrates replied, 'I thought you knew that the gods have just as much control over agricultural matters as they do over warfare. I imagine you are aware that people engaged in war propitiate the gods and use sacrificial victims and omens to

1. See *Memoirs*, 3.4.8 (p. 144); and pp. 335–6 on Ischomachus' treatment of slaves.

inquire what they ought and ought not to do before they embark on hostilities. Do you think it is any less necessary to ask the gods for mercy where agricultural affairs are concerned? Sensible farmers, I can assure you, worship and pray to the gods about their fruits, grain, cattle, horses, sheep – yes, and all their property.'

6

'Well, Socrates, I think you're right to tell me to try to bring the gods in at the start of any business, since the gods have authority over affairs conducted in peacetime just as much as they do over affairs in times of war. And that's what we will try to do. But could you return to where you broke off from the discussion of estate-management and try to explain the relevant issues? I mean, even from what you've said so far, I think I now have a clearer insight than before into what I must do to make a living.'

'All right,' said Socrates. 'So why don't we start by running through all the agreed points in our discussion, with a view to trying also to reach the same unanimity, if we can, as we go through the points which remain?'

'Yes, let's,' said Critobulus. 'It's nice when business partners don't fall out in their dealings; it is equally nice for us, who are partners in conversation, to agree on topics as we deal with them.'

'Well then,' said Socrates, 'we agreed that "estate-management" is the name of a branch of knowledge; that it is this knowledge which enables people to increase their estates; that an "estate" is the same as the sum of one's property; that "property" is whatever is beneficial in a person's life; and that beneficial things are those which one knows how to make use of. Now, we agreed that it is impossible to master all branches of knowledge, and we concur with our countries in rejecting the so-called manual crafts, because they seem to ruin people's bodies and soften their minds. We said[1] that the clearest evidence of this would be if, on the

1. Not in our text (see pp. 300–301); however, it is perhaps implicit in the argument that farmers would defend the land (pp. 306–7).

occasion of a hostile invasion of the country, one were to divide the farmers and the craftsmen into separate groups, sit them both down, and ask them to decide whether to defend the country or to give up the land and guard the fortified towns. We reckoned that in this situation those involved with the land would vote for defending it, while the craftsmen would vote for not fighting, but for sitting tight without effort or risk, as they have been conditioned to do. We judged that agriculture is the best work and the best branch of knowledge for a truly good person, because it supplies people with the necessities of life. We decided that it is the easiest work to learn and the most gratifying to do; that it makes people physically as attractive and fit as possible; and that it affords their minds the maximum possible opportunity for giving attention to their friends and countries. We agreed that agriculture also contributes towards promoting toughness in the people who work at it, since the crops that it grows and the livestock that it tends are situated outside the town fortifications. These are the reasons, we decided, why this means of making a living is held in the highest esteem by States, because it apparently turns out ideal citizens, who are extremely loyal towards the community.'

'Socrates,' said Critobulus, 'I certainly think I am sufficiently convinced that agriculture provides the finest, best and pleasantest life. But you said[1] that you understood the reasons why some farm in such a way that their farming gains them all they need and more, while the result of others' labour is that their farming fails to make a profit. I'm sure I'd be glad to hear what you have to say about these two cases, so that our activities are advantageous rather than detrimental.'

'All right, Critobulus,' said Socrates. 'What if I tell you from start to finish about an encounter I once had with someone who, in my opinion, really was one of those people who deserve to be called "truly good"?'

'I'd certainly like to hear about it,' said Critobulus, 'since I'd love to earn that description myself.'

1. See p. 296.

'I'll tell you, then,' said Socrates, 'how I came to be interested in him. It didn't take me at all long to visit our builders, smiths, painters, sculptors and so on, and see those products of theirs which are reckoned to be fine. But I had a passionate longing to meet one of those people who have this awesome designation of being "truly good"; I wanted to find out what they produced to make them deserve the name. Now, because "fine" is added to "good",[1] my starting-point was that whenever I noticed someone fine, I approached him and tried to discover whether I could observe goodness attached to his fineness. This was not the case, however. Instead, I discovered that, in my opinion, some people with fine exteriors have very obnoxious minds. I decided, therefore, to ignore what was fine to look at, and to visit someone who was called "truly good". So when I heard Ischomachus being called "truly good" by everyone – men and women, foreigners and Athenians – I decided to try to meet him.[2]

7

'Some time later, I saw him sitting in the portico of the temple of Zeus Eleutherios; he didn't seem busy, so I went and sat next to him and said, "What are you doing sitting here, Ischomachus? You're usually busy. I generally see you in the agora, either busy about something or at any rate not really with time on your hands."

1. The phrase translated here and throughout this book as 'truly good' is *kalos kagathos* – literally 'fine and good' (see also p. 159). The word 'fine' covers a vast range of commendable attributes (see p. 252, n. 2), but here Socrates chooses external good looks, on the common Greek assumption that a good exterior is a good interior shining through. The phrase 'fine and good' or 'truly good' is vague, but represents Xenophon's moral ideal: see pp. 59–62.
2. That Ischomachus was a historical person is attested by his being mentioned in other contemporary authors (more than one Ischomachus may be involved, however: see pp. 285–7). The orator Lysias reports (19.46) that while at one time Ischomachus was worth seventy talents, he only managed to leave twenty to his sons when he died; and the comic playwright Cratinus (Fragment 328, *c.* 425 BC), no doubt with the usual comic exaggeration, makes Ischomachus out to be stingy. In view of this, some of Xenophon's idealized portrait might seem misguided.

'"You wouldn't have seen me now, Socrates," said Ischomachus, "if I hadn't arranged to wait here for some people from out of town."

'"I'd be very grateful if you could tell me something," I said. "When you're not engaged like this, where do you spend your time, and what do you do? You see, I want very much to find out from you what activities have gained you the reputation of being truly good. For, as I can also tell from looking at your physical condition, you don't spend time indoors."

'Ischomachus smiled at my question as to what he did to have gained the reputation of being truly good (I got the impression that he was pleased), and said, "I don't know whether people call me that when they're talking to you about me. When I am summoned to an exchange of property, where the issue is financing a trireme or a chorus,[1] no one goes looking for 'Truly Good', but the summons calls me plain 'Ischomachus', the name my father gave me! Anyway, Socrates," he went on, "to answer your question, I don't spend any time at all indoors: my wife is perfectly capable of managing my household affairs by herself."

'"I've got a question on this too, Ischomachus," I said. "I'd be very glad if you could tell me whether you personally taught your wife how to be a model wife, or whether, when you were given her by her parents, she already knew how to manage her sphere of responsibility."[2]

'"How on earth could she know that when I received her, Socrates?" he asked. "She wasn't yet fifteen years old when she came to me, and in her life up till then considerable care had been taken that she should see and hear and discover as little as possible. Don't you think one should be content if all she knew when she came was how to turn wool into a cloak, and all she'd seen was

1. See p. 294, n. 2, on financing choruses etc. When someone was called upon by the State to perform some such duty, he had the right to summon someone else, who had not been asked, to an 'exchange of property': he challenged the other person, whom he considered better off, either to exchange property with him or to undertake the duty.
2. Compare 3.11–16 (pp. 299–300).

how wool-spinning is assigned to the female servants? I was content, Socrates," he added, "because when she came, she'd been excellently coached as far as her appetite was concerned, and that seems to me to be the most important training, for the husband as well as the wife."

'"What about all the other things she needed to know, Ischomachus?" I asked. "Did you personally teach your wife how to be capable of looking after them?"

'"Well, at any rate not, you can be sure, until I had made a sacrifice to the gods," said Ischomachus, "and had prayed that I would teach and she would learn what was best for both of us."

'"And did your wife join in your sacrificing, and offer up the same prayers?" I asked.

'"She certainly did," said Ischomachus. "She made many vows to the gods, and prayed that she might become a model wife. It was obvious that she would be a responsible pupil."[1]

'"Please tell me where you started, Ischomachus," I said. "What did you teach her first? I'd rather hear you describe this than the most spectacular athletic competition or horse-race!"[2]

'"All right, Socrates," said Ischomachus in reply. "I waited until she'd been broken in and was tame enough for a conversation, and then I asked her something along the following lines: 'Tell me, my dear: have you realized yet why I married you and why your parents gave you to me? I mean, I know, and it's clear to you too, that it wouldn't have been difficult for each of us to have found someone else to share our beds. But for my part, I was considering whom it was in my interest to get as the best person to share my home and my children, and your parents had your interests at heart; so I chose you, and your parents apparently preferred me to all other eligible candidates. Now, as far as

1. What follows is Xenophon's idealized picture of Ischomachus' nameless wife; for a possible alternative picture, and a name, see pp. 285–7.
2. The following conversation is likely to make the twentieth-century believer in equality for women cringe. It reflects ancient Greek attitudes, however, and one should not make the mistake of thinking that Xenophon's Socrates is teasing Ischomachus by having him reveal his bigotry.

children are concerned, we will wait to see if God grants us any before thinking about how best to bring them up: one of the advantages we will share with each other is having them to support us and look after us as well as they can when we grow old. But what we share now is this home of ours, and we share it because I make all my income available for both of us, and you have deposited all that you brought with you in the same common pool. There's no need to tot up which of us has made the greater contribution quantitatively, but we must appreciate that whichever of us is the better partner contributes more qualitatively.'

'"To this, Socrates, my wife replied: 'What assistance can I be to you? What can *I* do? It's all up to you: my mother told me that my job was to be responsible.'

'"'Yes, my dear, of course,' I said. 'My father gave me the same advice. But you should know that responsible people of either sex should act in such a way as to ensure that their property is in the best possible condition and is increased as much as fair and honest dealings permit.'

'"'And what can I do to increase our estate?' asked my wife. 'Can you see anything I can do?'

'"'Yes, indeed I can,' I replied. 'You can try to utilize to the best of your ability the talents which the gods have implanted in you and society approves.'

'"'What talents do you mean?' she asked.

'"'Ones which, in my opinion,' I said, 'are far from worthless – unless the jobs over which the queen bee of a hive presides are worthless! I'll tell you what I'm getting at, my dear. I think that the gods exercised especially acute discernment in establishing the particular pairing which is called "male and female", to ensure that, when the partners cooperate, such a pair may be of the utmost mutual benefit. In the first place, this pairing with each other is established as a procreative unit so that animal species might not die out. In the second place, human beings, at any rate, are supplied with the means to have supporters in their old age as a result of this pairing. In the third place, human life, unlike that of other animals, which live in the open, obviously requires shelter. But if people are to have something to store in this shelter, then they need someone to work out in the open: ploughing, sowing, planting and pasturing are all open-air jobs, and they are the sources of the necessities of life. Now, when these necessities have been brought under cover, then in turn there is a need for someone to keep them safe and to do the jobs for which shelter is required. Looking after new-born children requires shelter, as does making bread from corn and clothes from wool.

'"'Since both of these domains – indoor and outdoor – require work and attention, then God, as I see it, directly made woman's nature suitable for the indoor jobs and tasks, and man's nature suitable for the outdoor ones. For he made the masculine body and mind more capable of enduring cold and heat and travel and military expeditions, which implies that he ordained the outdoor work for man; and God seems to me to have assigned the indoor work to woman, since he made the female body less capable in these respects. And knowing that he had made it the woman's natural job to feed new-born children, he apportioned to her a greater facility for loving new-born infants than he did to man. And because he had assigned to the woman the work of looking after the stores, God, recognizing that timidity is no disadvantage in such work, gave a larger share of fearfulness to woman than he did to man. And knowing that it would also be necessary for the one who does the outdoor work to provide protection against potential wrongdoers, he gave him a greater share of courage. But because both sexes need to give as well as receive, he shared memory and awareness between them both, and consequently you wouldn't be able to say whether the male or the female sex has more of these. He also shared between them both the ability to be suitably responsible, and made it the right of whichever of them, the man or the woman, is better at this to reap more of its benefits. In so far as the two sexes have different natural talents, their need for each other is greater and their pairing is mutually more beneficial, because the one has the abilities the other lacks.

'"'So, my dear,' I said, 'we must recognize what God has

assigned to each of us, and try our hardest to carry through our respective responsibilities. Society approves of this too, since it pairs a man and a woman together. Just as God has made men and women share in procreation, so society makes them share in estate-management. Moreover, where God has implanted in either sex greater ability, there custom gives its blessing. For it is better for the woman to stay indoors than to go out, but it is more reprehensible for the man to stay indoors than to look after the outside work. And if a man acts contrary to the talents God has implanted in him, then the chances are that the gods notice his disobedience and punish him for neglecting his own duties or doing the woman's work. And I think,' I concluded, 'that the queen bee works away at similar tasks as God has assigned her.'

'"'How are the queen bee's tasks similar to the ones I should do?' asked my wife.

'"'In that although she stays in the hive,' I replied, 'she doesn't allow the bees to be idle: those whose duty it is to work outside she sends out to their work. She also acquaints herself with everything that every bee brings into the hive, receives it and keeps it safe until it is required; when the time comes for it to be used, she distributes a fair proportion to each bee. She also oversees the construction of the honeycomb in the hive, making sure that it is constructed correctly and quickly; and she looks after the growing brood, making sure that it reaches maturity. When it does so and the youngsters are capable of working, she sends them out to found a colony, with a queen to rule the company.'[1]

'"'So I too will be required to do these things?' asked my wife.

'"'Yes,' I said. 'You will have to stay indoors and send out the servants who have outdoor jobs, and oversee those with indoor jobs. You must receive the produce that is brought in from outside and distribute as much of it as needs dispensing; but as for the proportion of it which needs putting on one side, you must look ahead and make sure that the outgoings assigned for the year

1. Reading ἑπομένων with the manuscripts.

are not dispensed in a month. When wool is brought in to you, you must try to make certain that those who need clothes get them. And you must try to ensure that the grain is made into edible provisions. One of your responsibilities, however,' I added, 'will probably seem rather unpleasant: when any servant is ill, you must make sure that he is thoroughly looked after.'

'"'No, no!' said my wife. 'That will be quite the opposite of unpleasant, provided that those who are well looked after turn out to be grateful and to grow in their loyalty.'

'"I was delighted at this reply of hers. So I said, 'It is attentive actions like these on the part of the queen in the hive too which make the attitude of the bees towards her such that, when she leaves the hive, not a single bee thinks of abandoning her, but they all go with her. Don't you think, my dear, that such actions are the reason for this?'

'"'I would think it likely,' said my wife, 'that the actions of a leader like the queen bee are more applicable to you than to me. My storage and distribution of things indoors would look pretty absurd, I think, if *you* weren't trying to make sure that produce is brought in from outside.'

'"'On the other hand,' I replied, 'my bringing produce in would look absurd without someone to keep what was brought in safe! Don't you see how those who pour water into a leaky jar, as the proverb puts it, are pitied for their useless effort?'

'"'Yes, and pity is what they deserve, of course,' said my wife, 'for doing it.'

'"'Anyway,' I said, 'some of your specific responsibilities will be gratifying, such as getting a servant who is ignorant of spinning, teaching it to her and doubling her value to you; or getting one who is ignorant of housekeeping and service, teaching her to be a reliable servant, and ending up with her being of inestimable value; or having the right to reward those in your household who are disciplined and helpful, and to punish anyone who turns out to be bad. And the most gratifying thing of all will be if you turn out to be better than me, and make me your servant. This will mean that you need not worry that, as the years pass, you will have less standing in the household; instead you will have grounds for believing that, as you grow older, you will have more standing in the household, in proportion to the increase in your value to me as a partner and to our children as a protector of the home. For it is virtue rather than the physical beauty of youth that increases true goodness in human life.'[1]

'"That, Socrates, as near as I can remember, was my first conversation with her."

8

'"Ischomachus," I asked, "did you find that she was motivated towards taking more responsibility as a result of what you said?"

'"She most certainly was," replied Ischomachus. "And I know that she was annoyed and highly embarrassed because once, when I asked for something from the stores, she couldn't give it to me. When I saw that she was cross, I said to her, 'Don't worry, my dear, if you can't give me what I happened to ask for. It is certainly unsatisfying not to be able to use something you need; but not being able to have something you're looking for is less distressing than not looking in the first place because you know you haven't got it! Anyway, I'm to blame, not you: I entrusted things to you without telling you where they should all be put, so how could you know where to put them and where to get them from? There is nothing in human life as useful or as fine as orderliness, my dear. I mean, consider a dance-troupe, which is a collection of people: when each of its members acts at random, chaos ensues and it's not a pleasant spectacle; but when these same people act and sing in a disciplined way, then, I think, they are worth seeing and hearing.

'"'Or take the case of an army, my dear,' I went on. 'When it is in disarray, nothing is more chaotic, it's no problem for the enemy to overcome it, and it's an ignominious sight for those

1. As Socrates also discovered (p. 310), the Greek idea that external beauty is a reflection of internal beauty is not necessarily right.

who wish it well and of no use to them at all – it's a jumble of donkeys, hoplites,[1] baggage-carriers, light-armed infantry, cavalry and carts. How can they move like that, when they get in one another's way – walkers impeding runners, runners being frustrated by those who have stopped, carts hindering cavalry, donkeys in the way of carts, baggage-carriers obstructing hoplites? And suppose they need to fight – how could they manage to fight in this state? The contingents who have to withdraw from the advancing enemy[2] are quite capable of trampling on the hoplites. An orderly army, however, elates its watching supporters, but strikes gloom into its enemies. I mean, who – if he's on the same side – could fail to be delighted at the sight of massed hoplites marching in formation, or to admire cavalry riding in ranks? And who – if he's on the other side – could fail to be terrified at the sight of hoplites, cavalry, peltasts,[3] archers, slingers, all arranged and following their commanders in a disciplined way? When they march in formation, even if there are thousands upon thousands of them, still they all proceed without confusion, as if they were a single individual, because any gap that is created is filled by the man behind.

'"'Moreover, the only time a trireme packed with men strikes fear into the enemy, but is a wonderful sight for people on the same side, is when it is moving fast through the water. And why do the crew not get in each other's way? Only because they are seated in an orderly way, lean forward and pull back in an orderly way, and embark and disembark in an orderly way. Disorder strikes me as being like this: suppose a farmer were to put barley, wheat and pulse all together in the same place; then, when he wanted cake or bread or a savoury, he would have to sift instead of having them nicely separate and ready for use.

'"'So, if you want to avoid such chaos, my dear, and would like to be able to manage our belongings without making mis-

1. Heavily armed infantry.
2. The light infantry or the cavalry might be used to ambush the enemy and then withdraw.
3. Light infantry or cavalry.

takes, and to have easily available for use anything you require, and to please me by giving me anything I ask for, then let's decide on the appropriate place for everything and, once we've put them there, let's tell the housekeeper that that's where to get them from and where to return them. This will enable us to know which of our belongings are safe and sound and which are not, because the place itself will cry out for anything that's not there; our eyes will spot anything that needs attention, and knowing where each thing is will make it readily available so that there are no obstacles to our making use of it.'

'"The finest and most precise ordering of objects that I think I've ever seen, Socrates, was when I went on board the great Phoenician ship to inspect it.[1] There I saw a huge number of items all separately packed away in the least possible space. I mean, a ship, as you know, uses a lot of wooden objects and ropes when it docks and sets sail, and a lot of rigging, as it is called, when it is sailing; it carries a lot of devices to defend itself against enemy ships, a lot of weaponry for the crew and all the implements which people use in a house on land for each group of men who mess together. Apart from all this, it is filled with all the goods which the ship's owner is transporting for profit. And all these things I've mentioned are kept not in some over-large space, but in a hold which is comparable in size to a ten-couch dining-room. I observed that all these objects were stored in such a way that they didn't obstruct one another, didn't need a search-party, and weren't either so loosely or so tightly packed as to cause a delay when there was an urgent need for something. I found out that the helmsman's subordinate, who is called the prow-man of the ship, knows everything's location so well that even when he's not in the hold he can say where everything is and how many objects there are, just as someone who's literate can say how many letters there are in 'Socrates' and where in the word each letter comes. Nevertheless, I saw this same prow-man using his spare time to inspect all the ship's necessities. I was surprised that he was

1. Presumably a familiar sight in the Piraeus, Athens' port.

making such an inspection, and I asked him what he was doing. 'Sir,' he replied, 'I am inspecting the ship's equipment to see if anything is missing or awkwardly stored. I am doing this in case something unforeseen happens. You see, when God whips up a storm at sea, searching for an essential item or handing over something which is lying awkwardly is out of the question. God guarantees retribution for stupidity and punishes it. If God merely refrains from destroying innocent people, they have much to be grateful for; and even if you've done your job excellently and you are spared, it is the gods who must be profusely thanked.'

'"Anyway, since I'd seen the tidiness of this equipment, I said to my wife, 'If people on ships – even on small ships – can find space, can keep things tidy even when they are being tossed about in a violent storm, and can lay their hands on what they want even when they are terrified, then it would be very stupid for us, when our house has large, separate store-chests for everything and rests on solid ground, not to be able to find a correct and accessible place for each of our things. Wouldn't that be highly idiotic of us? What an advantage it is to have one's stock of equipment well ordered! I have already remarked on this, and how easy it is to find a suitable place to put everything in a house. What a fine impression is given by footwear of all different kinds when it is kept in rows! What a wonderful sight is clothing of all kinds, and blankets, and metalware, and tableware, when each item is stored separately! What a wonderful sight is a regular display of jars all kept nicely separate! (I know it particularly provokes superficial people to mockery, but profound people agree.) This regularity explains why everything else too looks more beautiful when it is arranged and ordered. We are faced with a dance-troupe of utensils, and the unobstructed space between them all is beautiful too, just as the dancers in a circle-dance are not only beautiful to watch themselves, but the space in the middle also looks beautiful and clear. We can test the truth of what I say, my dear, with nothing to lose and little effort.

'"'Also, my dear, you don't need to worry about its being difficult to find someone to learn where everything lives and to remember to put each item in its place. I mean, we are both, of course, aware that Athens as a whole has ten thousand times the possessions we do, and yet none of our servants has any difficulty in buying and bringing back home from the agora anything you tell him to get, which proves that they all know where to go to get anything. And the reason for this is precisely that everything is kept in its appointed place. On the other hand, one often gives up looking for a person, even though he may be looking for you too, before finding him; and this happens precisely when there is no appointed meeting-place.'

'"That, as far as I remember, was my conversation with her about arranging utensils and making them usable."

9

'"And what happened, Ischomachus?" I asked. "Did your wife give you any indication that she was taking seriously any of the points you'd been at pains to teach her?"

'"Of course. She promised to give them her attention, and she was obviously extremely delighted, as if she'd found the solution to a problem, and she begged me to make the kind of arrangements I'd described as soon as possible."

'"And how did you organize things for her, Ischomachus?" I asked.

'"Well, naturally, the first step that occurred to me was to show her the house's potential. You see, the rooms have not been ornately decorated,[1] Socrates, but have been purpose-built as the most functional containers possible of the things intended for them: consequently, each room tended to invite what was appropriate for it. The storeroom, being secure in the inner part of the house, invited the most valuable coverings and utensils; the dry rooms called for the grain, the cool rooms for the wine, the bright rooms for any objects and utensils which require light. I showed her that the house has rooms for people to pass time in

1. See *Memoirs*, 3.8.9–10 (pp. 159–60).

(these have been decorated), which are cool in summer, but warm in winter; and I showed her that the whole house lies open to the south, with the obvious result that it is sunny in the winter and shady in the summer. I also showed her the female servants' quarters, which are divided from the men's quarters by a bolted door, to prevent items being unnecessarily removed from the house and to stop the servants breeding without our permission. I mean, when good servants have children, their loyalty is usually increased; but when bad ones are paired together, their criminal activities are increased.

'"When we'd finished this," he continued, "the next step was for us to divide our movable property into categories. We began by gathering together the things we use in worship. Next, we took out the decorative attire women wear for festivals, and the men's festive and military clothing; here the bedclothes for the women's quarters, there the bedclothes for the men's quarters; here women's footwear, there men's footwear. Another category consisted of weapons, another of utensils for spinning, another of bread-making utensils, another of washing utensils, another of utensils used for kneading, and another of tableware. This latter category as a whole we subdivided into implements in constant use and those for special meals. We also set aside the goods that would be used up month by month, and made a separate category of the goods estimated to last for a year: this is the way to increase one's knowledge about what the situation will be at the end of a period of time.

'"When we had divided all the movable property into separate categories, we distributed each and every item to its appropriate place. Then we showed the servants, since they are the ones who use them, the proper places for all the utensils they use on a daily basis (for example, utensils for bread-making, savoury-making, spinning and so on); we entrusted these utensils to them and told them to keep them safe. But as for the utensils we use for festivals or parties or other occasional events, we entrusted these to the housekeeper, showed her their places and, once we'd counted them and made an inventory, told her that they were to be given to whoever needed them, and that she was to remember to whom she'd given them, get them back from that person and return them to the place she'd got them from.

'"We had appointed as housekeeper the woman whom we considered, after looking into the matter, to be the most self-disciplined with regard to food, drink, sleep and sex, and who, in addition, struck us as having the best memory and being most likely to avoid incurring our disfavour by neglecting her duties, and as most likely to think about how she could please us and so earn rewards from us. We taught her to be loyal to us by sharing with her the occasions which made us happy, and by getting her involved in things which upset us too; and we taught her to be prepared to work hard for the increase of our estate by making her aware of its nature and by sharing its successes with her. We also instilled justice in her, by rewarding right, not wrong, among the servants and by showing her that justice leads to a wealthier and freer life than injustice. And then we gave her the job.

'"Once all this was behind us, Socrates, I told my wife that none of it would be any good unless she made herself responsible for everything staying tidily arranged. I informed her that in countries with orderly constitutions the citizens don't stop at enacting a fine legal code, but also elect guardians of the law to keep an eye on things and to commend or punish legal or illegal actions respectively. So I instructed my wife to think of herself as a guardian of the law in our household. I told her to inspect our utensils, when she had a mind to do so, just as the commander of a garrison inspects his troops; and to assess whether or not each item was in a good condition, just as the Council assesses the cavalry and their mounts; and to behave like a queen who, on the basis of the authority that is hers, commends and rewards anyone who deserves it, and reprimands and punishes when necessary. I also told her that, where our property was concerned, she shouldn't be annoyed at my giving her more jobs to do than I gave the servants; I pointed out that servants' involvement in their master's assets is limited to fetching, looking after and protecting, but, unless their master lets them, they don't have the right actually to make use of any of the assets – it is only the master's right to make use of anything he wants. Therefore, I explained, the person who profits most if assets are safe and sound, but loses most if they are destroyed, should take the most responsibility for those assets."

'"Now, Ischomachus," I said, "once your wife had heard what you had to say, what did she do about it?"

'"Well," he replied, "she told me, Socrates, that I'd got it wrong if I thought that I was giving her an onerous task by telling her it was her duty to look after our property. She said that the duty of looking after what was good for her personally would be far less of a burden than if I'd told her to neglect what belonged to her. I think," he added, "that when she said that she thought it was more gratifying for a responsible woman to care for her own possessions (which please her because they belong to her) than to neglect them, she was expressing the same natural law which makes it easier for a responsible woman to care for her own children than to neglect them."

10

'When I heard this answer of his wife's,' said Socrates, 'I exclaimed, "Good heavens, Ischomachus! On your evidence, your wife has a mind as good as a man's!"

'"Yes," said Ischomachus, "and I'd like to tell you about other instances of her considerable conscientiousness, where I only had to say something once and she took to heart what I said."

'"Tell me, please," I said. "What did she do? I'd much rather hear about virtue in a real live woman than have Zeuxis show me a portrait of one, however beautiful."[1]

'So Ischomachus continued as follows: "Well, Socrates, I once noticed that she had rubbed a lot of white lead into her skin, to make herself seem even paler than she was, and also a lot of

1. Zeuxis was one of the best-loved painters of the fifth century.

alkanet, to make her cheeks redder than they were naturally,[1] and was wearing raised shoes, to appear taller than her actual height. 'Tell me, my dear,' I said, 'would you love me more, as your partner in our assets, if I showed you my belongings for what they are without pretending that I've got more than I have and without hiding any of them either, or would you love me more if I tried to deceive you by claiming to have more than I do, and by showing you counterfeit money and fake jewellery, and if I told you that clothing dyed with purple that will soon fade was the genuine article?'

'"She didn't hesitate, but exclaimed in response: 'What a dreadful thing to say! Don't you ever behave like that! I couldn't love you from my heart if you were like that.'

'"'Well, my dear,' I said, 'our marriage means that we are also partners in each other's bodies, doesn't it?'

'"'So people say, at any rate,' she replied.[2]

'"'So would you think me a more lovable physical partner,' I said, 'if I tried to present myself to you with a good natural complexion by ensuring that my body is healthy and fit, or if I presented myself to you after making up with red lead and smearing foundation cream under my eyes, so that, when we were together, I was deceiving you and making you see and touch red lead instead of my skin?'

'"'I'd rather touch you than red lead,' she replied, 'and I'd rather see your complexion than foundation cream, and I'd rather see your eyes naturally healthy than made up.'

'"'The same goes for me too, my dear,' I said. 'Don't think that I prefer the colour of white lead or alkanet to your own colouring. The gods have made horses attract horses, cows cows and sheep sheep. Human beings are no different: they find an unadorned human body the most attractive. It is possible that artifice like this

1. Alkanet roots produce a red dye which was commonly used as rouge in ancient times; white lead (presumably with all its poisonous consequences) was used like powder today.
2. I think this reply is meant to show her modesty: she wouldn't say such a thing herself.

may deceive outsiders, but it is inevitable that people who spend all their time together will not get away with trying to deceive each other. There are several possibilities: they'll be caught out when they get out of bed in the morning before getting dressed, or the truth will be revealed by sweat or tears or washing.'"

'"Please tell me," I said, "what reply she made to this."

'"Well," he said, "she never did anything like that ever again! Instead she set about presenting herself in an unadorned and tasteful manner. She did ask me, however, if I had any advice to offer on how she could make herself truly beautiful, instead of just appearing to be beautiful. Now, my advice to her, Socrates, was to avoid constantly sitting down, which is what slaves do, and to try, with the gods' help, to act like the mistress of the house and, when she approached the loom, for instance, to stand there and teach or learn, depending on whether she knew something better or worse than others; or again, I advised her to watch over the bread-making, to stand by the housekeeper when she's telling the servants their budgets, and also to walk around checking whether everything is in its proper place. My thinking was that these activities combine industry with walking. I also told her that there was good exercise to be provided by mixing water and flour and kneading dough, or by shaking and folding clothes and bedding. I pointed out that, if she exercised like this, she would enjoy her food more, be healthier and bring a genuine bloom to her complexion. As for what she looks like – when there's a decision to be made between her and a servant girl, then because she is less made up and more tastefully dressed, she becomes an object of desire, and especially because she is granting her favours willingly, whereas the servant has no choice but to submit.[1] But women who put on airs and sit around are inviting comparison with tarted-up seductresses. Anyway, Socrates," he concluded,

1. The master of the house did, of course, have the right to sleep with his servants. It is often dangerous to quote sentences from orators out of context, but Demosthenes (59.122) may well be expressing a common Greek sentiment when he says, 'We have courtesans for pleasure, concubines for our physical needs, and wives for the procreation of legal issue.'

"you can be sure that my wife's lifestyle and appearance now conform to my injunctions and the description I've been giving you."

11

'Next I said, "Ischomachus, I think I've heard enough for the time being about what your wife does – and it reflects very well on both of you. But why don't you tell me now what *you* do? You'll have the pleasure of explaining the reasons for your excellent reputation, and I'll get a thorough and comprehensible account (if my abilities allow me to understand it) of what a truly good man does, for which I'll be very grateful."

'"Yes, Socrates," said Ischomachus, "I will indeed be truly delighted to tell you what I spend my time doing, so that, if you think that anything I do is not right, you can set me straight."

'"I don't know about that," I said. "I don't see how it could be right for me to correct a man who is perfectly and truly good, when my reputation is of being a windbag with his head in the clouds,[1] and – though this seems to me to be the silliest criticism imaginable – I am also called impecunious! Actually, Ischomachus, I would have been very depressed by this criticism, if it were not for an encounter I had the other day: I saw the horse belonging to Nicias the foreigner surrounded by people gawping at it, and I overheard some of them having a long discussion about it. Well, I went up to the groom and asked him if the horse had a lot of money. He looked at me as if I was out of my mind for asking such a question, and said, 'How can a horse have money?' I breathed a sigh of relief at hearing that it was not out of the question for an impecunious horse to be a good horse (assuming that it does have a good temperament). So, since my becoming a good man is not entirely out of the question, do please tell me all about what you do, and then, in so far as I can understand what you say, I'll be able to try to follow suit, which is what I'll do, starting from tomorrow morning. For tomorrow is a good day for embarking on a life of virtue."

1. See especially Aristophanes, *Clouds*.

'"Despite your joking, Socrates," said Ischomachus, "I'll tell you what I try to the best of my ability to spend my life doing. One thing I think I understand is that the gods have ruled out success for people who don't know either what they ought to do or what steps they should take to achieve what they ought to do. Nevertheless, prosperity is given to only some of those who do have this knowledge and do take the proper steps. Therefore, I begin by worshipping the gods, and what I try to aim for in what I do is to make it possible for them to grant my prayers for physical health and strength, public recognition, goodwill from my friends, honourable survival in war and increasing wealth, blamelessly earned."

'When he'd finished, I said, "Ischomachus, do you really desire wealth – and all the bother of looking after large assets once you've got them?"

'"Yes," replied Ischomachus, "I certainly do desire these things. For it pleases me, Socrates, to give generously in worshipping the gods, to help my friends when they are in need, and to use my assets for beautifying the city as much as I can."

'"These are admirable reasons, Ischomachus," I said, "and anyone with outstanding ability should, of course, have such aims. The vast majority of people are either incapable of living within their means or are happy if they can make ends meet. So of course those who are able not only to provide for their own households, but also to create a surplus, with which to beautify their cities and alleviate their friends' burdens, are regarded as impressive and formidable men. However, I am far from being the first to find it easy to eulogize such people. Why don't you go back to the beginning and tell me how you look after your health and your strength, and how you guarantee honourable survival in war? After that," I said, "I'd be glad to hear about your financial affairs."

'"But all these things are interconnected, Socrates, I think," said Ischomachus. "You see, when someone has enough to eat and takes the correct amount of exercise, he will stay healthy and get stronger, in my opinion; and, if his exercise includes training in the martial arts, his survival will be more honourable; and, if he applies himself properly and keeps fit, he is more likely to increase his estate."

'"I can follow you so far, Ischomachus," I said. "You're saying that exercise and practice and training increase a person's chances of success. But I'd be glad to find out from you what sort of exercise you take to keep fit and strong, and how you train in the martial arts, and how you go about creating a surplus so as to help your friends and improve your city."

'"All right, Socrates," said Ischomachus. "I usually get up early enough in the morning so that, if I happen to need to see someone, I can find him still at home. If I have to do some business in Athens, I use it as an opportunity to take a walk; if there's no need for me to be in Athens, then my slave takes my horse on ahead to my farm, and I use the journey out of town as an opportunity for a walk – and this is probably better exercise for me, Socrates, than walking in my courtyard. Out on my farm I may find planting, ploughing, sowing or harvesting taking place, and I oversee all aspects of the labour and make any changes I can to improve on what's going on. Next, I usually mount my horse and put him through his paces: since I imitate as closely as I can the equestrian skills needed in battle, I don't steer clear of uneven or steep ground, or ditches or streams – although I do try as hard as possible not to lame my horse during these exercises. When this is over, my slave lets the horse have a roll and then takes him back home along with anything we need in town from the country. I walk some of the way home and run the rest, and then scrape myself clean with a strigil. Finally, Socrates, I eat enough to see me through the day without being either empty or too full."

'"Ischomachus," I said, "your activities seem faultless to me, I swear. You contrive to be healthy, you take steps to keep fit, you train for war, you look after your wealth – and you put all this into practice at one and the same time! I find it thoroughly commendable. And you are living and sufficient proof that you go about each of these pursuits in the right way. For we can see that you are on the whole (as much as the gods grant to any man) healthy and fit, and we know that you have the reputation of being one of the best horsemen and wealthiest people in Athens."

'"Anyway, Socrates," he said, "the result of my doing all this is that I am frequently slandered by sycophants,[1] though you perhaps thought I was going to say that I am frequently described as 'truly good'!"

'"Actually, Ischomachus," I said, "I was going to ask you whether you also do anything about ensuring that you can hold your own in an argument, should the occasion arise."

'"Socrates," he replied, "don't you think that I have constantly been preparing for precisely that[2] – to argue in my own defence that I do wrong to no one, but in fact often benefit people to the best of my ability? And don't you think that I prepare for arguing as a prosecutor too, by observing those individuals who often wrong not only private citizens but also the State, and never do good to anyone?"

'"Yes, Ischomachus," I said, "but I'd still like to hear whether you practise actually expressing all this verbally."

'"I never stop practising that, Socrates," he replied. "Sometimes I get one of my servants to play the role of prosecutor or defendant, and I listen to his speech and then try to refute it; sometimes I criticize or praise someone before a jury of his friends; sometimes I reconcile some of my acquaintances with one another by trying to explain that it is in their interests to be on good terms, not bad; sometimes we get together and pick holes in a general's conduct,[3] or speak in defence of someone who has been accused despite being innocent, or in impeachment of someone wrongly appointed to political office. Moreover, we often act like members of the Council, and recommend a course of action we approve of, or criticize one we don't approve of. And

1. See p. 133, n. 3.
2. Compare *Defence*, 3 (p. 41) and *Memoirs*, 4.8.4 (p. 215).
3. Ischomachus is still talking about role-playing, but in real life in Athens the office of general or military commander (*strategos*) was political, and at the end of his year of office a general could expect to have his conduct examined in court.

often, Socrates, I have even been singled out and sentenced to pay some appropriate penalty or fine!"

'"By whom, Ischomachus?" I asked. "I didn't know that had happened."

'"By my wife!" he said.

'"And what are you like at arguing your case?" I asked.

'"Not bad at all, when it is a matter of telling the truth; but when I'd be better off lying, Socrates, there's absolutely no way I can make the weaker argument into the stronger one."[1]

'"That, Ischomachus," I said, "is probably because you are incapable of making lies true!"

12

'"But don't let me detain you, Ischomachus," I went on, "if you want to get away."

'"No, no, Socrates," he replied. "I can't go until the agora is completely clear."

'"Good heavens!" I said. "You certainly take a great deal of care that you keep your reputation for being truly good. I mean, there's all your plentiful property requiring your attention, yet you are waiting here for your visitors from out of town, since you promised to do so, and you're not about to break a promise!"

'"As a matter of fact, Socrates," Ischomachus said, "I'm not neglecting my property either, because I have foremen on my farms."

'"What do you do when you need a foreman, Ischomachus?" I asked. "Do you watch out for a man with the right skills, and then try to buy him (just as I'm sure that, when you need a builder, you would watch out for a skilled builder and then try to get hold of him)? Or do you train your foremen by yourself?"

'"I try to train them myself, of course, Socrates," he replied. "I mean, since I want someone who is capable of looking after things in my place when I'm not there, he needs to know exactly what I

1. See p. 78, n. 2.

know. And if I have the competence to supervise the labour, I would surely be capable of passing that knowledge on to someone else too."

'"If he is to be capable of deputizing for you," I said, "it must be of prime importance that he is loyal to you and your property, since *any* foreman's knowledge is no good at all without loyalty, is it?"

'"Of course not, none whatsoever," said Ischomachus. "And in fact the first thing I try to inculcate is loyalty to me and my property."

'"Do please tell me," I said, "how you teach whoever it may be to be loyal to you and your property."[1]

'"By being his benefactor, of course," Ischomachus said, "when the gods grant us some great good fortune."

'"You're implying, then," I said, "that loyalty to you, and the willingness to act to your advantage, are the result of your sharing the benefits of your good fortune, aren't you?"

'"Yes, Socrates; the way I see it, that's the best means of securing loyalty."

'"But does loyalty to you by itself result in a competent foreman, Ischomachus?" I asked. "Isn't it obvious that almost everyone is loyal to himself, but people are still often not prepared to make themselves responsible for getting the good things they want to have?"[2]

'"Yes, of course," said Ischomachus. "So when I want to make people like that into foremen, I also teach them responsibility."

'"How on earth do you do that?" I asked. "I really thought that it was altogether impossible to teach people responsibility."[3]

'"In fact it isn't possible to teach it to absolutely everyone," he said.

1. There are obvious parallels in what follows with Ischomachus' training of the housekeeper in 9.11–13 (p. 323). Both, of course, reflect the Socratic theme of self-discipline.
2. That is, they expect good things to fall into their laps. For what follows, compare 1.18 ff. (pp. 292–3).
3. See p. 160, n. 1.

'"So what kind of people can be taught it?" I asked. "Please give me a thorough and clear description of them."

'"Well, in the first place, Socrates," he said, "you can't teach people to be responsible if they have a weakness for alcohol, because their drunkenness makes them forget everything they're supposed to do."[1]

'"Is this the only weakness that prevents responsibility," I asked, "or are there others?"

'"There most certainly are others," Ischomachus replied, "for instance, being ruled by sleep. I mean, it's impossible for someone to perform his duties or to delegate them if he's asleep!"

'"Well, are these now the only kinds of people who can't be taught responsibility," I asked, "or are there others as well?"

'"Yes," replied Ischomachus, "I think that people who are obsessed with a lover are incapable of being taught to take responsibility for anything except the object of their infatuation. It isn't easy to find a source of more pleasant anticipation or effort than attending to a loved one! And when the sexual act is imminent, it isn't easy to find a worse punishment than being kept from one's lover! So I refuse even to try to inculcate responsibility in people I recognize as being like that."

'"What about people who are in love with making money?" I asked. "Is there no hope of them being taught to take responsibility for farm matters?"

'"Quite the contrary," Ischomachus replied. "They are very easy to train for this work: you only need to show them that, if they take responsibility, they'll make money!"

'"What about the rest of mankind," I asked, "people who are not slaves to the influences you've been telling me about, and are only moderately fond of making money? How do you teach them to be responsible for the work you give them?"

'"It's very simple, Socrates," he replied. "When I see that they are behaving responsibly, I make sure I congratulate them and

1. Compare *Memoirs*, 1.2.21–23 (pp. 76–7).

reward them; when I see irresponsibility, I make sure my words and actions are caustically critical."

'"Ischomachus," I said, "can we change tack now? Instead of talking about those actually being trained in responsibility, could you explain a general educational issue to me: is it possible for someone who is himself irresponsible to make others responsible?"

'"No, it certainly is not," Ischomachus replied. "You might just as well expect someone tone-deaf to teach people to be musicians! It's difficult to learn to do something well when your teacher is giving you bad lessons; and it is difficult for a servant to learn responsibility when his master is giving lessons in irresponsibility. In a nutshell, I don't think I have found any cases of good servants with a bad master; I have seen cases of bad servants with a good master, however – but the servants didn't get away with it! Anyone who wants to make people capable of being responsible must be capable of supervising and scrutinizing the work, must be prepared to show gratitude for work performed well, and must not be afraid of administering punishment when irresponsibility demands it. The story about the Persian's answer is a good one, I think: the king of Persia happened to get a good horse, and wanted to fatten it up as quickly as possible. So he asked a recognized expert on horses what it is that fattens up a horse most quickly. 'The master's eye,' replied the man, as the story goes.[1] And I think, Socrates, that the same is true elsewhere: the master's eye is the most effective way of producing good work."

13

'"When you have conclusively demonstrated to someone that he must be responsible for the work you give him," I asked, "is he now capable of being a foreman, or is there more that he needs to learn before being a competent foreman?"

1. Pseudo-Aristotle, *Oeconomica*, 1345a4–5, tells the same story, but adds another nice one too: a Libyan, when asked what was the best fertilizer, replied, 'The master's footsteps.'

'"Yes, there certainly is," said Ischomachus. "He still needs to know what to do, and when and how. A foreman without this knowledge is as useless as a doctor who works from dawn to dusk at looking after a patient, but doesn't know what regimen will do the patient good."

'"All right, then," I went on. "If he learns how to do the work, will he still be inadequate in any respect, or will he now be a perfect foreman for you?"

'"I think he needs to learn how to wield authority over the workforce."

'"So do you also teach your foremen how to be capable of this?" I asked.

'"I try to," said Ischomachus.

'"Please," I said, "do tell me how you teach them to be good at wielding authority."

'"It's so straightforward, Socrates," he replied, "that you'll probably laugh when I tell you."

'"No," I responded. "This issue's not a laughing-matter, Ischomachus. For the ability to make people good at wielding authority obviously entails the ability to teach them mastery, and the ability to make people masters entails the ability to make them kings. So anyone who can do this deserves a high degree of respect, in my opinion, not scorn."

'"Well, Socrates," he said, "there are two ways in which the rest of the animal kingdom learns obedience – by being punished when they attempt to be disobedient, and by being rewarded when they willingly do what they're supposed to do. For instance, colts learn to obey their trainers because something nice happens to them when they are obedient and because they get into trouble when they are disobedient, and this goes on until they submit to the trainer's will. Or take puppies: although their intelligence and speech are negligible compared to a human's, the same method can still teach them to run around in circles and turn somersaults and so on, because, when they do as they're told, they get something they want, and when they don't listen, they are punished. Human beings can be made more obedient just by force of argument, by proving that it is in their interest to obey; but, where slaves are concerned, the training which is apparently designed only for lower animals is very effective for teaching obedience; for you'll get plenty of results by gratifying their bellies in accordance with their desires.[1] Those of them with ambitious temperaments can also be motivated by praise: I mean that some have an innate appetite for praise, just as others have for food and drink. Anyway, by using this training method, I think the people I deal with become more obedient, so I use it for those I want to appoint as foremen; I also back them up in situations like the following. You see, I am bound to supply my labourers with clothing and footwear, but I have some of these articles made better than others rather than making them all the same; then I can reward better workers with the better articles, and give worse workers the inferior articles. My reason, Socrates, is that I think good workers get very depressed when they see that, although they're the ones doing all the work, the others get the same as them, despite making no effort and being unprepared to face danger, if need be. So I don't think it is at all right for the better ones to get the same as the worse ones, and when I see that my foremen have assigned the best-quality articles to the most valuable workers, I congratulate them; on the other hand, if I see a worker receiving special favours as a result of sweet-talking a foreman or as a result of pleasing him in any other useless way, I don't turn a blind eye, Socrates, but I reprimand the foreman and try to explain that this sort of thing isn't even to his own advantage."

14

'"So when he has become capable of wielding authority, Ischomachus," I asked, "and consequently can make people obey him, do you think that he is then a perfect foreman? Is someone who

1. Even Aristotle spends a long time wondering whether slaves are capable of rational thought (*Politics*, 1259b–1260b); see also 1253b–1255b on slaves as 'animate tools'.

has all the abilities you've mentioned still inadequate in any respect?"

'"Yes, he most certainly is," replied Ischomachus. "He needs to be able to keep his hands off his master's property and not to steal. If the overseer of the crops ventures to steal them, and thus removes the source of the business's profit, then what advantage could there be in using his industry to run the farm?"

'"Do you, then, also undertake to teach honesty in this respect?" I asked.

'"Yes, indeed I do," said Ischomachus, "though I find that not everyone is prepared to take this lesson to heart! Still, I draw on both Draco's and Solon's legal codes and try to point my servants towards honesty.[1] I think that Draco and Solon established many of their laws precisely to educate people in this kind of justice. For instance, the laws state that people who try to steal are to be punished, imprisoned and executed, if they are caught in the act. Now, obviously, they enacted these laws with the intention of making dishonest gain unprofitable for the criminals. Anyway, by making use of some aspects of their laws, and also by availing myself of some aspects of the royal Persian laws, I try to make my servants honest in their handling of property. I use this combination because Draco's and Solon's codes merely punish transgression, whereas the royal Persian code not only punishes criminals, but also benefits those who are law-abiding,[2] and this has the effect of showing that honesty is more lucrative than dishonesty, so that often, even if they are mercenary, people staunchly persevere at avoiding dishonesty. Now, if I've treated someone well but nevertheless find him still inclined towards dishonesty, then I regard him as incurably avaricious, and I make no further use of him; if, on the other hand, I find someone who is moved to

1. Draco and Solon were the two great legislators of Athens. Draco's code (621 BC) was effectively the first thorough set of laws; thirty years later Solon repealed most of them (many were harsh – hence the term 'Draconian') and established a revised set of laws and a new democratic constitution for Athens.
2. See 4.7–11 (pp. 301–2) for a possible example of how the Persian code benefits the law-abiding (though there are better examples in *Cyropaedia*).

be honest not only because he wants to profit by his honesty, but also because he wants to earn my praise, then I treat him as I would a free man, in the sense that I don't just reward him financially, but also give him the recognition due to a truly good person. You see, Socrates, I think that the difference between a man who wants recognition and a man who wants profit lies in the fact that the former is prepared to accept approbation and recognition as reasons for working hard at his duties, facing danger and avoiding dishonest gain."

15

'"All right," I said. "So now you've got a man in whom you have bred the desire for your welfare and the ability to be responsible for bringing this about; you have also made him possess knowledge of how every aspect of the business is to be done so as to increase its utility; you have also made him capable of wielding authority; and on top of all this, it is just as much his pleasure to maximize the crop yield for you as it is yours to do the same for yourself. I no longer need to ask whether your man is inadequate in any respect: I think that such a man would be an extremely valuable foreman. But please, Ischomachus, don't ignore that aspect of the discussion which has been touched on, but has not been developed at all."

'"Which aspect do you mean?" asked Ischomachus.

'"You said, as you will remember," I continued, "that it was absolutely crucial to learn how each part of a task is to be done; otherwise, you claimed, if someone lacks the knowledge of what is to be done and how to do it, even his applying himself to the task is no good at all."

'"Are you now prompting me to explain the actual technical details of agriculture, Socrates?" asked Ischomachus.

'"Yes, I am," I said, "because the chances are that knowledge of the technical details makes people rich, whereas those who don't know them can expend plenty of effort but still live a life of poverty."

'"Well now, Socrates," he said, "I shall also show you how altruistic this art is,[1] because, in addition to being very profitable and pleasant work, and in addition to being very attractive and congenial to both gods and men, it is also very easy to learn. Who, then, could fail to find it generous? As you know, we call even animals generous when they are attractive, important and useful, and are also kind to people."

'"Well," I said, "I think I have grasped this latter point[2] well enough, Ischomachus, in so far as you described the method required to train a foreman: I mean, I think I understood how you said you make him loyal to you, and how you make him take responsibility and wield authority and be honest. But you also said that for someone to apply himself successfully to agriculture, he must learn *what* to do, and *how* and *when* to do it; and this is the aspect of the discussion which I think has been touched on, but has not been developed. It's as if you were to say that, for someone to be capable of writing down a dictation or reading something written, he must know the alphabet. If you'd told me that, I'd have heard that I must know the alphabet, but my appreciation of this point would not, I think, bring me any closer to actually knowing the alphabet. The present situation is just the same: I have no difficulty in being convinced that, for someone to apply himself successfully to agriculture, he must know agriculture, but my appreciation of this point does not bring me any closer to knowing how farming must be done. Instead, if I made a firm decision right now to become a farmer, I would be no different from the doctor we mentioned,[3] who goes around examining his patients, but is completely ignorant of what regimen will do his patients good. I don't want to be like that," I said, "so please explain to me the actual tasks involved in agriculture."

'"All right," he said, "but in fact, Socrates, agriculture isn't like other skills, where the pupil has to spend an exhausting amount of

1. See 5.1–17 (pp. 305–7).
2. Presumably, that agriculture is easy to learn; but the text is badly constructed here, and has possibly suffered from displacement or omission.
3. See p. 335.

time at his lessons before his work is of a high enough quality to earn him a living. No, agriculture isn't awkward to learn like that: all you need is to watch people working at some aspects of it, and listen to people explaining other aspects, and then you'd understand it – well enough even to explain it to someone else, if you wanted. I also think that you yourself know considerably more about it than you think you know. And the fact is that, whereas experts in other areas in a sense keep the most vital parts of their particular skills secret, among farmers the best planter likes nothing more than having someone watch him, and the same goes for the best sower. Whatever you ask him about work he has done well, he will tell you the method without keeping anything secret. Do you see, Socrates, how very generous agriculture apparently makes the characters of those who are involved in it?"

'"You have delivered a brilliant introduction to the subject," I said, "and one which is designed to sustain the interest of your audience. Now explain the actual subject to me, and all the more thoroughly because it is easy to learn. I mean, you won't lose face if you teach an easy subject, but I'll lose face far more if I don't know it, especially if the subject happens to be useful too."

16

'"All right, then, Socrates," he said. "The first thing I want to prove to you is that no real difficulty is involved in that aspect of farming which is called the most complex by people who give the most detailed verbal account of farming, but never actually work on a farm. For they say that a necessary prerequisite to successful farming is knowledge of the land."

'"And they're right," I said, "since ignorance of what the land can grow would, I imagine, entail ignorance of what ought to be sown or planted."

'"Well," said Ischomachus, "this knowledge can be gained by looking at the crops and trees on somebody else's land to find out what the land can and cannot grow. And when you've found this out, of course, fighting against the gods starts to seem inexpedient. For you'll gain more produce by sowing and planting what the land readily grows and nurtures than by sowing and planting what *you* want. But if the land you examine can't show you its potential because the people who own it have not worked it, then, rather than questioning a local person, it is often possible to get more accurate information from a local piece of land! But in fact even uncultivated land still shows its quality: if it allows wild plants to flourish, then, when cultivated, it is also capable of bearing flourishing domesticated plants. Thus, even people without much experience of agriculture can still discern quality in land."

'"Well, as far as this matter is concerned, Ischomachus," I said, "I think I am now confident enough not to feel I have to avoid agriculture from fear that I won't recognize the quality of the land. In fact, I am reminded of what fishermen do. They work on the sea and don't stop for a look or, while moving, interrupt their activities, but simply glide past the fields; nevertheless, when they see crops growing on land, they do not shrink from expressing their views about which land is good and which is bad, but they condemn the one and praise the other. Moreover, I notice that the views they express about the good land usually coincide to a high degree with those of experienced farmers."

'"So where would you like me to start, Socrates?" he asked. "How shall I remind you of what you know about agriculture? I'm sure that you already know a great deal of what I'll tell you about farming methods."[1]

'"A philosopher's job is above all to learn, Ischomachus," I said, "so I think the first thing I'd like to learn is how I could work

1. This is the second time we've met this point and it will recur in what follows. The assumption that we already know more than we realize is implicit in the Socratic technique of questioning, which Ischomachus here employs to some extent: the questioning is designed to bring latent knowledge out of the answerer. Plato is the master at portraying this technique, and provides speculative back-up for it in his famous Theory of Recollection: all so-called learning is recollection of knowledge previously acquired, and ultimately acquired before birth (see, for example, *Meno*, 81a–86b, *Phaedo*, 72e–78b). Here, however, the issue is not pre-natal knowledge, but what one has seen and assessed by common sense, but forgotten.

the land (supposing I wanted to) to maximize the crops of wheat and barley I can get from it."

'"Well, here's something you know, don't you? That fallow land must be ploughed up to be ready for sowing?"

'"Yes, I know," I said.

'"So," he asked, "if we were to set about ploughing the land in winter . . . ?"

'"Then the land would be waterlogged," I replied.

'"But what do you think about ploughing in summer?"

'"The ground will be too compact for the plough to turn."

'"This job should probably be undertaken in the spring, then."

'"Yes," I said, "since it is reasonable to suppose that at that time of year the soil will break up most as it is being turned."

'"Moreover, Socrates," he added, "at that time of year the weeds which are turned over act as fertilizer for the land, but haven't yet shed their seeds, and so won't grow. I mean, I think you already know that if fallow ground is to be good, it must be clear of weeds and baked as much as possible in the sun."

'"Yes, I have little doubt that this is another crucial factor," I said.

'"So do you think there is any other way of achieving this than by turning the soil as often as possible during the summer?" he asked.

'"I'm absolutely sure," I replied, "that the best way for the weeds to be brought to the surface and withered by the heat, and for the soil to be baked by the sun, is to plough up the ground in midsummer – and at midday too!"

'"And if people use spades to work the fallow, then isn't it obvious that they must separate the weeds from the soil?"

'"Yes, and they must spread the weeds on top of the ground, so that they wither," I added, "and must turn the soil, so that the moist part of it is baked."

17

'"You can see, Socrates, that both of us are of one mind where fallow ground is concerned," he said.

'"Yes, apparently," I replied.

'"Now, what do you think about the season for sowing, Socrates?" he asked. "Would you disagree with the season which past experience has universally shown, and present experience is universally confirming, to be the best for sowing? I mean, when autumn approaches, everybody, so to speak, looks to God, to see when he will dampen the ground with rain and thus let them sow."

'"Furthermore, Ischomachus," I said, "it is also universally agreed that sowing in dry ground is to be avoided if you can, obviously because people have had to contend with a great deal of retribution if they sow before God gives the go-ahead."

'"So there is universal unanimity on this point," said Ischomachus.

'"Yes," I said, "God's injunctions lead to unanimity. For example, everyone prefers to wear thick clothing during winter, if they can, and to light a fire, if they have wood."

'"But there is an aspect of sowing," said Ischomachus, "about which there is considerable difference of opinion, and that is whether it is best to sow early in the season, in the middle of it, or right at the end."

'"God orders the year unpredictably," I said. "In one year it is best to sow early, in another in mid-season, and in another right at the end of the season."

'"Well, Socrates," he asked, "do you think it is better to choose just one of these times, whether a small or a large quantity of seed has to be sown, and do one's sowing then, or do you think that sowing should carry on from the very beginning of the season to the very end?"

'"In my opinion, Ischomachus," I replied, "it is best to make use of the whole sowing-season, because it is far preferable to have a constant supply of sufficient food than to have too much at one time and too little at another."

'"Here again, Socrates," he said, "you and I – pupil and teacher – have the same view, even though you expressed your opinion before having heard mine!"

'"What about actually scattering the seed?" I asked. "Is there a complicated technique involved?"

'"Let's look into this question too, Socrates, by all means," he replied. "I'm sure you are aware that the seed must be scattered by hand."

'"Yes, I've seen that," I said.

'"But some people can scatter it evenly, some can't," he said.

'"In that case," I remarked, "we find that here too, as in playing the lyre, the hand needs practice, so that it can obey the mind's directions."

'"Quite so," he said. "But what if some of the soil is lighter than normal and some heavier than normal?"

'"What do you mean?" I asked. "By 'lighter' and 'heavier' do you mean 'weaker' and 'stronger'?"

'"That's right," he said. "And my question is whether you would assign an equal amount of seed to both kinds of soil, or a greater quantity to one rather than the other."

'"Well," I replied, "I think that the stronger the wine, the greater the quantity of water which ought to be added to it, and the stronger the man, the greater the weight which ought to be loaded on to him, if there were things that needed carrying; and if feeding people were the issue, I would arrange for the number of people anyone fed to increase in proportion to his ability to do so. Can you tell me, however," I added, "whether the more seed it takes in, the stronger weak soil becomes? After all, this is what happens with farm animals."

'Ischomachus laughed and said, "There's many a true word spoken in jest, Socrates; I'll have you know that, if you put seed in the ground and then, when it has sprouted (and picking a time when the ground is still getting plenty of nourishment from the skies), you plough the seed back in again, it turns into food for the soil, and the soil *does* in a sense become strong thanks to the seed. On the other hand, if you allow the soil to give its nourishment to the crops all the way through from seed to fruition, then, if the soil is weak by the end of this process, you are unlikely to get much of a crop, just as it is difficult, of course, for a weak sow to give nourishment to a lot of healthy piglets."

'"Do you mean that the weaker the soil, the less seed ought to be put into it, Ischomachus?" I asked.

'"Precisely, Socrates," he replied. "And this agrees with your suggestion that lesser loads are to be assigned to weaker creatures."

'"Now, Ischomachus, what about hoers?" I asked. "Why do you get them involved with the corn?"

'"I'm sure you are aware," he said in reply, "that there is a lot of rain during winter."

'"Of course."

'"Well then, let's suppose that some of the corn has got covered to a certain extent by mud streaming down over it thanks to the rain, and that some of the roots have been exposed by flooding. And, of course, weeds often spring up among the corn, as you know, thanks to the rain, and choke it."

'"These are all likely events," I said.

'"So don't you think the corn needs some assistance at this point?" he asked.

'"Yes, I certainly do."

'"And what do you think should be done to help the corn which has been swamped by mud?"

'"The weight of the soil should be reduced."

'"And what about the corn which has its roots exposed?" he asked.

'"Soil needs heaping up on top of the roots."

'"And what if weeds have sprung up and are choking the corn and depriving it of its nourishment – like useless drones depriving the bees of the stuff which they have industriously stored as food?"

'"The weeds must be cut down and removed from the source of nourishment,[1] of course," I said, "just as the drones must be removed from the hives."

1. Reading τῆς τροφῆς with Thalheim.

'"So do you think it sensible of us to get hoers involved?" he asked.

'"I certainly do," I said. "But you know, Ischomachus, I am mulling over the significance of introducing similes at appropriate points, because when you mentioned drones, you made me very angry about the weeds, far more angry than when you were talking just about the weeds."

18

'"But anyway," I went on, "the next stage is probably the harvest; so please tell me anything you can about this too."

'"I will – provided that we don't find that you already know what I know about this topic too," he said. "Anyway, I'm sure you are aware that the corn must be cut."

'"Of course."

'"Now, while you are cutting it," he said, "would you stand facing the direction in which the wind is blowing, or facing into the wind?"

'"I wouldn't face into the wind," I said, "because I think your eyes and hands would suffer if you harvested with your body turned towards straw and husks."

'"And would you cut off just the heads, or would you cut close to the ground?" he asked.

'"If the stems were short," I replied, "I'd cut them low down, to have a better chance of getting enough straw; but if the stems were long, I think I'd be right to cut them halfway down, so as not to provide the threshers or the winnowers with unnecessary matter which would make their work more troublesome. I suppose that what is left in the ground could enrich the soil by being burned, and could increase the amount of fertilizer by being added to it."

'"Do you see, Socrates," he said, "that you have been caught in the act? You already know what I know about harvesting too."

'"It looks that way," I said. "Now I want to see if I know about threshing too."

'"Well, here's something I'm sure you know," he said, "that draught-animals are used to thresh the corn."

'"Of course I do," I said. "And 'draught-animals' is a general term for oxen, mules and horses."

'"Do you think that trampling on the corn as they are being driven along represents the sum total of these creatures' knowledge?" he asked.

'"Yes, what else could draught-animals know?"

'"And who has the job of seeing that they crush what they ought, Socrates," he asked, "and that the corn to be threshed is spread evenly?"

'"Obviously the threshers do," I replied. "They keep tossing the corn, and throwing the unthreshed corn under the animals' hoofs, and it is clear that, while they are doing this, they are keeping the threshing-floor as evenly spread as possible and are getting the work done as quickly as possible."

'"So you know just as much about this as I do," he said.

'"Well, the next stage will be for us to winnow the impurities out of the corn," I said.

'"Tell me this, Socrates," said Ischomachus. "Do you appreciate that if you start from the windward part of the threshing-floor, your chaff will be blown across the whole threshing-floor?"

'"Inevitably."

'"So it's likely that it will actually fall on to the corn," he said.

'"Yes," I said, "because the bare part of the threshing-floor is beyond the corn – a long way for the chaff to be blown."

'"What if the winnowing is started from the leeward part?" he asked.

'"Obviously," I said, "the chaff will pretty soon find itself in the trough designed for it."

'"And when you've got halfway across the threshing-floor in cleaning the corn," he said, "will you leave the corn scattered like that while you winnow the rest of the chaff, or will you first gather the cleaned corn together into as narrow as possible a line along the diameter of the floor?"[1]

1. The threshing-floor is circular.

'"I'll certainly gather the clean corn together first," I said, "so that the chaff is blown over it into the bare part of the threshing-floor; otherwise, I'll have to winnow the same chaff twice."

'"So then, Socrates," he said, "you could teach somebody else how to clean corn in the quickest way possible!"

'"Well, I hadn't been aware of this knowledge of mine. In fact, I've been wondering for some time whether I also know how to smelt gold and play the pipes and paint pictures, but wasn't aware of it. I mean, no one[1] has taught me these subjects, but then I've never been taught agriculture; but just as I see people farming, so I see people working at other arts and crafts."

'"You can see now," said Ischomachus, "why I told you some time ago[2] that agriculture was the most generous art, because it is the easiest to learn."

'"All right, Ischomachus, I do have this knowledge," I said. "I just hadn't realized that I knew all about sowing corn."

19

'"But, anyway, is planting trees also part of the art of agriculture?" I continued.

'"Yes, it is," replied Ischomachus.

'"Then how can I know all about sowing, and yet be ignorant about planting?"

'"You mean you don't know about planting?" said Ischomachus.

'"How could I?" I said. "I don't know what kind of soil is right for planting, nor how deep or wide a hole to dig, nor how much of the plant to put in the hole, nor what arrangement of the plant in the soil best allows it to grow."

'"All right, then," said Ischomachus, "now's your chance to fill any gaps in your knowledge. I'm sure you've seen what kinds of holes are dug for the plants."

1. Reading μέν with Thalheim.
2. See p. 339.

'"Yes, often."

'"So have you ever seen one more than three feet deep?"

'"No, and in fact I've never seen one more than two and a half feet deep either."

'"And have you ever seen one more than three feet wide?"

'"No, not more than two feet wide, in fact."

'"All right. Now tell me this too: have you ever seen one less than a foot deep?" he asked.

'"No, not less than one and a half feet, in fact," I said. "I mean, when digging goes on around the plants, they'd be dug out of the ground, if they'd been planted too close to the surface like that."

'"Then here is something which you do know well enough, Socrates," he said, "that the holes are dug no deeper than two and a half feet and no shallower than one and a half feet."

'"Yes, I know that," I said. "I'm bound to notice something so obvious."

'"Now, can you also use your eyes to recognize drier and damper soil?" he asked.

'"Well, I suppose that the ground near Lycabettus and any similar ground is dry," I said, "and the ground in the Phalerian marsh and any similar ground is damp."[1]

'"In which would you choose to dig a deep hole for your plant – the dry ground or the damp ground?" he asked.

'"The dry ground, of course," I replied, "because if you were to dig a deep one in damp ground, you'd meet water, and then you couldn't proceed with your planting."

'"I think you're right," he said. "Now, once the holes have been dug, under what conditions is it preferable to place the plants in the ground?[2] Have you ever noticed this?"

'"Definitely," I said.

'"So, given that you want the plants to grow as quickly as possible, do you think that if you were to put worked soil under

1. Lycabettus was a hill north-east of Athens, famous for its olive trees; Phalerum was a low coastal region.

2. The text is corrupt here: I read ὅπῃ νικᾷ [omit δεῖ as a gloss] τιθέναι ἐν τῇ γῇ τὰ φυτά.

the cutting, the new shoots would reach firm soil more quickly through this loose soil or through unworked soil?"

'"Obviously," I said, "it would shoot more quickly through the worked soil than it would through unworked soil."

'"Then soil must be put under the plant."

'"Of course," I said.

'"And do you think the cutting would take root better if you put the whole plant upright, pointing towards the sky, or if you bend some of it under the soil which you've put under the plant, making it like an upside-down gamma?"[1]

'"The latter alternative would surely be better, because more of the plant's buds would be underground; I can see that shoots grow from the buds of plants above ground, so I assume that the buds below ground have the same function, and that, the more shoots there are growing underground, the more rapidly and strongly the plant will grow."

'"So on this matter too," he said, "we find that you know as much as I do. But would you only heap soil up around the plant, or would you also pack it very firmly?"

'"I would pack it, of course," I said. "Otherwise, I'm sure that the soil would turn soggy when it rained, or the sun would make it dry right down to the bottom, and consequently the plants would probably be rotted by moisture or withered by desiccation as their roots heat up."

'"Now, all this is relevant to planting vines, Socrates," he said, "and we find that you know as much as I do on the subject."

'"And do the same points apply to planting fig trees?" I asked.

'"Yes," said Ischomachus, "and to all other fruit trees too, in my opinion. I mean, when you've got a good method for planting vines, why reject it as a method for planting other types of tree?"

'"And what's the method for planting olive trees, Ischomachus?" I asked.

'"You're just putting me to the test," he said, "since you know this too perfectly well. You can see, because there's non-stop

1. So that it would look like an L.

digging going on alongside the roads, that a deeper hole is dug for olives; you can see that there are stumps adjacent to all the suckers; and you can see that mud is put on the tops of all the plants and that part of every plant which is above ground is wrapped up."[1]

'"Yes, I've noticed all these things," I said.

'"Well, if you've noticed them," he replied, "then of course you know all about them. Or do you not know how to put the potsherd up there on the mud, Socrates?"

'"No, there's certainly nothing among the things you've mentioned that I don't know, Ischomachus," I said. "In fact, I've been wondering for some time why on earth, when you asked me earlier the general question whether I knew how to plant trees, I said that I didn't. I mean, I didn't think I'd have anything to say about how planting ought to be done; but then you set about asking me particular questions, and I find that, as you say, I come up with answers which correspond to what you know, and you are an acknowledged expert at agriculture. Is questioning an educational process, Ischomachus? I'm asking because I've just understood your method of questioning me. You take me through points that I know, you show me that these points are no different from points I'd been thinking I didn't know, and thus you convince me, I think, that I do know the latter points too."

'"Does it follow," asked Ischomachus, "that if I'd asked you whether or not a coin was sound, I could convince you that you knew how to distinguish sound and counterfeit coinage? And if I'd asked you about pipe-players, could I convince you that you knew how to play the pipes, and so on for painting and other such skills?"

'"I wouldn't put it past you," I replied, "since you have convinced me that I know how to farm, even though I am aware that I've never had a teacher in this area of expertise."

1. A common method of propagating olives was to cut pieces off a vigorous tree and plant these stumps in the ground: the suckers that grew would become the next generation of trees. The mud and the wrapping protected the stump against disease; a tile or potsherd protected the mud (see Theophrastus, *De Causis Plantarum*, 3.5.5).

'"That isn't so, Socrates," he said. "I told you before that agriculture is such an altruistic and kind art that one only has to watch and listen for the result to be knowledge of it. And in many respects, agriculture itself teaches the best agricultural methods. A vine climbs up trees, if there are any near by, and immediately teaches us to support it; while the bunches of grapes are delicate, the vine spreads its leaves around them, and teaches us to protect its exposed parts from the sun throughout that period; but when the time comes for the grapes to be sweetened by the sun, the vine sheds its leaves and teaches us to defoliate it and to ripen its fruit; because of its fecundity the vine produces ripe grapes while other bunches are still relatively unripe, and teaches us to pluck those that are swollen at any time, just as one does figs."

20

'At this point I asked, "If the business of farming is so easy to learn, Ischomachus, and everyone has equal knowledge of the necessary jobs, why are people's achievements not equal? Why do some farmers make an exceptionally good living, while others are unable to supply themselves with the necessities of life, and even run up debts?"

'"I'll tell you, Socrates," said Ischomachus. "What is responsible for the fact that some farmers do well, whereas others get into difficulties, is not their knowledge or ignorance. You won't hear anyone trotting out an argument that his estate has been ruined because the sower failed to sow the seed evenly, or because the trees weren't planted in straight lines, or because someone's ignorance of vine-bearing soil made him plant the vines in infertile ground, or because someone didn't know that fallow ground should be ploughed to be ready for sowing, or because someone didn't know that the land should be fertilized. Instead, you're far more likely to hear that the reason so-and-so fails to get crops from his fields is that he neglected to sow it or fertilize it; or the reason so-and-so has no wine is that he neglected to plant vines or to ensure that his existing vines bear fruit; or the reason so-and-so has no olive oil or no figs is that he was irresponsible and didn't make sure that he got them. These are the sorts of factors, Socrates, which make some farmers better than others and achieve better results – and far more outstanding results than people who invent some apparently clever device for the work.

'"The same goes for military commanders too: there are some aspects of military matters in which commanders differ in the sense that some are better than others, not by virtue of intelligence, but obviously because they take responsibility. I mean, there are matters which all commanders know (as do most civilians), but not all of them put their knowledge into practice. For instance, they all know that it is better for soldiers who are passing through enemy territory to do so in the formation which will best allow them to fight, if they have to. Anyway, despite knowing this, not all of them put it into practice. They all know that it is better to post guards in front of their encampment all day as well as during the night; but here too, whereas some of them make sure that this happens, others don't. Or again, you're not likely to find someone who is unaware that it is preferable to occupy the vantage points before advancing through a pass, are you? But here too, whereas some of them make sure that this is done, others don't.

'"So, for instance, although everyone acknowledges that fertilizer is essential in farming, and although they can see that it is a natural product and can be absolutely certain how it is produced, and although it is easy to get plenty of it, nevertheless here too, whereas some people make sure they have a stock of it, others are remiss. And yet God on high supplies us with water, and all hollows become pools of water, and the earth supplies all kinds of weeds, which must be cleared off the land before sowing; and if the stuff which is removed and thrown out were to be put into the water, then time by itself would make matter which enriches the land. For there is no way in which weeds and earth, left in standing water, do not turn into fertilizer. And everyone also knows all the treatment the land needs: if it is too damp for sowing or too salty for planting, they know how water is drained off and how salty soil is corrected by having all kinds of non-salty substances, whether liquid or solid, mixed in with it. Yet, again, not everyone actually does something about treating the land.

'"Imagine someone who is completely unaware of what the land is capable of growing, and who can neither see its crops and trees, nor hear any accurate information about it. Even so, isn't it far easier for any person to find out about the land than about a horse, and isn't it far easier than finding out about a human being? For when the land shows something, it doesn't do so in order to deceive, but in a straightforward fashion it gives clear and accurate information about what it is and is not capable of. And I think that, because the land makes everything easy to know and learn, there is nothing better at exposing people who are bad rather than good.[1] You see, it is not like the other arts, where it is possible for people to plead ignorance if they fail to achieve anything: everyone knows that if you do good to the land, you will achieve good results, so failure on the land is a clear indictment of a bad character. For no one persuades himself that human life is not sustained by certain essentials: so someone who is not prepared to be a farmer, and knows no other skill by which he could earn money, is evidently planning to make a living by being a thief or a burglar or a beggar – or else he is a complete imbecile.

'"Farming may or may not be profitable; now, given that there are labourers, the crucial difference is that one person makes sure that his workers, even if there are rather a lot of them, are hard at work when they should be, while another person doesn't make sure of this. For if even one man in ten is doing his full complement of work, that makes all the difference; and the scales can be tipped the other way by someone leaving work early. So allowing the workforce to take it easy all day long easily halves the total amount of work done. When two men are travelling, their relative progress might differ so much that, on a journey of 200 stadia,[2] one will be 100 stadia ahead of the other, because, even though both of them are young and fit, one is walking to reach a

1. Reading τοὺς κακοὺς πρὸς τοὺς ἀγαθούς.
2. A stadium is 185 metres or about 200 yards.

goal, while the other has a casual attitude and stops to gaze around by streams and in places sheltered from the sun, and looks for routes where balmy breezes blow. Exactly the same goes for agricultural labour too: it makes a great deal of difference to the end-result when people do the work they've been given, rather than finding excuses for not working and being allowed to take it easy. So making sure that the work is done well rather than badly tips the scales no less than the work being done rather than left undone. Suppose digging is going on to clear vines of weeds: if the result of the digging is that the weeds multiply and flourish, wouldn't you be forced to describe this as unproductive work?

'"So these factors are far more responsible for the collapse of estates than cases of excessive ignorance. Although the estate has its full quota of expenses, the work is not being carried out to bring in more than is being spent: so there is no longer any reason to be surprised if this situation results in a shortfall instead of surplus. However, those who are capable of applying themselves and of working hard at farming[1] find no more effective way of making money than agriculture, as my father found by engaging in the business himself, and as he taught me too. He never used to let me buy land that had been farmed, but he used to recommend me to buy land which, because of the owners' neglect or inefficiency, was unworked and unplanted. He claimed that farmed land was expensive and could not be developed; and he reckoned that land which couldn't be developed couldn't give one anything like the same amount of pleasure – which was maximized, in his opinion, by the improvement of any object or creature. And nothing is more capable of improvement than land which is being transformed from an unworked state to full fertility. You should know, Socrates, that between us we have by now greatly increased the original value of many plots of land. And this scheme is so lucrative, Socrates, and also so easy to grasp that, having

1. Note the verbal echo of 2.18 (p. 296), where the topic of why some are successful, when others are not, was first raised; as usual, Ischomachus is confirming Socrates' thoughts from earlier in the dialogue: see p. 283.

been told it, you will go away knowing it just as well as I do, and can teach someone else, if you want to. In fact, my father didn't learn it from anyone else and didn't have to think long and hard to come up with the scheme: he claimed that it was because he loved farming and wasn't afraid of hard work that he wanted land that would enable him simultaneously to keep busy and to have the pleasure of making a profit. I tell you, Socrates, I think that no Athenian has ever been naturally inclined to love farming as much as my father."

'Well, once I'd heard what he had to say, I asked him, "Did your father retain all the plots of land he'd worked, Ischomachus, or did he also sell them, if he had a good offer?"

'"Oh, he sold them, of course," said Ischomachus. "But because he was so fond of the work, he used straight away to buy another one, which was unworked, to replace any he sold."

'"From your description, Ischomachus," I said, "your father really was naturally inclined to love farming to the same degree that traders love corn. For suppose traders hear that there's a vast quantity of corn somewhere: because they love it so much, they sail there to get it, which might involve crossing the Aegean or the Euxine or the Sicilian sea.[1] Then, when they've got hold of the largest quantity they can, they transport it by sea, and do this by putting it into the same ship in which they themselves are sailing. When they want to make money, they don't casually get rid of the corn in any old place, but they take the corn to where they hear corn is fetching the highest price and the people's demand for it is the greatest, and sell it to them there.[2] And your father was apparently fond of farming in the same sort of way."

'"You may joke, Socrates," Ischomachus replied, "but I don't think it detracts from a person's love of building houses, say, if he

1. The Aegean and Sicilian seas were respectively to the east and west of Greece; the Euxine ('Hospitable') sea is our Black Sea.
2. There is a bitter undertone here: Athens itself was often badly in need of grain, yet Athenian entrepreneurs sold it elsewhere, if they could get a better price. Compare Lysias, 22.

sells them once he's finished building them, and then builds others."

'"Good heavens, no, nor do I, Ischomachus," I said. "I swear to you that I most emphatically believe you when you say that everyone is naturally inclined to love the things which they think will profit them."[1]

21

'"However," I continued, "I am reflecting on how well your hypothesis has been supported by the whole argument you have provided. Your hypothesis was that agriculture is the easiest to learn of all areas of expertise, and I am now convinced, as a result of everything you've said, that you are absolutely right about that."

'"Of course I am," said Ischomachus, "but there is one point I'll concede, Socrates: it has to do with the ability to wield authority, which is common to all activities, whether they are concerned with agriculture or politics or estate-management or warfare. I concede to you that some people's mental flair is far greater than others' in this respect. Consider what happens on board triremes, for example: when the rowers are out at sea and are supposed to complete a voyage within a day, some boatswains can speak and act in ways designed to stimulate the crew's willingness to work, while others lack this flair to such an extent that it takes them more than double the time to complete the same voyage. The crew of the first ship disembark all covered in sweat, with the officer congratulating his men and the subordinates just as pleased with their officer; the crew of the second ship arrive without having worked up a sweat, hating their boss and being hated in return.

'"This factor also distinguishes military commanders from one

1. The word used for 'profit' is neutral, and doesn't imply merely monetary gain. It is a standard tenet of Socratic ethics that everyone wants what they perceive to be good for them; the issue then is to find out what is *really* good for one. Is it money or morality?

another. Some fail to make their men prepared to work and face danger, and not only make them averse and reluctant to obey (unless it is absolutely unavoidable), but even have the effect of making them take pride in disobeying their officers; and these are precisely the commanders who fail to instil in their men a sense of shame at any dishonourable event that might occur. On the other hand, there are the divinely favoured, competent and knowledgeable commanders, who take over the same men (and, not infrequently, others too) and can make each and every one of them feel ashamed to do anything dishonourable, can make them prefer obedience and take pride in it, and[1] can make them work at their duties and do so happily. Just as some civilians are innately fond of work, so also a whole army can be imbued by good commanders not only with love of work, but also with the desire to be seen by the commander to be acting with honour. It is leaders whose followers have this attitude towards them who make strong commanders; it is certainly not those soldiers who are physically the most capable, or who are the best spearmen or archers, or who own the best horses and so face danger like perfect cavalrymen or peltasts.[2] No, strong commanders are those who can impress upon their troops that they must be followed even through fire or danger of any kind.[3] It would be right to ascribe great flair to these men – men whom people follow because they recognize their qualities; it would be reasonable to say that a man like this goes to war with strength in his hand, since so many hands are prepared to obey his mind's directions; and great indeed is the man who can use his mind rather than his physical might for great achievements.

'"The same applies to non-military matters as well. Whether the person in charge is a foreman on a farm or an administrator in the city, it is anyone capable of making people work enthusiastically, energetically and consistently, who promotes good results

1. Reading καὶ πονεῖν with Richards.
2. Light-armed infantry or cavalry.
3. See p. 304 on Cyrus the Younger.

and creates a substantial surplus. But suppose the master puts in an appearance at work, Socrates: he is the one who is most capable of hurting a bad labourer and rewarding an enthusiastic one, and, if his appearance fails to make the workers act in a noticeably different manner,[1] I for one could not admire him; but, if his appearance stimulates the workers and inspires each of them with purpose and with eagerness to outdo one another and with desire to be the best, then I would say that his character has some kingly quality. And this, in my opinion, is the most crucial factor in any work which depends on human endeavour – and that includes agriculture.

'"However, I should stress that I am not saying that this kingly quality too can be learned by someone who just sees it, or is told about it once;[2] my position is rather that anyone who is to have this ability requires training and must also be naturally talented and above all favoured by the gods. For I'm not quite convinced that this gift of wielding authority over willing subjects is entirely human rather than divine: it is clearly granted to those who are true initiates in self-discipline. On the other hand, it seems to me that the gods give tyranny over reluctant subjects to those who they think deserve a life like that of Tantalus in Hades, who is said to spend eternity in fear of a second death."'[3]

1. See also the tale of 'the master's eye' on p. 334.
2. As agriculture can (see pp. 339–40); Xenophon is here correcting the impression he gave us on pp. 335–6 that the ability to wield authority requires only training.
3. There are several versions of the Tantalus story, but Xenophon seems to be following the most common version, in which Tantalus' punishment for transgressing against the gods was to stand in a pool of water with fruit-laden branches above his head: whenever he stooped for a drink, the water receded and, whenever he stretched for some fruit, the branches withdrew (hence 'tantalize'). In addition, a rock hung poised above him, threatening at any moment to crush him. Similarly, all tyrants must fear the stab in the back.

BIBLIOGRAPHY

There is no longer any need for me to provide a lengthy bibliography on Xenophon's Socratic works. I can simply refer the reader to D. R. Morrison, *Bibliography of Editions, Translations and Commentary on Xenophon's Socratic Writings, 1600–Present* (Mathesis Publications, Inc., 1988). However, as the title suggests, Morrison lists chiefly works on Xenophon, whereas many relevant aspects of Socrates may be contained in works on, say, Plato. Morrison's bibliography should, therefore, be supplemented by referring to the bibliographies in T. J. Saunders (ed.), *Plato, Early Socratic Dialogues* (Penguin, 1987), and in W. K. C. Guthrie, *A History of Greek Philosophy*, vol. 3: *The Fifth-century Enlightenment* (Cambridge University Press, 1969). This latter work was also issued by the same publishers in two paperback volumes in 1971, entitled *The Sophists* and *Socrates*.

I here append the briefest of bibliographies, a selection of which should get the reader started. All these works are fairly accessible to the non-specialist reader.

XENOPHON'S LIFE AND WORK

J. K. Anderson, *Xenophon* (Duckworth, 1974)

HISTORY OF THE TIMES

J. B. Bury and R. Meiggs, *A History of Greece to the Death of Alexander the Great*, 4th edn (Macmillan, 1975)

J. K. Davies, *Democracy and Classical Greece* (Fontana/Collins, 1978)

N. G. L. Hammond, *A History of Greece to 322 B.C.*, 3rd edn (Oxford University Press, 1986)

BIBLIOGRAPHY

ATHENIAN SOCIETY

A. Andrewes, *Greek Society* (Penguin, 1971)
C. M. Bowra, *Periclean Athens* (Weidenfeld & Nicolson, 1971; Penguin, 1974)
T. B. L. Webster, *Athenian Culture and Society* (Batsford, 1973)

GREEK RELIGION

W. Burkert, *Greek Religion* (Harvard University Press, 1985)
F. M. Cornford, *Greek Religious Thought* (J. M. Dent & Sons, 1950)
W. K. C. Guthrie, *The Greeks and Their Gods* (Methuen, 1950)
M. P. Nilsson, *A History of Greek Religion*, 2nd edn (Oxford University Press, 1949)

GENERAL CLIMATE OF BELIEFS

K. J. Dover, *Greek Popular Morality in the Time of Plato and Aristotle* (Basil Blackwell, 1974)
L. Pearson, *Popular Ethics in Ancient Greece* (Stanford University Press, 1962)
B. Snell, *The Discovery of Mind in Greek Philosophy and Literature* (Dover Publications, Inc., 1982)

SOCRATES' PHILOSOPHICAL PREDECESSORS

J. Barnes, *Early Greek Philosophy* (Penguin, 1987)
W. K. C. Guthrie, *A History of Greek Philosophy*, vols. 1–3 (Cambridge University Press, 1962, 1965, 1969)
E. Hussey, *The Presocratics* (Duckworth, 1972)
G. B. Kerferd, *The Sophistic Movement* (Cambridge University Press, 1981)

SOCRATES

F. M. Cornford, *Before and After Socrates* (Cambridge University Press, 1932)
N. Gulley, *The Philosophy of Socrates* (Macmillan, 1968)
W. K. C. Guthrie, *A History of Greek Philosophy*, vol. 3: *The Fifth-century Enlightenment* (Cambridge University Press, 1969)

CONVERSATIONS OF SOCRATES

T. J. Saunders (ed.), *Plato, Early Socratic Dialogues* (Penguin, 1987)
A. E. Taylor, *Socrates: The Man and His Thought* (Doubleday Anchor Books, 1953)
H. Tredennick, *Plato, The Last Days of Socrates* (Penguin, 1954)

SOCRATICS OTHER THAN PLATO

G. C. Field, *Plato and His Contemporaries*, 2nd edn (Methuen, 1948)
H. D. Rankin, *Sophists, Socratics and Cynics* (Croom Helm/Barnes & Noble, 1983)

INDEX OF PROPER NAMES

The page numbers printed in bold type refer to portions of the translations; the other page numbers refer to introductions and footnotes.

PENGUIN CLASSICS

THE CONSOLATION OF PHILOSOPHY
BOETHIUS

'Why else does slippery Fortune change
So much, and punishment more fit
For crime oppress the innocent?'

Written in prison before his brutal execution in AD 524, Boethius's *The Consolation of Philosophy* is a conversation between the ailing prisoner and his 'nurse' Philosophy, whose instruction restores him to health and brings him to enlightenment. Boethius was an eminent public figure who had risen to great political heights in the court of King Theodoric when he was implicated in conspiracy and condemned to death. Although a Christian, it was to the pagan Greek philosophers that he turned for inspiration following his abrupt fall from grace. With great clarity of thought and philosophical brilliance, Boethius adopted the classical model of the dialogue to debate the vagaries of Fortune, and to explore the nature of happiness, good and evil, fate and free will.

Victor Watts's English translation makes *The Consolation of Philosophy* accessible to the modern reader while losing nothing of its poetic artistry and breadth of vision. This edition includes an introduction discussing Boethius's life and writings, a bibliography, glossary and notes.

Translated with an introduction by Victor Watts

PENGUIN CLASSICS

PROMETHEUS BOUND AND OTHER PLAYS
AESCHYLUS

Prometheus Bound/The Suppliants/Seven Against Thebes/The Persians

> 'Your kindness to the human race has earned you this.
> A god who would not bow to the gods' anger – you
> Transgressing right, gave privileges to mortal men'

Aeschylus (525–456 BC) brought a new grandeur and epic sweep to the drama of classical Athens, raising it to the status of high art. In *Prometheus Bound* the defiant Titan Prometheus is brutally punished by Zeus for daring to improve the state of wretchedness and servitude in which mankind is kept. *The Suppliants* tells the story of the fifty daughters of Danaus who must flee to escape enforced marriages, while *Seven Against Thebes* shows the inexorable downfall of the last members of the cursed family of Oedipus. And *The Persians*, the only Greek tragedy to deal with events from recent Athenian history, depicts the aftermath of the defeat of Persia in the battle of Salamis, with a sympathetic portrayal of its disgraced King Xerxes.

Philip Vellacott's evocative translation is accompanied by an introduction, with individual discussions of the plays, and their sources in history and mythology.

Translated with an introduction by Philip Vellacott

PENGUIN CLASSICS

THE PERSIAN EXPEDITION
XENOPHON

'The only things of value which we have at present are our arms and our courage'

In *The Persian Expedition*, Xenophon, a young Athenian noble who sought his destiny abroad, provides an enthralling eyewitness account of the attempt by a Greek mercenary army – the Ten Thousand – to help Prince Cyrus overthrow his brother and take the Persian throne. When the Greeks were then betrayed by their Persian employers, they were forced to march home through hundreds of miles of difficult terrain – adrift in a hostile country and under constant attack from the unforgiving Persians and warlike tribes. In this outstanding description of endurance and individual bravery, Xenophon, one of those chosen to lead the retreating army, provides a vivid narrative of the campaign and its aftermath, and his account remains one of the best pictures we have of Greeks confronting a 'barbarian' world.

Rex Warner's distinguished translation captures the epic quality of the Greek original and George Cawkwell's introduction sets the story of the expedition in the context of its author's life and tumultuous times.

Translated by Rex Warner with an introduction by George Cawkwell

PENGUIN CLASSICS

HOMERIC HYMNS

'It is of you the poet sings …
at the beginning and at the end
it is always of you'

Written by unknown poets in the sixth and seventh centuries BC, the thirty-three *Homeric Hymns* were recited at festivals to honour the Olympian goddesses and gods and to pray for divine favour or for victory in singing contests. They stand now as works of great poetic force, full of grace and lyricism, and ranging in tone from irony to solemnity, ebullience to grandeur. Recounting significant episodes from mythology, such as the abduction of Persephone by Hades and Hermes' theft of Apollo's cattle, the *Hymns* also provide fascinating insights into cults, rituals and holy sanctuaries, giving us an intriguing view of the ancient Greek relationship between humans and the divine.

This translation of the *Homeric Hymns* is new to Penguin Classics, providing a key text for understanding ancient Greek mythology and religion. The introduction explores their authorship, performance, literary qualities and influence on later writers.

'The purest expressions of ancient Greek religion we possess … Jules Cashford is attuned to the poetry of the Hymns' Nigel Spivey, University of Cambridge

A new translation by Jules Cashford with an introduction by Nicholas Richardson

THE GREEK SOPHISTS

'In the case of wisdom, those who sell it to anyone who wants it are called sophists'

By mid-fifth century BC, Athens was governed by democratic rule and power turned upon the ability of the individual to command the attention of the other citizens, and to sway the crowds of the assembly. It was the Sophists who understood the art of rhetoric and the importance of being able to transform effective reasoning into persuasive public speaking. Their inquiries – into the gods, the origins of religion and whether virtue can be taught – laid the groundwork for the next generation of thinkers such as Plato and Aristotle.

Each chapter of *The Greek Sophists* is based around the work of one character: Gorgias, Prodicus, Protagoras and Antiphon among others, and a linking commentary, chronological table and bibliography are provided for each one. In his introduction, John Dillon discusses the historical background and the sources of the text.

Translated by John Dillon and Tania Gergel with an introduction by John Dillon

PENGUIN CLASSICS

THE RISE OF THE ROMAN EMPIRE
POLYBIUS

'If history is deprived of the truth,
we are left with nothing but an idle, unprofitable tale'

In writing his account of the relentless growth of the Roman Empire, the Greek statesman Polybius (*c.* 200–118 BC) set out to help his fellow-countrymen understand how their world came to be dominated by Rome. Opening with the Punic War in 264 BC, he vividly records the critical stages of Roman expansion: its campaigns throughout the Mediterranean, the temporary setbacks inflicted by Hannibal and the final destruction of Carthage in 146 BC. An active participant in contemporary politics, as well as a friend of many prominent Roman citizens, Polybius was able to draw on a range of eyewitness accounts and on his own experiences of many of the central events, giving his work immediacy and authority.

Ian Scott-Kilvert's translation fully preserves the clarity of Polybius' narrative. This substantial selection of the surviving volumes is accompanied by an introduction by F. W. Walbank, which examines Polybius' life and times, and the sources and technique he employed in writing his history.

Translated by Ian Scott-Kilvert
Selected with an introduction by F. W. Walbank

read more

PENGUIN CLASSICS

THE ODYSSEY
HOMER

'I long to reach my home and see the day of my return. It is my never-failing wish'

The epic tale of Odysseus and his ten-year journey home after the Trojan War forms one of the earliest and greatest works of Western literature. Confronted by natural and supernatural threats – shipwrecks, battles, monsters and the implacable enmity of the sea-god Poseidon – Odysseus must test his bravery and native cunning to the full if he is to reach his homeland safely and overcome the obstacles that, even there, await him.

E. V. Rieu's translation of *The Odyssey* was the very first Penguin Classic to be published, and has itself achieved classic status. For this edition, his text has been sensitively revised and a new introduction added to complement E. V. Rieu's original introduction.

'One of the world's most vital tales. *The Odyssey* remains central to literature'
Malcolm Bradbury.

Translated by E. V. Rieu

Revised translation by D. C. H. Rieu, with an introduction by Peter Jones

THE STORY OF PENGUIN CLASSICS

Before 1946 ... 'Classics' are mainly the domain of academics and students, without readable editions for everyone else. This all changes when a little-known classicist, E. V. Rieu, presents Penguin founder Allen Lane with the translation of Homer's *Odyssey* that he has been working on and reading to his wife Nelly in his spare time.

1946 *The Odyssey* becomes the first Penguin Classic published, and promptly sells three million copies. Suddenly, classic books are no longer for the privileged few.

1950s Rieu, now series editor, turns to professional writers for the best modern, readable translations, including Dorothy L. Sayers's *Inferno* and Robert Graves's *The Twelve Caesars*, which revives the salacious original.

1960s The Classics are given the distinctive black jackets that have remained a constant throughout the series's various looks. Rieu retires in 1964, hailing the Penguin Classics list as 'the greatest educative force of the 20th century'.

1970s A new generation of translators arrives to swell the Penguin Classics ranks, and the list grows to encompass more philosophy, religion, science, history and politics.

1980s The Penguin American Library joins the Classics stable, with titles such as *The Last of the Mohicans* safeguarded. Penguin Classics now offers the most comprehensive library of world literature available.

1990s The launch of Penguin Audiobooks brings the classics to a listening audience for the first time, and in 1999 the launch of the Penguin Classics website takes them online to a larger global readership than ever before.

The 21st Century Penguin Classics are rejacketed for the first time in nearly twenty years. This world famous series now consists of more than 1300 titles, making the widest range of the best books ever written available to millions – and constantly redefining the meaning of what makes a 'classic'.

The Odyssey continues ...